Religion and Radical Empiricism

SUNY Series in Religious Studies
Robert C. Neville, Editor

Religion
and
Radical
Empiricism

Nancy Frankenberry

State University of New York Press

"Bernard Meland: Empirical Realism and Lived Experience"
in Chapter Four of this work appeared in a slightly different
version in the *American Journal of Theology & Philosophy,* vol. 5,
nos. 2 and 3.

Published by
State University of New York Press, Albany

For information, address State University of New York Press,
State University Plaza, Albany, N.Y., 12246

Library of Congress Cataloging in Publication Data

Frankenberry, Nancy, 1947-
    Religion and radical empiricism.

    (SUNY series in religious studies)
    Includes index.
    1. Experience (Religion)   2. Empiricism. I. Title.
II. Series.
BL53.F66   1987   200'.1   86-16558
ISBN 0-88706-408-6
ISBN 0-88706-409-4 (pbk.)

10   9   8   7   6   5   4   3   2   1

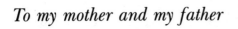

To my mother and my father

Contents

Preface

For some time now, the decisive question facing contemporary philosophy of religion has been, in one form or another, the general question of the justifiability of religious belief. How are religious truth-claims justified? What evidence could count for or against such claims? If no empirical data could conceivably falsify religious truth-claims, how can such claims be meaningful? A whole generation of philosophers of religion has foundered again and again on these questions, and with good reason. They have no simple answers.

I have come to think that what are now the most widely discussed approaches to these questions are fundamentally untenable. More recently, I have come to see that the discipline of philosophy of religion itself can no longer be undertaken exclusively within the context informed by Anglo-American philosophical interests and Western religious practices. In proposing a new approach to the question of the justifiability of religious belief, I am concerned less with the content of traditional religious belief than with the empirical dimension of religous, particularly theistic, belief. Although my argument, like all work in the philosophy of religion, consists of rational reflection on certain data, the mode of justification I am contending for is, in the last analysis, an empirical one rather than a strictly rational or logical one. In sum, I am attempting to offer a rational account of how and why reflection on religious truth-claims must seek justification of those claims finally in terms of empirical criteria.

The selection of what is to count as empirical criteria is, of course, never philosophically neutral. Empiricism has always stood for the justificatory need to ground all knowledge in experience. But as such it is a thesis in search of an adequate *theory* of experience. "Experience" is not an easy word to introduce into today's intellectual climate, however. It is so slippery and overworked, at the same time. It is one of those words that, as Humpty Dumpty noted, ought to be paid overtime because it does so much work.

I have written from the perspective of radical empiricism about the nature and role of experience in religion, presenting radical empiricism more as a necessary complement than as a stark alternative to other methods in the study of religion. Drawing upon radical empiricism in the work of William James, especially as this has been developed by several American religious empiricists and elaborated in the direction of a naturalistic metaphysics by Whiteheadian and Buddhist philosophy, I hope to lay the groundwork for moving beyond some of the typical impasses that arise in current analytic philosophy of religion.

Chapter One begins with a selected survey of the contemporary scene in the philosophy of religion. After clarifying some of the issues embedded in current arguments about experience, justification, and theism, I conclude with a need for a carefully specified and comprehensive theory of experience in terms of which these issues can be systematically addressed.

Chapter Two analyzes four major forms of empiricism, namely, classical empiricism, logical empiricism, linguistic empiricism, and neopragmatic American empiricism. Although I make some effort to assess the merits of each of these respective positions, their net yield for a contemporary empirical philosophy of religion is judged deficient.

Chapter Three presents radical empiricism, whose theory of the nature of experience I find most adequate and compelling. As proposed by William James and augmented by John Dewey, radical empiricism also offers a fresh perspective for considering the religious dimension of experience. The point is not to gerrymander zones of experience so as to garner votes for a specific religious interest group, but to depict a quality that may characterize any experience of any individual.

Chapter Four continues the analysis of radical empiricism by considering the work of three American religious empiricists who have explored a range of theistic options hardly attended to at all by recent philosophers of religion. Henry Nelson Wieman, Bernard E. Meland, and Bernard M. Loomer do not share the sweeping dismissals of theism current today, although they have little use for many of the forms in which theism has been and is found. My discussion of their interpretations of theism could have been given one of the more startling titles that abound in recent books, such as "Beyond Theism" or "Post-Theistic Theology." But I have resisted that move on the grounds that it acquiesces in the standard conception of theism as normative and static.

Chapter Five concludes this study by carrying to the fully explicit metaphysical level the theory of experience presupposed by James and Dewey and by the American religious empiricists. The metaphysical perspective I find most consonant with radical empiricism is one that has been summarized and transformed by Whitehead, and which is represented and reinforced by Buddhist religious philosophy as well. My account obviously does not aim to be exhaustive, only to propose a way forward. Thus, the discussion in Chapter Five is presented as a test case, lifting out and applying a radically empirical theory of experience to engage a quite different empirical theory found in Abhidharma Buddhism.

Although I have become convinced that philosophy of religion in our time must be conducted in a comparative context, I have made only a partial beginning on that task. The historical-analytic scope of this book is but the necessary first step toward a constructive-comparative project that I hope to address in another volume. But I cannot end without reiterating my conviction that the discipline of the philosophy of religion must seek to become a philosophy of religion*s* in the future. For no more than Christian theology can continue to confine its attention to Christianity alone, no longer can Anglo-American philosophy of religion continue to restrict its study to typically Western philosophical problems and practices. The need to engage critically and appreciatively the religious insights of Eastern cultures is an important concern in every aspect of religious scholarship today. Within the discipline of the philosophy of religion, radical empiricism may yet constitute the basis for developing a new standpoint for work in comparative religious philosophy.

Acknowledgments

I am grateful to my colleagues, my friends, in the Department of Religion at Dartmouth College. For the ten years of our association, Fred Berthold, Ronald Green, Robert Henricks, Robert Oden, Hans Penner, and Charles Stinson have given me support, encouragement, and the example of exacting standards. More recently in that splendid department I have welcomed the collegiality of Arthur Hertzberg and Kevin Reinhart.

I have been stimulated and helped by conversations with William Dean, Charley Hardwick, Robin and William Matthews, Bernard Meland, Marjorie Suchocki, Terrence Tilley, and Thomas West. In particular, the insights of Robin Matthews and Terrence Tilley, each in different areas of expertise, were invaluable to me at various stages of writing this book. Terrence Tilley read, and heroically re-read, the entire manuscript, offering extensive comments from which I benefitted immeasurably.

A Dartmouth College Faculty Research Grant helped defray expenses in the preparation of the final manuscript. Frances Dupuis and Gail Patten deserve singular thanks for their expert typing and unflappable patience. Nick Humez prepared the index.

To Robert Neville, editor of this series in religious studies, I and many others owe a special salute. Both in his brilliant and innovative writings and in his generous interest in the work of newer authors, he epitomizes the model of responsible and imaginative scholarship.

To good friends who bore with me over the last three years, especially Mary and Robert Kelley in Hanover, and those friends in the Lake Michigan area whose laughter and perspective punctuated my summer exertions, I remain, as they know, permanently thankful. My deepest gratitude goes to Sasha and Paula Jaudes for affording such gracious summer hospitality during the time when this work was conceived and finally completed.

N.F.
Hanover, NH

Chapter One

Experience, Justification, and Theism

Rarely in modern times has religion been associated with empiricism except to its own peril. At the turn of the century, William James predicted optimistically: "Let empiricism once become associated with religion, as hitherto, through some strange misunderstanding, it has been associated with irreligion, and I believe that a new era of religion as well as of philosophy will be ready to begin."[1] James himself was hoping to clear the ground for the doctrine he called "radical empiricism." But in the years since James's clarion call, empiricisms of very different sorts have flourished on American soil. Most of these have done more to discredit religious belief than to justify it. Even among those who have sought to carry on the task begun by James, considerable disagreement has arisen as to just what "empiricism" is and what sort of "association" of empiricism with religion is most fruitful.

The one feature common to all schools of modern empiricism, in contrast to rationalism, has been a commitment to the proposition that something called "experience" is the touchstone of all theories and all claims to knowledge. In this form, however, the thesis can receive quite different philosophical emphases and refinements, as we will discover in the next chapter. For now, I want to note several complications that the problem of definition poses at the very outset. "Empiricism" is used roughly in three ways. First, the term "empirical" may refer very loosely to the general temperament or attitude of a thinker, to what William James called the quality of "tough-mindedness." In this way, "to describe a temper as empirical is to express in summary fashion the fundamental bias by which it is dominated, the bias for stubborn facts, immediate values, shifting forms, flexible standards, cautious opinions, disillusioned aspirations."[2] Such a use of the term is no doubt as vague as the frequent use of the term "realistic" to

1

mean essentially the same thing. If the "association of religion with empiricism" is to be understood in this form, the empirical philosopher of religion will need to examine more precisely the exact nature of those "stubborn facts," "immediate values," and "flexible standards" that dominate the empirical temper in religion.

Second, the term "empiricism" has been used to denote a method of inquiry, a way of getting at or organizing and interpreting the data of investigation that is broadly instrumental, operational, or experimental. Such a method is usually patterned after those working procedures that have been deemed so successful in the natural sciences. When the empirical method is conceived in this manner, it is usually distinguished from rationalist or dialectical forms of inquiry by its emphasis on what is publicly observable, verifiable, communicable, and controllable, involving a concern with a *posteriori* hypotheses and induction rather than logical analysis or *a priori* arguments. But it is no longer a very useful device, if it ever was, to depict the history of philosophical thought in terms of "empiricists" on the one hand and "rationalists" on the other hand. Even if something of methodological import is nevertheless captured by this distinction, few philosophers since Kant have been inclined to employ the distinction very sharply.

The exact import of empirical methodology as applied to the philosophy of religion, therefore, has become particularly complex and has tended to yield widely divergent results. For a whole generation of religious scholars in America prior to World War II, the influence of James's plea for an association of religion with empiricism was at work in the development of works as various as D. C. Macintosh's *Theology as an Empirical Science* (1919), E. S. Brightman's *The Problem of God* (1930), W. E. Hocking's *The Meaning of God in Human Experience* (1912), and H. N. Wieman's *Religious Experience and Scientific Method* (1927). But as James Alfred Martin's study of this period shows, all of these representative attempts to construct empirical religious philosophies involved "divergent methodological assumptions, interpretive schema, and personal religious convictions, implicit and explicit, which are the presuppositions rather than the results of their 'empirical' inquiries."[3]

In the period after World War II, empirical methodology came to be advocated among members of the "Chicago School" as the foundation of an explicit theological movement. According to Bernard M. Loomer, one of its leading advocates, empirical method in theology was to be understood as

> . . . a methodology which accepts the general empirical axiom that all ideas are reflections of concrete experience, either actual or possible. All propositional or conceptual knowledge originates from and is

confirmable by physical experience. The limits of knowledge are defined by the limits of the experienceable, by the limits of relationship. Reason functions in the service of concrete fact and experience.[4]

Similarly, the assumption underlying Bernard E. Meland's unique empirical method of focusing theological inquiry was that "faith is to be understood not simply as a legacy of belief inherited from the past, but as a vital response to realities inhering within the immediacies of experience as a resource of grace and judgment."[5] As each statement indicates, adopting an empirical method in theology was closely entangled with a concern for "concrete experience," the "limits of the experienceable," or the "immediacies of experience." In each case the identification of that which was taken as "concrete" or as "limits" or as "immediacies" proceeded from and was relative to specific philosophical theories about the nature of experience in general.

This brings us to the third broad meaning of "empiricism." Most often, empiricism has signified an "appeal to experience" in the establishment and justification of claims—a concern for the "given," variously construed. But in this case, the ambiguity is simply pushed back to the question of what constitutes "experience." The difficulty, needless to say, of making empirical appeals to experience has much to do with the fact that "experience" itself has become an increasingly problematic term. Indeed, the term "experience" lately seems to have joined "reality" and "truth" in the class of words which can no longer be written unless apologized for by inverted commas.

Appeals to experience, always to experience understood or interpreted in some particular way, pose a peculiar problem in religion. As John E. Smith has observed, so important and personal an affair as religion can scarcely be expected to live *without* experience, and yet when we consider some of the claims being made in the name of experience, it might seem that religion cannot live *with* it.

Clearly, if we are to pursue James's recommended "association of religion with empiricism" in any of these three forms today, we confront fresh terminological difficulties concerning the nature of the temper, the methodology, and the appeal to experience involved in the empirical task. But the terminological difficulties are at bottom philosophical ones that combine to force the questions at the very heart of our present perplexities in the philosophy of religion. How is religious belief justified? What role does an appeal to experience properly play in the validation or vindication of religious truth-claims, particularly theistic ones? In fact, does theism in any form admit of empirical justification at all?

These questions, stated so broadly, surely must be subject to clarification before they are even considered. While it might be facetious to reply to the question "Is life worthwhile?" by pointing out that it all depends on what one means by "while," there is a more serious reason for insisting that to the question "Does theism admit of empirical justification?" the only straightforward reply is "It all depends on what one means by 'theism,' by 'empirical,' and by 'justification'." This chapter examines each in turn.

The Problem of Justification

Like the multivalent term "empirical," the term "justification" requires close scrutiny. The dominant interest of much philosophy of religion in the modern period has been a concern with issues of justifiability and true belief. In these discussions, to "justify" has been taken to mean an indefinite variety of practices, including "to verify, confirm, make firmer, strengthen, validate, vindicate, make certain, show to be certain, make acceptable, show probable, cause to survive, defend particular contexts and positions." These understandings of justification, whatever their degree, usually have had one thing in common: the assumption that the task of justification requires securing firm foundations, whether rational or empirical, in order to ground belief or knowledge.

This is exactly the assumption I wish to call into question here. To do so, I want first to sketch the argument that made the foundational metaphor seem attractive to many philosophers in the past, and then to present an alternative, nonfoundational theory of justification currently emerging in epistemological discussions. The implications of the critique of foundationalism for contemporary philosophy of religion will become apparent later.

Foundationalism

In brief, foundationalism is the thesis that our beliefs can be warranted or justified by appealing to some item of knowledge that is self-evident or beyond doubt. In the history of philosophy, it has been associated with a predilection for searching out so-called indubitable, incorrigible foundations, on the assumption that nothing short of some rockbottom "given" or self-certifying premise or unassailable datum will suffice to do the job of justification. As one author has observed:

> The central idea of modern empiricism has been that, if there is to be such a thing as justification at all, empirical knowledge must be seen as resting on experiential 'foundations.' To claim that knowledge rests on foundations is to claim that there is a privileged class of beliefs the members of which are 'intrinsically credible' or 'directly evident' and which are able, therefore, to serve as ultimate terminating points for chains of justification.[6]

The history of modern epistemology from Descartes on has provided such unpromising candidates as particulars, or universals, or essences, or sense data, or atomic facts, or synthetic *a priori* propositions, or even givenness itself as the foundation for knowledge. The assumption throughout has been that, without such a foundation, we are condemned to vicious circularity, infinite regress, or self-defeating skepticism.

In recent years different variants of foundationalism have been distinguished as "strong" or "weak," "Cartesian" or "minimal,"[7] but in any case the central assumption has been that unless some knowledge is foundational in the required sense, nothing else we believe could be justified at all. The most decisive argument in favor of foundationalism, one that has made it seem that *some* version of foundationalism must be true, is the epistemic regress argument. As formulated by Anthony Quinton, this argument is as follows:

> If any beliefs are to be justified at all, . . . there must be some beliefs that do not owe their . . credibility to others. For a belief to be justified it is not enough for it to be accepted, let alone merely entertained: there must also be good reason for accepting it. Furthermore, for an inferential belief to be justified the beliefs that support it must be justified themselves. There must, therefore, be a kind of belief that does not owe its justification to the support provided by the others. Unless this were so no belief would be justified at all, for to justify any belief would require the antecedent justification of an infinite series of beliefs. The terminal . . beliefs that are needed to bring the regress of justification to a stop need not be strictly self-evident in the sense that they somehow justify themselves. All that is required is they should not owe their justification to any other beliefs.[8]

The argument then is that the threat of the regress obliges us to recognize that certain empirical beliefs possess a degree of independent epistemic justification that does not derive from inference or coherence relations. The regress can be escaped only by admitting the existence of beliefs that can be justified without their justification accruing to them from further beliefs. Whether these beliefs are called "intrinsically credible" or "basic beliefs" or "directly evident" the metaphor of foundations and the architectonic picture insinuates itself as essential to discovering the nature of ultimate justification. And as long as "ultimate justification" involves an appeal to an ultimate stopping point, which is itself claimed to be self-justifying, foundationalism incurs the reproach of dogmatism.

Nonfoundationalism

Among the many critics of empiricist foundationalism, the arguments of Wilfrid Sellars, W. V. Quine, Wittgenstein, Thomas Kuhn, and, recently, Richard Rorty, have been especially effective in shaking down the foundationalist approach to traditional epistemological questions. These authors have suggested an alternate picture of knowledge and justification to that offered by the foundational view and its comrade-in-arms, the doctrine of the given. Instead of the picture of knowledge as an edifice resting on fixed and immutable foundations, they have offered the picture of human knowledge as an evolving social phenomenon within a web of belief. Belief systems are discovered within a contextual matrix that is itself groundless, and justification becomes a matter of accommodating beliefs that are being questioned to another body of accepted beliefs, not to "raw chunks of reality" and not to anything "intrinsically indubitable." Any belief may be questioned, though not all at once. If no particular set of statements is immune to refutation, then none is irrevocably at the foundation of empirical justification. In that case, regardless of whatever theories we might have about anything that is "given" in experience, epistemic justification will not have "*the* given" at its foundation.

Especially challenging to empiricist foundationalism is Karl Popper's basic argument that the acceptance of a proposition on the basis of experience is not the same thing as its justification. To inquire in what manner one has reached a particular conclusion is quite different from showing in what manner this conclusion can be justified. In order to justify a proposition, according to Popper, one can only refer to other sentences, and this procedure is, he thinks, without end. Therefore, no sentences, neither theoretical nor empirical, can constitute an unquestionable, fully justified basis on which our knowledge is built.

Other critics of foundationalism believe it is time to halt the search for indubitable, incorrigible foundations of knowledge. They handle the worries of the strong foundationalists simply by noting that the position adopts an absurdly severe criterion of certainty that deprives the concept of any sensible use. They dispose of radical skepticism, the specter that has haunted the entire Cartesian episte-mological legacy, by showing that the idea of knowledge it relies on is not worth preserving. Finally, they slough off the worries of even minimal foundationalism by denying the claim that the no-founda-tions view is committed to the existence of a (potential) infinite regress of justification. If we ask what the cash value of this criticism is, the answer is perhaps only this: that, according to the non-foundationa-list, there are no privileged classes of beliefs such that justification "ultimately" terminates with beliefs belonging to these classes.[9] The epistemic regress argument may have *prima facie* plausibility, but it suffers the disadvantage of resorting to a fallacious inference. From the fact that each attempt at justification must come to an end some-where, it does not follow as a conclusion that there must be some privileged class of intrinsically credible basic beliefs with which all attempts at justification must necessarily terminate. In order to escape the regress of justification, all that is needed is the presence of *some* beliefs one has no good reason to doubt at the time, *not* the postulation of intrinsically credible foundations for all time.

Adopting this rationale leads to a radical contextualization of the notions of justification and doubt. It leads to replacing the metaphor of foundations of knowledge with the metaphor of Neurath's boat: we are afloat on the open sea and can repair some planks of the ship only by standing, however temporarily, on others.[10]

Justifications in the Philosophy of Religion

Leaving aside for now the details of the debate between founda-tionalists and the non-foundationalists, and turning to the ways in which issues of justification have figured in the history of religious thought, we can note an interesting parallel. The story of much of modern religious thought can be told to a large extent in terms of an opposition between those who have endeavored to secure the intellec-tual grounding of religious beliefs by exhibiting sufficient reasons and evidential bases, and those who have urged that faith has no need of such foundations. The entire tradition of natural theology, from

Aquinas to Hartshorne, has taken the first approach, while Kierkegaard, Barth and their followers have pursued the second. Both projects have suffered in common an irreparable loss of cogency in late
twentieth century intellectual life, insofar as it is generally taken for
granted by many now that natural theology cannot be carried out
successfully and that sheer fideism is not a viable option.

In significant respects, radical empiricism in religion stands between these two traditions, offering what I believe is an important
non-foundational view of justification, without the relativistic, fideistic, and rationalistic elements found in other positions. This makes it a
striking alternative to three positions on the problem that have been
offered by contemporary philosophers of religion: (1) the Wittgensteinian fideist view that no ultimate justification of frameworks, standards, or forms of life is *possible*; (2) Alvin Plantinga's argument that
no justification is *needed*; and (3) Charles Hartshorne's logical and
ontological justification of theism. In surveying these positions, I will
examine their strategies from the perspective of radical empiricism.
But since that perspective itself will not come into focus until a later
chapter, my critical remarks will be very general. I suggest that none
of these positions leaves adequate room for the category of experience
and so, in all three, the possibility of undertaking a radically empirical
justification of theism is either ignored or directly rejected.

A Fideistic Mode of Justification

Over the last fifteen years it has become fashionable in some
circles of the philosophy of religion to attempt to evade the issue of the
justification of religious belief altogether. Many philosophers who
strenuously reject any attempt to justify religious beliefs have treated
disagreements about religion as falling outside the category defined
by the reasonable/unreasonable distinction. The view that religious
beliefs are commitments that as such cannot be justified, and that a
justification of anything must always presuppose a previous commitment, bears familiar enough echoes of Kierkegaard, but it is chiefly
through the influence of Wittgenstein's later philosophy that this approach has taken hold today.

The inspiration for the current fideism comes directly from
Wittgenstein's celebrated point that language-games, like forms of
life, cannot and need not be justified. Wittgenstein's own argument, it
should be noted, never mentions *religious* language-games in this connection and is restricted instead to a discussion of certain framework
principles such as the continuity of nature or the assumption that

material objects do not cease to exist without physical cause. In these examples, Wittgenstein is interested in countering those who mistakenly hanker after certainty and justifications. Thus Wittgenstein writes that "attempts at justification need to be rejected" when speaking of material objects that must simply be accepted.[11] Some language-games are simply given, or, as Wittgenstein says, "the language-game is .. something unpredictable. I mean: it is not based on grounds. It is not reasonable (or unreasonable). It is there—like our life."[12] In certain spheres of life we reach a point where the search for justification must finally give way to accepting certain basic modes of behavior and human reactions:

> If I have exhausted the justifications I have reached bedrock, and my spade is turned. Then I am inclined to say: 'This is simply what I do.' . . . Our mistake is to look for an explanation where we ought to look at what happens as a 'proto-phenomenon.' That is where we ought to have said: *this language-game is played.*[13]

How far Wittgenstein himself would apply this view to interpretations of religious belief and religious truth is unclear. In his reconstructed lectures on religious belief, for instance, Wittgenstein remarks:

> Suppose somebody made this guidance for his life: believing in the Last Judgment. Whenever he does anything, this is before his mind. In a way, how are we to know whether to say he believes this will happen or not?
>   Asking him is not enough. He will probably say he has proof. But he has what you might call an unshakeable belief. It will show, not by reasoning or by appeal to ordinary grounds for belief, but rather by regulating for all in his life.[14]

This suggests that, for Wittgenstein, statements of what is believed in a religious way are not to be taken as statements about historical or other empirical facts. A sentence like "There will be a Last Judgment" expresses a certain attitude to life. If one does not have this attitude, it seems that for Wittgenstein there is not much one could say about the Last Judgment.

> Why shouldn't one form of life culminate in an utterance of belief in a Last Judgment? But I couldn't say either 'Yes' or 'No' to the statement that there will be such a thing. Nor 'Perhaps' nor 'I'm not sure.' It is a statement which may not allow of any such answer. . . If an atheist says, 'There won't be a Judgment Day,' and another person

says there will, do they mean the same?—Not clear what criterion of meaning the same is. They might describe the same things. You might say, this already shows that they mean the same.[15]

In a case like the Last Judgment, Wittgenstein's treatment may be fairly noncontroversial, but David Pears sees in these expressions a generalized account of Wittgenstein's view of the whole of religious language. Pears sums it up by saying:

> A religious tenet is not a factual hypothesis, but something which affects our thoughts and actions in a different way. This sort of view of religion fits very naturally into [Wittgenstein's] later philosophy: the meaning of a religious proposition is not a function of what would have to be the case if it were true, but a function of the difference that it makes in the lives of those who maintain it.[16]

Norman Malcolm and D. Z. Phillips, among others, have attempted to press these strands of Wittgenstein's thought into the service of philosophy of religion by developing the view that religious concepts are *sui generis* and that, consequently, criteria of intelligibility are to be found only within the particular language-games themselves. The language-game of religion has its own autonomy and hence can neither be justified nor proscribed on independent grounds. Malcolm concludes that "one of the primary pathologies of philosophy is the feeling that we must *justify* our language-games. We want to establish them as well-grounded. But we should consider here Wittgenstein's remark that a language-game 'is not based on grounds. It is there— like our life'."[17] Malcolm claims that religious and scientific frameworks are on a par here. He even states that "the attitude toward induction is belief in the sense of 'religious' belief—that is to say, an acceptance which is not conjecture or surmise and for which there is no reason—it is a groundless acceptance . . . Religion is a form of life . . . Science is another. Neither stands in need of justification, the one no more than the other." Understood as an interpretive framework or way of looking at the world, religious belief "does not rise or fall on the basis of evidence or grounds."[18]

Similarly, D. Z. Phillips has claimed that "the criteria of [religious] meaningfulness cannot be found *outside* religion" and that the meaning of terms like "real," "unreal," "rationality," and "corresponding to reality" differs with context.[19] We must look to various uses of language within the religious language-game if we are to clarify the confused contents of our thought. Analysis of the depth grammar of the ontological argument, for example, shows, according to Phillips, that "to have the idea of God is to know God."[20] From here it develops that "to have the idea of God" means not only knowing how to use the word "God," but also means *to know God.* Thus Phillips, in what must surely be one of the most remarkable assertions of recent times, states that

> The religious believer must be a participant in a shared language. He must learn the use of religious concepts. What he learns is religious language; a language which he participates in along with other believers. What I am suggesting is that *to know how to use this language is to know God . . . He is to be found in the language people learn when they come to learn about religion.*[21]

Implicit in these and other accounts of what has come to be called "Wittgensteinian fideism" are what I consider several dubious assumptions. These are that: (1) forms of life considered as a whole are not amenable to criticism; (2) each mode of discourse is in order as it is, for each has its own criteria and sets its own norms of intelligibility, reality, and rationality; (3) there is no Archimedean point in terms of which a philosopher can relevantly criticize whole modes of discourse; so, (4) commitment is prior to understanding, intracontextual criteria take precedence over extracontextual considerations, and confessional functions can supplant cognitive meaning.

Against this development, it seems important, from the standpoint of rational concerns, to point out several major drawbacks. First, Wittgensteinian fideism does not come to grips with the fact that many people understand religious discourse of one kind or another but still find it incoherent for one reason or another, whereas, for example, no one finds first-order material object talk incoherent. Second, while it is true that one must place religious concepts in their proper context and see the way religious people use them if one wishes to understand them, it does not, however, follow that religious concepts are actually coherent. Third, religious discourse is part of all reasonable human discourse, and logical criteria pertain to such discourse (*e.g.,* consistency) that can be used to appraise religious discourse too. Fourth, in our Western "form of life," religion and science are part of the same interrelated conceptual structure, and hence, it is not clear why considerations or modes of thought that are at home in science, common sense, or other forms of life should have no bearing upon our assessment of the truth or rationality of religious belief. Finally, appraising whole forms of life (*e.g.,* witchcraft) is itself a well-established practice; *i.e.,* that game too is played.

Furthermore, even on its own terms, this strategy is simply not capable of evading the issue of the truth or falsity of the religious language-game or form of life once it is recognized that the truth-claims which are made by different religions conflict with one another. One has only to note, for example, the conflicting claims of Islam and Christianity concerning the doctrine of the Incarnation, or the strikingly different modes of discourse employed by Hindus and Buddhists concerning the existence or inexistence of the soul or ultimate reality. If, on the assumption of Wittgensteinian fideism, there are no criteria that transcend particular religious traditions and that can be used to appraise disputes of this kind, then, as Patrick Sherry notes, the whole status of religious "truth" or "knowledge" is called into question. Sherry is right to argue that we cannot evade questions of justification simply by labelling religion as a "form of life" since the question is not about "religion" but about *particular* religions; and in any case it is probably more faithful to Wittgenstein's usage to say that religion *includes* forms of life than to say that it *is* one.[22] Similarly, Roger Trigg is right to complain that the conceptual relativism into which Wittgensteinian fideism easily slides sweeps aside all questions of objective truth and falsity, and all distinctions between genuine religion and superstition.[23] Emphasis on the relativity of rationality in an extreme form makes any basic commitment or religious faith seem totally blind and arbitrary. And John Whittaker is surely correct in pointing out that when Wittgenstein's defense of commonsensical beliefs in the face of philosophical scepticism is used to invite a similar defense of religious beliefs in the face of religious doubts, the comparison is too simple to sustain in any final analysis of religious truth claims and their logic.[24] Hardly anyone doubts the reality of the physical world, but many people question the existence of God. Demands for justification are misguided with regard to the class of beliefs Wittgenstein called "certainties," but hardly so with regard to the peculiar features of religious assertions that cannot be immunized against doubts as easily.

From the standpoint of radical empiricism, even more decisive objections can be made against Wittgensteinian fideism. The complex phenomena hidden under the fairly simplistic model of "forms of life" and the equally obscure idea of "language-games" cry out for clarifications and concrete content that religious Wittgensteinians have not even begun to supply. The notion that religious systems have their own autonomous principles of judgment and their own distinct decision procedures (calling for all-or-nothing forms of commitment) forfeits their dependent relation with other aspects of human experience. But, by common consent, religious language and belief involve more than simply making acceptable moves in a propositional game, having no more descriptively appropriate relation to the actual world than to any other possible world. Indeed, it is the inability of Wittgensteinian fideism to explain *how* religious language-games are at all related empirically to our forms of life, or *why* we choose some language-games over others, that marks its most serious limitation. In addition to learning or explaining the meaning of religious concepts by relating them to other concepts, sooner or later we must establish their connection to human experience; to facts about human nature, life, and history; or to characteristics of the universe.

This fact suggests that there is more to the matter of using religious language than understanding and adopting the internal workings of some specialized linguistic system that is not answerable to anything outside itself. There is also more to the matter of making "commitments." If they are not entirely arbitrary and contentless, they will be embedded in something far more specific than autonomous "forms of life," which are viewed as not capable of being put into question. In short, I am arguing that a corrective is needed. As important as it has been for philosophers of religion to show that religious language and literature employ humanly created conventions, it is now at least as important that they rescue some sense in which these conventions and the commitments they serve to express can be appraised critically and transformed continuously. Otherwise, as a tool in the hands of religious Wittgensteinians, the notion of "forms of life" and "language-games" is nothing other than an ideological shelter for protecting religious beliefs from examination, refutation, or revision. Whatever one makes of Wittgenstein's own dictum that forms of life "must be accepted," the work of his fideistic followers is clearly dominated throughout by roughly the same conservative attitudes that also characterize evangelical Christianity. In the end, both embed their arguments in assumptions that reinforce dogmatism and serve to insulate from criticism precisely those well-entrenched already-established standards, frameworks, or activities that have come to be most controversial.

A Basicalist Mode of Justification

While the strategy of religious Wittgensteinians has been to emphasize that questions of justification *cannot* be raised, another strategy is to argue that questions of justification *need* not be raised. Alvin Plantinga has essentially adopted this tack in a series of recent articles.[25] Plantinga's original and contemporary work in the philosophy of religion combines three outstanding features: an analytic philosophical orientation, an assertion of the cognitive meaningfulness and epistemic autonomy of religious belief, and an attempt to turn the failure of foundationalism to theistic advantage.

In contrast to religious Wittgensteinians, Plantinga has argued that theistic belief is a cognitive belief, rationally justifiable because "belief in God is properly basic." Unlike Malcolm or Phillips, for instance, Plantinga holds that the absence of reasons or evidence for belief in God does not necessarily lead to the conclusion that such belief is groundless or gratuitous or without justifying circumstances. By "properly basic," Plantinga means a belief that need not be based on or justified by other beliefs; therefore, he might appear to be involved in some sort of foundational move. Interestingly, however, in the series of articles which I examine next, his thesis is tied to a critique of foundationalism as self-referentially incoherent.

In an article entitled "Is Belief in God Rational?" Plantinga lays out the main lines of his argument against classical foundationalism and concludes that it does not give us a good reason for supposing that belief in God is not properly basic. He takes as a "splendid if somewhat strident" example of foundationalism the famous essay "The Ethics of Belief" by the nineteenth century philosopher W. K. Clifford. For Clifford, anyone who believes in the existence of God does so clearly on the basis of insufficient evidence and therefore sins against the ethics of belief. Clifford summed up his views in the ringing statement that, "It is wrong always, everywhere, and for everyone to believe upon insufficient evidence." William James heard in these words a "tone of robustious pathos." Plantinga sees in them a paradigmatic expression of the monumentally difficult and slippery questions of rationality and evidence in relation to belief. What is essential to the Cliffordian foundationalist, in Plantinga's view, is the position that there is a set of propositions F such that a person's belief in God is rational if and only if it is evident with respect to F. Plantinga calls the assemblage of beliefs a person holds, together with the various logical and epistemic relations that hold among them, that person's "noetic structure." Then the set F will constitute the foundations of a person's noetic structure, and for each person S, a proposition p will be rationally acceptable for S only if p is evident with respect to F.

The question of foundationalism is whether belief in God is evident with respect to F. Plantinga's strategy is to ask at this point whether belief in God may not itself be a member of F, and be itself part of the foundations of a rational noetic structure. The Cliffordian foundationalist, he believes, would reject this suggestion because the only propositions that properly belong in the foundations are those which are self-evident or evident to the senses.

Now the question becomes, what is "self-evidence?" Plantinga's reply is that self-evidence is relative to persons, so that what is self-evident to one need not be self-evident to another. Furthermore, he finds both an epistemological and a phenomenological component to self-evidence. A proposition is self-evident only if it is known immediately (the epistemic component); and a self-evident proposition has about it what Locke called "evident luster" and Descartes called "clarity and distinctness" (the phenomenological component).

From this Plantinga builds to the question, how does the foundationalist know—how does anyone know—that, indeed, a given proposition *is* self-evident? For not everything that seems self-evident turns out to be, and the lesson of Russell's paradoxes is that one cannot sensibly hold that *whatever* appears self-evident, really is. How is the foundationalist to justify the appeal to self-evidence? Only, Plantinga points out, by accepting some such proposition as "whatever seems self-evident is very likely true" or "most propositions that *seem* self-evident *are* self-evident (and hence true)." But why should we accept these? Plantinga draws attention to the problem that neither proposition is self-evident, nor evident to the senses. So their acceptance, he argues, violates the foundationalist's canon of rationality: they are accepted as basic without reason. In other words, the foundationalist, in accepting them, uses them to determine the acceptability of *other* propositions; they are thus members of the foundationalist's noetic structure. But since they are neither self-evident nor incorrigible, the foundationalist appears to be, in Plantinga's pointed cliché, "hoist with his own petard."

In another form of the argument against foundationalism, Plantinga claims that it is no more than a bit of intellectual imperialism to hold that *only* self-evident and incorrigible propositions are properly basic for S. The foundationalist is committed to reason and to nothing more, declaring irrational any noetic structure that contains more—belief in God, for example—in its foundations. But Plantinga shows that the dictum that belief in God is not basic in a rational noetic structure is itself neither apparently self-evident nor apparently incorrigible. Nor is it a deductive consequence of what is self-evident or incorrigible. Is there then, Plantinga asks, any reason at all for holding that a noetic structure including belief in God as basic is irrational? If so, it remains to be specified.

By way of conclusion Plantinga makes the following point:

> The mature theist does not typically accept belief in God tentatively, or hypothetically, or until something better comes along. Nor, I think, does he accept it as a conclusion from other things he believes;

he accepts it as basic, as a part of the foundations of his noetic structure. The mature theist *commits* himself to belief in God; this means that he accepts belief in God as basic. Our present inquiry suggests that there is nothing contrary to reason or irrational in so doing.[26]

But there is something wrong with this statement as it stands. Even if Plantinga were correct in his description of the nature of mature theistic belief, the psychological claim he is making here does not support his philosophical position. It comes suspiciously close to saying that the "mature theist" is *very, very convinced* of the existence of God, but this obviously does nothing to settle the question of the epistemic status of that conviction.

Despite his contribution to our understanding of certain limitations with foundationalism, Plantinga's progress toward answering the question of the justifiability of theism is minimal. Even if one agrees with him that classical foundationalism fails because its criteria for properly basic beliefs are neither self-evident nor incorrigible, supposing that Plantinga's own less restrictive version succeeds in warranting belief in the existence of God is premature. And even if one agrees that theism involves "nothing contrary to reason or irrational," much more would be needed to show that it is rational to accept or adopt theism.

But perhaps the most troubling aspect of Plantinga's argument here is that if it works, it works too well. Why may it not be applied with equal elegance to belief in any proposition at all? Nothing that Plantinga has shown here would rule out W. K. Clifford's having a noetic structure that included among its foundations "there is no God." Suppose that one does not hold, as Clifford unfortunately did, that only self-evident and incorrigible propositions can properly be included in the foundations. There is, on Plantinga's showing so far, nothing epistemically infelicitous about the proposition that a noetic structure which includes disbelief in God as basic is rational. In other words, it seems that Plantinga's "not yet shown to be irrational" strategy of defending theism could be used in defense of atheism as well.

In another essay, "Is Belief in God Properly Basic?," Plantinga has explicitly considered an objection of this sort. If belief in God is properly basic, why can't *just any* belief be properly basic? What about the belief that the Great Pumpkin returns every Halloween, he asks? Could we take *that* as basic? And if we can't, why can we properly take belief in God as basic? The best answer he has to such a question is to repeat that in fact we have no revealing necessary and sufficient conditions for proper basicality which follow from clearly self-evident premises by clearly acceptable arguments. Therefore, the proper way to arrive at such a criterion, Plantinga says, is, broadly speaking, inductive. This means that, "We must assemble examples of beliefs and conditions such that the former are obviously properly basic in the latter, and examples of beliefs and conditions such that the former are obviously *not* properly basic in the latter."[27] Plantinga thinks we must have the capacity to recognize particular cases prior to claiming any general criterion for proper basicality, otherwise there will be no chance of arriving at a general criterion at all. Hence we can't decide which beliefs are properly basic (*e.g.*, God) and which are not (*e.g.*, the Great Pumpkin) on the basis of a general criterion. And in the absence of such a generally established criterion, Plantinga tells us, we have no reason for *denying* that belief in God is properly basic while belief in the Great Pumpkin is not.

This, of course, leaves the matter at a stalemate, since not everyone will agree on the examples. Plantinga seems satisfied with this, and in the face of the fundamental disagreements between theists and skeptics he is able only to say that,

> . . . there is no reason to assume, in advance, that everyone will agree on the examples. The Christian will of course suppose that belief in God is entirely proper and rational; if he doesn't accept this belief on the basis of other propositions, he will conclude that it is basic for him and quite properly so. Followers of Bertrand Russell and Madelyn Murray O'Hare may disagree, but how is that relevant? Must my criteria, or those of the Christian community, conform to their examples? Surely not. The Christian community is responsible to *its* set of examples, not to theirs.[28]

From this it should be clear that Plantinga's basicalist mode of justification is a variation on the theme of Wittgensteinian fideism. Both positions stress that either (1) believers and unbelievers inevitably find themselves dealing with some principles, criteria, or frameworks that are basic and can only be "justified" by circular arguments or inconsistent ones; or (2) demands for justification, evidence, or warrants occur within whole systems of thought and cannot be answered or imposed from outside.

But there is another, and distinctive, feature of Plantinga's position that separates it from those who take the position that religious belief is groundless belief. The argument is so undeveloped that it is unclear, but Plantinga seems to hold that even though a proposition can properly be accepted by someone without evidence from other propositions, it does not follow that there is nothing that justifies it.

For there may be certain "circumstances" that occasion or "call forth" a belief and that can be singled out as the ground or the justification for accepting the belief as properly basic. For example, in the case of perceptual beliefs, memory beliefs, and beliefs which ascribe mental states to other persons, there are characteristic types of experiences that have a crucial role in the formation and justification of beliefs such as (1) I see a tree, (2) I had breakfast this morning, and (3) that person is angry. According to Plantinga, "We might say this experience, together, perhaps, with other circumstances, is what *justifies* me in holding it; this is the *ground* of my justification, and, by extension, the ground of the belief itself."[29] Analogously, in the case of belief in God, Plantinga points to the existence of several conditions and circumstances that "call forth" belief in God: guilt, gratitude, danger, a sense of divine presence, and perception of various parts of the universe. The circumstances, including experiences, are not construed as *evidence*, only as grounds, because Plantinga's aim is only to acquit the believer of the charge of irrationality, not to *prove* proper basicality. The grounds consist in the circumstances within which accepting beliefs without reasons is rational.

At this level of the argument, radical empiricists would introduce several objections to Plantinga's position. They would insist, first, that Plantinga needs to carry a fuller burden of proof to show that the two cases above are really analogous. In asessing so controversial a belief as the existence of God (with all the traditional content Plantinga embraces) something more must be done than simple comparison of it with examples of ordinary rational beliefs (perceptual beliefs, memory beliefs, etc.) that we commonly accept without reasons. The fact that reasons often *are not* given by people does not entail that no reasons *could be* given either for perceptual beliefs or for theistic ones. In keeping with the neo-Calvinistic epistemology he is developing, Plantinga does not want to hang the rationality of religious belief on the adequacy of *reasons*, so we should construe his mention of the justifying "ground" and "circumstances" of belief as a cause, not a reason, for belief formation. But this looks like a confusion of explanation with justification. Experience is given a role to play in connection with the acquisition of belief, but not with respect to adducing evidence.

A second issue between Plantinga and radical empiricism can be brought out by considering the difference between (1) the state or condition of *being justified* in one's beliefs, and (2) having or being able to *give a justification* for one's beliefs. By restricting his attention entirely to (1), Plantinga can at best show that the believer is "within his intellectual rights in believing as he does," *i.e.*, he cannot be convicted of irrationality. But this very minimal intent fails to provide any account at all of (2) and it is (2) which is the only thing that will save Plantinga's basicalism from self-insulation. When justification is associated only with (1) and not with the difficult (and dialogical) task involved in (2), it is, of course, easier to take cover in the hard-nosed "agree to disagree" policy Plantinga apparently espouses.

This is the most serious issue between Plantinga's basicalism and radical empiricism. An arbitrary closure is at work in this justificatory recommendation that seems to preclude learning anything radically new religiously. The basicalist is only interested in epistemic justification within his or her own convictional community. Interconvictional conversations, whether with Bertrand Russell and Madelyn Murray O'Hare or with Buddhists, Muslims, or Hindus, would be quickly short-circuited. To this extent, Plantinga's approach cuts off one very good means by which transformation of one's noetic structure might occur. He can only agree to disagree with those who do not already share his noetic structure and he can not radically overhaul a belief so basic as to be unassailable.

Finally, arbitrary closure occurs at another level as well. To radical empiricists, Plantinga's concept of a properly basic belief looks like the epistemological equivalent of the old theological idea of an "unmoved mover"[30] and may prove just as difficult to comprehend. It is able to impart justificatory "motion" to other beliefs, but assumed to stand in no such need of having justification conferred on it. Familiar theological paradoxes lurk here. Why should the unmoved (or self-moved) mover not be itself in motion? Why bring the series of "why" questions to rest just *here*? Why suppose that "belief in God as properly basic" is epistemically self-moved? From the perspective of radical empiricism, we may well wonder whether *any* properly basic beliefs exist at all.

A Metaphysical Mode of Justification

If one rejects both Wittgensteinian fideism and Plantinga's basicalism, a number of other approaches to, or arguments for, the justification of religious belief can be found. Several influential directions have been explored by writers whose primary concern has been with establishing the rational consistency and coherence of arguments for the existence of God and with demonstrating the place of metaphysical claims as a distinct logical type essentially different from scientific language. Charles Hartshorne's work stands out as indicative of the importance, as well as the limitations, of the rationalist approach to questions of justification in religion. In attempting to telescope his views in a limited space, I call attention to the limitations of this work, from the viewpoint of radical empiricism, rather than to the original and perceptive aspects of the discussion contributed by Hartshorne.

More than any other living philosopher, Charles Hartshorne has devoted himself to the analysis and defense of logical arguments for the existence of God, giving sustained discussion to the ontological argument. Preeminently among contemporary philosophers of religion, Hartshorne has long maintained the position that empirical evidence is irrelevant to acceptance or rejection of theism. An adequate conception of God, in Hartshorne's view, means that belief in the existence or nonexistence of such a being can in no way depend on empirical evidence. The existence of God, according to Hartshorne, must not only be compatible with the world we do in fact experience, but with any *logically possible* world. It is repugnant to the very meaning of "God" that theism should be subject to empirical confirmation or falsification.

By "empirical" Hartshorne intends the sharp sense developed by Karl Popper's method of empirical falsification in the philosophy of science. According to Poppers' insight, falsification, as a minimal condition for a claim to qualify as empirical, requires that there must be some evidence from experiment (experience) that would show the claim to be incorrect, and from which that claim could not be insulated. In endorsing Popperian empiricism, while at the same time stressing the suitability of the divine existence for religious worship, Hartshorne holds that "any god with whom facts could conflict is an idol, a fetish, correlative to idolatry, not to genuine worship."[31]

Hartshorne maintains that the "falsification" and "verification" hypotheses coincide with the modal distinction between "contingency" and "necessity." While the "falsification" hypothesis characterizes all empirical claims, the verification principle defines analytic (or for Hartshorne, metaphysical) claims. He elaborates this coincidence in the following manner:

> Metaphysics may be described as the study which evaluates *a priori* statements about existence. *A priori* is here used in a somewhat Popperian sense of contradicting no conceivable observation .. But I agree entirely with his [Popper's] claim that it is observational falsifiability which alone distinguishes empirical from metaphysical or *a priori* statements. This is a precious contribution to philosophical wisdom.
>
> The reason Popper is right here is so obvious that it seems almost silly. . . . If there are truths which are nonempirical, noncontingent, holding *a priori*, any experience must be compatible with

and, in so far corroborate, them. Thus agreement with experience could not possibly be the distinctive mark of *contingent* truths, but only of truth as such, whether contingent or necessary.

All truths will agree with experience, hence the difference between contingent and necessary truth can show itself only in this, that the former could while the latter could not *conflict* with any *conceivable* experiences.[32]

On this basis Hartshorne is able to argue that if the truth is metaphysical, it is embodied in any possible experience and therefore exerts no empirical, critical leverage. The ontological idea is, for Hartshorne, the statement of what is required for a rational understanding of anything whatsoever; the standards of perfection must be accessible, he assumes, to reason, and the absolute standard logically entails its own existence. As a process philosopher, Harthorne adheres to the doctrine of God's continual becoming, so that the "perfection" in question is that of a continually creative and surrelative perfection.

Hartshorne recognizes that his modal version of the ontological argument is a purely *a priori* argument, independent of empirical evidence and contingency, and a basis only for abstract thinking about necessary existence. This tells but half of the story, however. By adopting a dipolar form of theism in which the nature of God is conceived as irreducibly complex rather than as simple, Hartshorne is able to distinguish both an abstract and a concrete aspect to the divine perfection. It is only the abstract aspect which concerns the absolute, eternal, and necessary *existence* of God, knowable by metaphysical argument and logical proof. The concrete aspect is the dependent, related, and contingent *actuality* of the divine reality, inaccessible to rational proof but presumably knowable by direct, empirical observation or encounter. Hartshorne frequently reiterates his contention that the theistic arguments only demonstrate the bare *existence* of God (*that* God is) and that they tell us nothing whatsoever about the concrete *actuality* of God (*how* God is). The divine actuality can only be known through empirical observation and experience.[33]

This means that the bare existence of God, as correlative with the possibility of anything whatsoever, is the ultimate metaphysical abstraction. As such, it is totally nonspecific and capable of being correlated with any situation at all. Consequently, Hartshorne emphasizes that the *existence* of God is not any state of affairs that makes any recognizable difference in the world. Hence, there can be no empirical "proofs" or justification of God's existence. As necessary, God is exemplified in every fact and every experience, but there is no contingent state of affairs (*e.g.,* the existence of a particular sort of world) which is such that its existence would provide a good reason for God's existence and its nonexistence would weaken or destroy the case for theism.

At the same time, the concrete *actuality* of God is related to the actuality of all things at any given moment and may also be called the Supreme Fact or State of Affairs.[34] Even though for Hartshorne the fact *that* God is actualized is an eternally necessary abstract truth, the *how* of divine actualization is a contingently different fact each moment. But contingent facts, in Hartshorne's scheme, afford no basis for generating strictly valid claims that must be logically, necessarily true. Therefore, evidently nothing about the world or the experience of it could possibly either prove or disprove the existence of God. As a result, Hartshorne leaves only two extreme options: theism or positivism. If the ontological argument is valid, the possibility of God's nonexistence is thereby logically excluded. Then the only choice is either to affirm that "God" means necessary existence or else it means nothing at all (or is nonsense).[35]

The impressive logical rigor and rational consistency with which Hartshorne has pursued the logic of theism (and to which my summary does little justice) deserve full appreciation. His contribution to the discussion of theism is especially welcome in the face of fideisms offering only nonrational or noncognitive justifications of theism. Nevertheless, from the viewpoint of radical empiricism, there is much left to be desired, if not criticized, about Hartshorne's position. On issues of justifiability, radical empiricism finds two sources of dissatisfaction with Hartshorne's formulation of the "empirical," having to do with, respectively, the tautological conditions for establishing necessary existence and the negligible conditions for knowing the concrete divine actuality.

First, even assuming that Hartshorne's defense of the ontological idea is valid, some doubt exists as to what the argument proves. However much Hartshorne has succeeded in clarifying the conception of *a priori* truth as a modality of truth-claims, he has not, from the viewpoint of radical empiricism, shown that what we do in thinking about universal and necessary conditions of existence involves anything more than entertaining a conceivable hypothesis. In other words, even if Hartshorne has correctly shown the logical status of claims about God to be *a priori*, such that God is compatible with all possible worlds and falsifiable by none, it follows only that this is logically *how* we think the concept, not that this is *what* we are thinking about. We are thinking *about* an hypothesis. We may even say with Hartshorne that, if we are thinking it correctly, we are thinking it as a necessary truth, but that does not alter the fact that the status of that thought as an element of human knowledge is the status of an *hypothesis* which may or may not be true.

How are we to judge when we have a genuine candidate for an *a priori* truth? If the claim to have discovered a universal and necessary condition for any possible world is itself, as I am suggesting, a hypothetical claim *about* an *a priori* truth, how is that claim to be tested? Sheer logic is no help at this point. Logically, conceivable alternatives to any hypothesis that purports to interpret *all* experience can always be found. Or, stated more pointedly, the Whiteheadian-Hartshornian process categories are not the *only* available means for interpreting all experience.[36] Empirically, however, there is an indirect way of testing any hypothesis that claims to exhibit necessary features exemplified in all reality, and that is by finding, or by failing to find, some set of experiences *not* adequately covered by the hypothesis. If no such experiences are (as yet) discovered, then the hypothesis is rendered more plausible, but it is no less a hypothesis. We are back, then, to experience as the final judge.

But Hartshorne's notion of the "empirical" reduces to a *logical* category that is identical with "contingency" and *not* with "experience" as construed by radical empiricism. At the very least, Hartshorne's admission of an experiential dimension to the problem seems to be verbal only. That which is exemplified in all experiences and falsifiable by none turns out to be compatible with every experience and, therefore, may be suspected of being vacuous.[37] Furthermore, radical empiricists will note that a subtle and important methodological difference exists between "understanding seeking exemplification in experience" and "experience seeking understanding." To emphasize the former, as Hartshorne does, is to lock into a logical system that invariably fails to fulfill the radically empirical ideal of adequacy to experience. To emphasize the second, as radical empiricism does, is to arrive at ideas of what is universal and necessary, if at all, only by way of tentative descriptive generalization from what is contingent and particular.

Second, radically empirical theists have found a further source of dissatisfaction with Hartshorne's predominantly logico-rational justification of theism.[38] The concrete actuality of the divine existence receives very little elucidation in Hartshorne's work. Neoclassical metaphysics, as Hartshorne has developed it, contributes significantly to a rational understanding of the abstract pole of divine dipolar existence, but the problem of how to talk meaningfully of the concrete actuality of God has gone largely unaddressed. The question of what possible use the ontological argument is to our understanding of the world apart from our experience of that "most perfect being" which enters into every thought is, apparently, not a pressing problem for Hartshorne. Although he is able to affirm that "the highest knowledge is not metaphysical, but empirical . . . ,"[39] the question of exactly how God may be known empirically is simply dismissed in passing by Hartshorne. "The concrete whole," he tells us, "we are unable to know, but metaphysics can give us its most abstract principle, and with that, together with fragments of the whole which we get from science and personal experiences, we can be content."[40] On the whole, Hartshorne concludes that "our knowledge of the concrete divine reality is negligibly small."[41] In this case, if knowledge of the divine actuality gained from all available empirical sources is indeed so negligible, and if Hartshorne's veto against empirical theism is upheld, it follows that there can be no empirical justification of theism in any sense, either by showing how the idea of God is *derived from* experience or by showing how it is *verified by* experience. But if that is so, we may at least be justified in wondering what possible value metaphysical necessities of thought have unless *some* perceptual elements, correlated with them or deducible from them, can be discovered in experience.

The Problem of Theism

The brief survey I have given of contemporary philosophy of religion, as represented by the work of religious Wittgensteinians, Alvin Plantinga, and Charles Hartshorne, underscores the claim that "Rightly understood, the problem of God is not one problem among several others; it is the only problem there is."[42] In the view that I am recommending, the problem needs to be raised in entirely new terms today. From Plato to the present, human reason has struggled to give conceptual expression to what is meant by "God." Competing rational systems of thought have been constructed, skillful theistic arguments have been advanced, and bold speculative syntheses have been proposed. The long centuries of theological and philosophical attention to the problem of God have produced a plethora of abstract concepts by which historically "God" has been conceived in the West: as Ideal Good (Plato); Unmoved First Mover (Aristotle); The One (Plotinus); Subsistent Being or Pure Act (Aquinas); Substance Endowed with Thought and Extension (Spinoza); Absolute Spirit or Idea (Hegel); Ultimate Concern (Tillich); Process (Whitehead). In recent years, as the problem of God has shifted from the ontological to the linguistic level, questions have been raised as to the meaningfulness of all conceptions of God and the cognitivity of any assertive claims concerning God's existence, nature, attributes, and relation to the world. The shift, however, has been in direct continuity with the concern for conceptual clarification which has motivated the tradition of classical theology. Discussions of the ontological argument for the existence of God have given way to questions of whether "existence" is a predicate. Questions of the truth of revealed faith have been transposed to considerations of the justification of convictional utterances and requisite conditions for a "happy speech-act."[43]

Evident in both the older ontological approach and in the newer linguistic approach is a tendency to treat the problem of God primarily as a conceptual rather than as a perceptual problem. Whether it is approached ontologically or linguistically, the problem of God has been consistently viewed as a *conceptual* problem, having empirical and existential implications, rather than as an empirical and existential problem, having conceptual and logical implications. What has been forfeited, as philosophy of religion has steadily assumed more and more the status of logical and semantic explication, is any concerted or sustained attempt to describe empirically the structures pertaining to the actual operation of deity in human and natural existence.

What would be the effect of reversing the emphasis of the dominant order of inquiry? How might "the problem of God" be approached as an empirical question in our time? Clearly, such inquiry cannot be conducted in a conceptual vacuum nor with the aid of merely persuasive definitions. Some minimal definition or denotation of what is to serve as the "object" of inquiry when the problem of God is approached empirically is needed in order for inquiry even to begin.

At this point, two fundamental alternatives present themselves, and the choice between them is crucial. Essentially, it is the choice between traditional theological theism and revisionist philosophical theism. The latter option is the one I have chosen and its development will emerge in subsequent chapters. Currently, I am concerned with demonstrating why traditional theism does not provide either an inevitable or an adequate set of terms for launching inquiry. By "traditional theism" I mean that standard set of doctrines presupposed in Western theological thinking about God and found alike in such thinkers as Augustine, Anselm, Aquinas, Luther, Calvin, Descartes, Kant, and Kierkegaard. The central doctrines of traditional theism can be summed up in the set of descriptions which Richard Swinburne, among other contemporary defenders of theism, provides in his defense of *The Coherence of Theism*. According to Swinburne, this is the doctrine that God is

> a person without a body (*i.e.*, a spirit), present everywhere, the creator and sustainer of the universe, a free agent, able to do everything (*i.e.*, omnipotent), knowing all things, perfectly good, a source of moral obligation, immutable, eternal, a necessary being, holy, and worthy of worship.[44]

Arguments against the rational coherence and consistency of this list of attributes are so well known that it is unnecessary to review the literature here. What I wish to emphasize is the inadequacy of presupposing this set of descriptions in any attempt to develop an *empirical* justification of theism. The first thing to note is that Swinburne puts forward this definition as what a God must be to be "worthy of worship" and an "adequate object of religious attitudes." The underlying rationalism of this approach is evident by the way in which traditional theists typically proceed by first stating without question what a thing *must* be prior to inquiry, and then trying to demonstrate that God must conform to this prescription. One may wonder whether anything at all can be known on the basis of such an *a priori* procedure. An empirical approach would insist, to the contrary, that knowledge should come as a consequence of inquiry, not by prescribing before inquiry begins what it must discover. Inquiry, to be sure, needs to be guided by theory, but Swinburne's definition is not formulated as a theory. Like other similar versions, it is first developed to meet the demands of worship. These demands have in turn arisen in specific sectarian communities conditioned by a long religious tradition consisting of ceremonies, songs, myths, and rituals. Such factors may account for the emotional intensity and the cultural-psychological conditioning by which traditional ideas about God are maintained, but they hardly indicate that this God is, philosophically speaking, *worthy* of commitment.

The lingering grip that traditional theism continues to exercise upon the theological and philosophical imagination only serves to block the road of inquiry into a revisionist and more empirically adequate object of commitment. This is as true of the critics as it is of the defenders of traditional theism. Thus, when J. L. Mackie sets forth his case against *The Miracle of Theism,* he takes as his starting point the model of theism proposed in Swinburne's earlier summary definition of traditional theism and follows Swinburne in taking these descriptions fairly literally.[45] The only difference is that Mackie reaches the conclusion that the arguments against theism (so conceived) outweigh those in its favor, while Swinburne argues the exact opposite case. As long as these standard debating moves are repeatedly played out on traditional turf, they lead again and again to familiar impasses over the question of the rational coherence of theism.

From an empirical viewpoint, an even more serious objection to the *adequacy* of Swinburne's definition is found. Any one who would assert literally the full set of theistic doctrines as expressed in Swinburne's summary is, at some time, bound to confront the problem of evil in its most intractable form. In light of this consideration alone, one may well ask why traditional theism, when it has failed so miserably to deal with evil, should retain a privileged position. To continue according it special status is only to ensure, from the viewpoint of those especially sensitive to the problem of evil, that the traditional concept of God will seem infinitely remote from the world and the self as it is experienced.

In light of this, for several generations now Christian theologians themselves have been turning increasingly to a study of revisionist forms of theism that attempt to replace (or at least to reformulate) the traditional model of theism. By now, for a whole new generation of scholars it is no longer desirable or possible to rationalize the problem of evil in any way that leaves wholly intact the traditional perfection, goodness, and omnipotence of God.

At the same time, the various proposals for developing new and revisionist forms of theism have been met with obstinate criticism. If any revisionist form of theism is to succeed in gaining more of a hearing in our time, these criticisms must be carefully evaluated. The principal objection, voiced in one form or another by proponents of orthodox Christian theism, is that revisionary theism can at most have to do with a petty, finite entity that cannot possibly compare with the lofty majesty of the eternal, infinite, omnipotent Supreme Being worshipped for ages in the mainstream of the Christian tradition. I think three decisive replies can be made to this objection. First, whatever may be validly said of the "majority of the faithful," it is not at all clear that popular piety and actual worship has been fashioned according to this model. Rather, it seems more obviously and narrowly to be a model fashioned by an intellectual elite within ecclesiastical and scholarly western communities. Second, those who disdain revisionist forms of theism as "religiously unsatisfying" must assume a burden of proof here that cannot simply take for granted a fixed and agreed upon notion of "religiously satisfying." There is much scope for legitimate disagreement in this area, especially when revisionist forms of theism can be shown to offer distinct advantages over the former

model. Third, the notorious obscurities of traditional theism's notion
of a timeless deity count against allowing it pride of place in contemporary discussions. Very strong supporting arguments are required to
defend even the minimal intelligibility of this model, let alone its
superiority over competing alternatives. These arguments are, in my
view, conspicuously lacking.

Consequently, resorting to the either/or ploy exemplified by
Terence Penelhum in the following passage does little good:

> From time to time thinkers suggest that there is a God who is all-
> good but not all-powerful, or who is all-powerful but not all-good.
> Such suggestions clearly avoid the problem of evil; but we are merely
> bored by them. The alternatives are always tacitly restricted to two—
> either there is a God who is all-powerful and all-good, or there is no
> God at all. Christianity may not have convinced everybody, but it has
> certainly made us all very finicky . . . [T]he only God in whose exis-
> tence we can evince interest is one whom it would be proper to
> worship. And worship in the Western world does not mean the ap-
> peasing of an angry God or the encouragement of a weak one. It
> necessarily includes submission and moral reverence.[46]

Aside from the fact that such a restrictive imposition on the discussion
makes for a narrow, parochial treatment of divinity, it is doubtful that
Penelhum's references to "an angry God" or to "a weak one" cover the
existing alternatives fairly.

Equally weak is the argument advanced by J. N. Findlay who
finds it

> wholly anomalous to worship anything *limited* in any thinkable man-
> ner. For all limited superiorities are tainted with an obvious relativ-
> ity, and can be dwarfed in thought by still mightier superiorities, in
> which process of being dwarfed they lose their claim upon our wor-
> shipful attitudes.[47]

The obvious reply to this is that what matters is what actually exists,
not what is abstractly ideal. Findlay's ideal deity, which remains only a
conceivable ideal, is inferior to any actual-but-limited deity.

Another variation on this theme can be found in the criticisms
which Edward H. Madden and Peter H. Hare make of Alfred North
Whitehead's conception of God. Madden and Hare argue that a
"God" which fits the requirements of theism must be one who is able
to guarantee the "triumph of good in the actual world," by which they
mean "that good outweigh[s] or replace[s] evil in the production of
greater good, that the good will outlast evil, and so on."[48] With these
prescriptions in mind, the authors claim that it is difficult to see how

the ultimate triumph of the good can be ensured on the basis of any revisionist moves that would redefine or qualify the classical doctrine of omnipotence. Therefore, they conclude that process theism, as developed by theologians influenced by the work of Whitehead, is incompatible with the God of traditional theism. Indeed, Madden and Hare charge that in process theism God is so "weak" as to be

> unable to move toward an aesthetic end without an enormous cost in pain (his own and others'); he is apparently so weak that he cannot guarantee his own welfare. If he is that weak, obviously he is not able, as a theistic God should be, to *insure* the ultimate triumph of an end of his choice.[49]

But who has the burden of proof in this case? Revisionist theists who defend a more adequate and coherent conception of omnipotence than is found in the tradition? Or critics who defend an orthodox conception of what they hold to be intrinsic to any theism worthy of the name? While no unambiguous answers are found in this debate, it is interesting to note that what Madden and Hare take to be the hard-core of traditional theism's doctrine of omnipotence is actually quite arbitrary even from the standpoint of traditional theism. Their demand for the achievement of the maximum amount of good at a point *within the temporal process* seems more a product of utopianism than of orthodox Christian faith which, as Reinhold Niebuhr never doubted, "insists that the final consummation of history lies beyond the conditions of the temporal process."[50]

Forsaking these debates, it seems imperative that any philosophical theism that moves beyond the well-worn path of the traditional discussion will be a deliberately revisionist account of theism. If this choice introduces a whole set of new problems, they are hardly any worse than those imposed by a choice of the former option. One of the chief problems in formulating a contemporary revisionist theism is definitional. If there is to be an initial, minimum, definition of that which is designated "God," so as to focus inquiry, it will need to be one which is sufficiently general as to avoid metaphysical seepage and not to prejudice the outcome of the inquiry in advance. Further specification and elaboration of the definition will depend on the philosophical system supplied for its elaboration, but the starting point itself should be completely general.

A promising candidate for such a starting point was suggested by Henry Nelson Wieman who argued that:

> The goal of inquiry is not to find what conforms to some chosen traditional idea of God except the one essential in that tradition,

namely, what operates in human experience to create, save and transform toward greatest good.[51]

Wieman's work was notable for its pioneering efforts in the development of an empirical philosophy of religion. In one of his earliest attempts to bring a scientific method to bear upon the question of religious experience, Wieman raised an extremely important question that is still relevant to research today:

> Is our knowledge of God knowledge by acquaintance, or is it purely descriptive? Is God an object that enters into our immediate awareness, or is [God] only an object of speculation, known only through the logical consistency of propositions, which must be the form of all accurate knowledge, but known through a logical consistency which does not define any object entering our immediate awareness? Is [God] an object of possible experience, or is [God] purely a system of concepts? . . . Either God is an object of sensuous experience, or else [God] is purely a system of concepts and nothing more. All attempts to escape this dilemma must result in confusion and befuddlement, if not in actual superstition.[52]

Wieman was by no means denying that what is designated "God" can be known through a system of concepts. His point was that if God is a datum of experience, then the system of concepts can be shown to have reference to felt qualities of experience, while if God is not a datum of experience, the concepts are experientially empty and useless. Wieman's presentation proved to be an overly simplified analysis in the long run, but at this stage in our inquiry he points to a useful preliminary distinction.

Finally, bearing in mind the historical nature of all thinking, we should be able to appreciate the way in which any description or definition of God uncovered by research, understood by interpretation, or proposed for contemporary judgment is historically conditioned—not only by the one who propounds the definition but also by the language one uses. One implication of this recognition is that all past definitions of "God" are adequate for the present only insofar as they correspond to the historicity of the present and are suited to the differentiations of experience of the present. Thus, in principle, no one definition, concept, or theological model of God will remain static for a very long period of time. The particular model of theism that radical empiricism employs is no more sacrosanct than others. But to object that such a concept of God bears no relation to the true God is to beg the question. We do not know the "true" God.

The Problem of Appeals to Experience

The problems I have been discussing in connection with issues of justification and with models of theism come to a head in a consideration of the question I want to pose now. What role does experience properly play in the formulation or testing of knowledge claims?

Since the beginning of the Enlightenment, Western thinking has been preoccupied with the appeal to experience. The analysis of what experience is and means has passed from classical British empiricism, through the criticism of Kant and Hegel, to the developments given in this century by pragmatism, phenomenology, and existentialism. Recently, critical theory in the style of Habermas and hermeneutics in the hands of Gadamer have added fresh refinements.

However, a fundamental dichotomy appears in the notion of experience as it has developed since the seventeenth century. It is a dichotomy that has played particular havoc with discussions of the nature of experience in Western religious thought. Thus, with respect to any experience, it has become typical to distinguish between (1) the experience taken as a psychological event or state in the person having the experience, and (2) the experience viewed as a form of awareness *of* some object.

Obviously, not every appeal to experience is an empirical claim. In everyday life finding people advancing appeals to experience rather recklessly is not unusual. What is not, after all, an experience of one kind or another for someone or other? Sensing, perceiving, willing, doing, wondering, feeling, inferring, imagining—surely all these and many more are modes of experience. Philosophers, however, especially if they are epistemologists, are less latitudinous, particularly when determining questions of truth, justification, and knowledge. With respect to these questions, ordinary appeals to immediacy, directness, or self-evidence in experience are considered very unreliable guides. In fact, the pervasive epistemological orientation of contemporary philosophy is decidedly inhospitable to appeals to immediate experience or claims to noninferential knowledge on the basis of experience. The notion of empiricism as involving a simple or direct consultation of what is "given" in experience has been subject to heavy criticism in this century, along with the philosophical motivation in making any appeal to "foundational" knowledge. Appeals to immediate experience, however the word is defined, are almost universally suspect on the grounds that they lead to unwelcome and exasperating claims to privileged access or self-confirming suppositions.

Transposed to the religious sphere where it has lately received attention, the principle that there is no uninterpreted experience carries the serious theological implication that there can be no immediate religious experience, no "self-authenticating" apprehension of the divine, no indubitable intuition from which description can be developed. There are, on this assumption, no immediate experiences of God; there are only experiences which are interpreted in a theistic manner. Accordingly, we have no unmediated access to reality or to any religious dimension of experience. All experience requires *some* interpretive form. All "knowledge by acquaintance" is conditioned by modes of description, intention, and expression. There is, then, no rock bottom knowledge or brute datum for the theologian to describe, any more than for the philosopher. Description is itself always an interpretation.

Particularly in the area of religion, where appeals to religious experience multiply faster than loaves and fishes, the use of the word "experience" is hardly neutral as to interpretive schemes. Historically, the appeal to religious experience in both scholarly and confessional writings has taken a bewildering variety of forms, ranging from experiences of mystical transport, beatific vision, or blinding ecstasy, to experiences of personal renewal, social transformation, and political justice. Judging from the vast array of recent studies on the topic of religious experience, one might conclude that the term itself has now become so diffuse as to be practically devoid of definite meaning. Indeed, John Moore argued more than forty years ago that the term "religious experience" had "outlived its usefulness" and that its popularity has rested in large measure on its vagueness and ambiguity.[53] By now it is obvious to many students of the subject that certain kinds of experiences are singled out and labelled "religious" at least partly on the basis of implicit theoretical assumptions that have been shown to be subject to criticism in their own right; and any talk of the "object" of religious experience has become, by all accounts, problematic and elusive.

But if the types of religious experiences appealed to in support of theistic arguments have varied enormously, the familiar challenges to the validity of such arguments are more easy to classify. The most common objections to Arguments to God from Religious Experience come from two directions. First, there is the verificationist objection, which contends that existence-claims always must be subject to verifying procedures involving tests and checks of a public kind. But appeals to experience of God or any other religious object cannot be verified in this way; therefore, it is not possible to decide whether anyone has had an authentic experience of God as opposed to an illusory one. Neither is it considered possible to fathom how far appeals to religious experience involve a bare record of an *immediate* encounter, as often purported, and how far those experiences have been *interpreted*, perhaps even misinterpreted, by the subject in the very attempt to make sense of them. From here it is an easy slide into a second familiar challenge, the psychological objection, typified for example by C. B. Martin who finds that the logic of the statement "I have direct experience of God and therefore know that he exists" is "very, very like" the logic of such admittedly psychological statements as "I have a funny feeling and therefore know that I have a funny feeling."[54] On this basis, all statements about experiences are considered psychological statements about our feelings, sensations, and mental events, and from these no inference to the existence of objective realities is valid. Just because I have certain subjective experiences I cannot conclude that there are real objects corresponding to them. Therefore, no experience, however self-convincing, can possibly establish that God or any other religious object exists. Thus, as Ronald Hepburn summarizes the situation:

> There seems no way, at the *experiential level,* of settling the really urgent questions, most of all the following: Do we have in theistic experience *mere* projection? Or do we have a projection matched by an objectively existing God?[55]

Given this reading of the problem, the debate concerning the validity of religious experiences appears not to have moved much beyond the kind of impasse which George Bernard Shaw recorded in *St. Joan*:

> Joan: I hear voices telling me what to do.
> They come from God.
>
> de Baudricourt: They come from your imagination.
>
> Joan: Of course; that is how the messages of God come to us.[56]

These are stock responses. Hepburn and St. Joan both illustrate an all too-common stalemate wherein proponents place beyond criticism precisely those claims that opponents seek to place in jeopardy. In order to make any improvement on these tedious terms of discussion, fundamentally new questions are needed. And a new epistemology will need to be fashioned. For this purpose, narrow empiricist appeals to arbitrary paradigm cases of knowledge are stultifying. Uncritical religious appeals to privileged standpoints are no less unsatisfactory.

The contemporary challenge to empirical philosophy of religion

consists in facing squarely the epistemological questions associated
with experiential claims without losing sight of the place of experience
within religion. I am suggesting, therefore, that several avenues need
to be opened in pursuit of William James's aspirations for a new
association of religion with empiricism, leading to "a new era of religion as well as of philosophy." There is, first, the need to move beyond
the tendency to identify experience with some merely subjective or
mental event as if to suggest that experiences in general and religious
experiences in particular take place independently of our interaction
with an environing objective world. The result of this tendency is that
religious experience is automatically assigned a noncognitive status in
which argumentation is irrelevant. A variation of this is the tendency
to treat religious experience as a matter of hearing voices, seeing
visions, or having bizarre and beguiling feelings. Second, and closely
related to the first point, there is the need to see an appeal to religious
experience as more than merely an appeal to an isolated experience or
single occasion by one person having no connections with the ongoing
experiences of one's life, history, and culture. Treated this way, appeals to experience are removed from any possibility of confirmation.
A variation of this is the inverse tendency to treat reports of religious
experience as *nothing but* interpretive products of a person's history,
culture, language, religious background, and so forth. Third, and
most crucially, there is the need for a carefully specified and comprehensive *theory* of experience in terms of which the religious dimension
of experience may be systematically related to an understanding of
the general dimensions of experience.

Implicit in my third point is the proposal that an empirical
approach to the philosophy of religion will recognize that, as John E.
Smith aptly declares, "no appeal to experience is naive, for every such
appeal carries with it a theory of experience, some principle indicating
what experience is and how much it is supposed to contain."[57] Therefore, part of the task of any endeavor to justify theism by appeal to the
nature of experience must include the process of making fully explicit
an interpretive theory of experience. The theory should strive to be
not only coherent and logically consistent, but also applicable and
adequate to the full range of experience. In the formulation of hypotheses, the interpretation of data, and in the extrapolation from
data, an inevitable element of theory attends every empirical inquiry.
But the goal is to formulate a general theory of what is ingredient in
experience and exemplified by it, not to impose an interpretive
scheme on the data of experience.

I began this chapter by pointing out that William James regarded it as "some strange misunderstanding" that empiricism has "hither-

to . . . been associated with irreligion." I am now suggesting that this may be the fault of the particular empiricisms and notions of experience which have arisen, more than it is an indictment of any alliance at all between empiricism and religion. In that case, the chief methodological problem to be faced by an inquiry into the possible empirical justification of theism is the formidable one of first having to deal with the equally challenging question, What is experience?[58] And, as we will see in the next chapter, there is reason to believe with Gadamer that "however paradoxical it may seem, the concept of experience seems to be one of the most obscure we have."[59]

Chapter Two

Shaking the Foundations
of Empiricism

Empiricism as a general philosophical position has become a many-splintered thing. When William James wrote that it was through "some strange misunderstanding" that empiricism had "hitherto been associated with irreligion," he had no way of foreseeing that the classical empiricism he was thinking of would soon give way, not to the radical empiricism he favored, but to logical empiricism, linguistic empiricism, and postpositivistic forms of neopragmatic empiricism. In the course of passing through these cycles, twentieth century empiricism has metamorphosed itself into something else James favored—a pragmatic theory of justification.

I can summarize much of this complex history by calling attention to a fundamental ambiguity in the statement of the empiricist thesis itself. It has been stated both as a "genetic thesis" about the origins of certain beliefs in experience, and as a "justificational thesis" about the proper criteria for testing claims to knowledge at the altar of experience. The genetic thesis assumes that all knowledge originates in and is derived from individual experiences of seeing, hearing, smelling, tasting, or touching. The justificational thesis urges that all knowledge, whatever its supposed source, is ultimately to be tested for its truth, soundness, or acceptability in terms of the evidence supplied by experience, where "experience" is variously construed.

Today, very little remains of empiricism as a genetic thesis. Largely as a result of challenges to it from the methodology and the results of scientific practice, empiricism has been led to reject or severely alter the picture of knowledge as *derived from*, and not just *verified by*, experience. In the work of contemporary empiricists of various stripes, a fundamental shift of interest *away from* concern with origins, causes, and antecedents of knowledge, and *toward* James's own pragmatic concern with consequences, workings, and outcomes has occurred.

But the shift from "genetic empiricism" to "justificational empiricism," as I am calling it, still involves contemporary variants of empiricism in an appeal to experience at some level. And as Alfred North Whitehead noted, "the word 'experience' is one of the most deceitful in philosophy."[1] Not only in ordinary language but also in the various forms of classical empiricism, logical empiricism, linguistic empiricism, and pragmatic or radical empiricism, the appeal to experience is always an appeal to some particular understanding or interpretation of experience. Appeals to experiential origins or to empirical facts are never advanced apart from general assumptions concerning the nature of experience, its scope, character, and ingredients. These assumptions may or may not be explicitly asserted. Where they are not made explicit and systematically examined, such assumptions tend to operate in unanalyzed and uncriticized ways and are likely to be naive, vague, or dogmatic. Sooner or later it seems that any serious empirical venture needs to confront the task of clarifying and articulating the general theory of the nature of experience it employs, involving some specifications as to the ways in which various aspects of experience are related to one another. For, in the absence of any general theory of the nature of experience, the empirical thesis that all ideas are to be tested by experience tells us very little until the precise meaning of "experience" is determined.

In this chapter, therefore, I intend to evaluate critically four forms of philosophical empiricism insofar as they bear on the problems of empirical philosophy of religion. The first three types, classical empiricism, logical positivism, and linguistic empiricism, are, in my view, finally inadequate, but they have the merit of focusing certain issues which need to be weighed very carefully. The fourth type, which can be called "neopragmatic American empiricism," represents a recovery and continuation of the pragmatic criterion James helped to introduce, and it has, I believe, important implications not previously explored for religious epistemology. But, as I will argue later in Chapter Three, none of these four variants of empiricism goes as far as radical empiricism in breadth and adequacy to actual experience.

David Hume and Classical Empiricism

Any discussion of the history of modern empiricism begins with the school of British empiricists, principally Locke, Berkeley, and

Hume. My attention here is on the thought of David Hume, in whom classical empiricism found its most influential expression. Hume's reading of the nature of experience shows up initially in the three rules that he enunciated in the *Treatise* and that, following Marjorie Grene's division, may be called: (1) the Genetic Principle; (2) the Atomistic Principle; and (3) the Associative Principle.[2]

The Genetic Principle

The first rule Hume stipulated in the *Treatise* concerns the origin of experience. This is the principle that "all our simple ideas in their first appearance are derived from simple impressions, which are correspondent to them, and which they exactly represent."[3] If all the contents of the mind are derived ultimately from experience, perceptions (or the mind's contents in general) may be analyzed as of two kinds: impressions (the immediate data of experience, such as sensations) and ideas (copies or faint images of impressions in reasoning).

This was the general principle with which Hume launched an empiricist assault on what he called "all that jargon which has so long taken possession of metaphysical reasonings and drawn disgrace upon them."[4] The challenge was briskly stated at the end of Section II of the *Enquiry*: "When we entertain, therefore, any suspicion that a philosophical term is employed without any meaning or idea (as is but too frequent), we need but inquire, *from what impression is that supposed idea derived?* And if it be impossible to assign any, this will serve to confirm our suspicion."[5] In this passage and in the frequently quoted "commit it then to the flames" passage at the end of the *Enquiry*, the genetic principle takes on the proportions of a dogmatic dictum for Hume.

Various difficulties arise with Hume's principle that ideas follow from and copy impressions. One is epitomized by the famous missing shade of blue, the case of a person who, by Hume's own account, could imaginatively supply the simple idea of a shade of blue he had never seen. Hume considered this exception to the general maxim "so particular and singular, that 'tis scarce worth our observing."[6] He failed to see that if this exception holds at all, it holds for the entire class of sensations. But once the exception is extended to sound, and to smell, and to all gradations of sensation, it becomes extremely hard to salvage the thesis that perception is prior to thought, at least in the rigid and doctrinaire form in which Hume stated his first rule.

Furthermore, the principle cannot be applied to complex impressions and complex ideas in any straightforward way. Imaginative freedom obviously plays a role here, but Hume restricted imagination

to "compounding, transposing, augmenting, or diminishing" the ma-
terials afforded by sense. In his explanation of how complex impressions and complex ideas are formed, Hume managed to conflate at
least three distinct notions that deserve closer analysis than he gave
them. There is, first, the "manner" or order in which many simples
constitute some one complex impression or idea; second, there is the
reason by which complex perceptions arise; and, third, a mere multiplicity of simples constituting the complex perception in a definite
manner. Concerning the first notion, Hume wrote that "the idea of
time is not deriv'd from a particular impression mix'd up with others,
and plainly distinguishable from them; but arises altogether from the
manner, in which impressions appear to the mind, without making one
of the number."[7] But is the particular "manner" or order of appearance of simples itself a simple idea or impression? Either it is, in which
case we find a final simple idea, or it is not, in which case another
"manner" of composition is required for the original manner, and so
on, indefinitely. The solution to this would be to admit, as Hume did
not, that there can be a novel simple idea conveying the novel "manner," which is not a copy of an impression. Elsewhere in searching for
manners of unity, whereby many simples become one complex impression, Hume found it in "a gentle force which commonly pre-
vails."[8] Other times the elusive "principle of union" was identified
with the chief part of the complex idea of substance.[9] Here it was
unclear whether this principle had to do with "manner" or with "efficacious reason," but in either case it was inconsistent with Hume's
assertion that the idea of substance is nothing but a collection of
simple ideas united by the imagination.

The Atomistic Principle

The second principle of Hume's empiricism involved an atomistic conception of experience. This presupposition was stated drastically in the *Treatise* in a clear but unconvincing passage:

> Whatever is clearly conceiv'd may exist; and whatever is clearly con-
> ceiv'd, after any manner, may exist after the same manner. This is
> one principle . . . . Again, everything which is different, is distin-
> guishable, and everything which is distinguishable, is separable by
> the imagination. This is another principle. My conclusion from both
> is, that since all our perceptions are different from each other, and
> from everything else in the universe, they are also distinct and sep-
> arable, and may be consider'd as separately existent, and may exist
> separately, and have no need of anything else to support their exis-

tence. They are, therefore, substances as far as this definition explains a substance.[10]

What are the implications of this reasoning? First, "different" implies "distinguishable" and "distinguishable" implies "separable." From this it is possible to deduce that "different" also implies "separable." It is, of course, analytically true that "what is different is distinguishable." But the next move is less innocent: "what is distinguishable is separable by the imagination." Here we need to know separable *in what respect?* In thought or in fact? Why should it follow that if *x* and *y* are distinct and separable by the imagination they are also capable of independent existence? If *x* is a geodesic dome and *y* is a polygon, they are separable to the extent that a geodesic dome is not a polygon and a polygon is not a geodesic dome; but we cannot conceive a geodesic dome apart from polygons. It follows that geodesic domes, although distinguishable from polygons, cannot be separated in fact or imagination from polygons. Likewise, perceptions, for all Hume showed, may be really distinct *and* really connected, that is, neither simply identified nor simply separated.

But there is an additional reason for not concluding with Hume that because all our perceptions are different they are therefore separate and capable of independent existence. This principle appears to collide with Hume's own way of distinguishing impressions from ideas in terms of his force-and-vivacity criterion. In the passages in which Hume described all perceptions as divided into impressions and ideas by the superior "force and vivacity" of impressions, it turns out that the absolute distinctness and separateness of our perceptions is very blurred indeed. Hume tells us that "those perceptions, which enter with most force and violence, we may name *impressions* . . . ," and "by the term 'impression' . . . I mean all our more lively perceptions . . ."[11] Now if we ask, more forceful and lively than *what*, the answer is of course *ideas*. How are ideas described? They are "less forcible and lively," as the "faint images of [impressions] in thinking and reasoning."[12] In other words, ideas are described *in terms of* other perceptions. If experience consists of atomistic, solitary impressions, how can the force-and-vivacity criterion as a means of discriminating perceptions from one another be intelligibly applied? Furthermore, if ideas are a faint image of impressions, it is inconsistent to hold that they require nothing else in order to exist. Hume allowed that we may be unsure in particular cases whether a perception meets or fails to meet the criterion of difference between impressions and ideas. But to be unsure of this means that we must be able to compare the perception in question with other perceptions. To do that we must view it *in relation to* other perceptions if we are even to attempt to apply the force-and-vivacity criterion to our perceptions. On Hume's own principles, therefore, perceptions, far from being isolated and discrete from other perceptions, cannot even exist without other perceptions.

The Associative Principle

The third major principle of Hume's empiricism concerns the association of ideas:

> The qualitites from which this association arises, and by which the mind is, after this manner, conveyed from one idea to another, are three, *viz. resemblance, continguity* in time or place, and *cause* and effect.[13]

In Hume's view, all reasoning in matters of fact, as contrasted with relations of ideas, is causal inference. "All reasonings concerning matters of fact," he said, "seem to be founded on the relation of cause and effect. By means of that relation alone we can go beyond the evidence of our memory and senses."[14] But Hume discovered, in employing his principle of atomism, that the concept of cause is neither *a priori* necessary nor required by immediate evidence. In focusing on those parts of experience that are most clearly perceived, Hume could find no element of causality. Impressions of sensation were free-floating qualitites that became attached to entities in the external world only by practice, custom, or habit. (However, they *were* attached to the mind or "soul." Hume thought that impressions of sensations arise "in the soul originally, from unknown causes."[15])With respect to the notion of causation, Hume then invited us to

> [s]uppose two objects to be presented to us, of which the one is the cause and the other the effect; it is plain that, from the simple consideration of one or both these objects, we never shall perceive the tie by which they are united, or to be able certainly to pronounce, that there is a connection betwixt them. It is not, therefore, from any one instance, that we arrive at the idea of cause and effect, of a necessary connection, of power, of force, of energy, and of efficacy.[16]

It follows, Hume concluded, that no single impression of necessary connection occurs and, thus, that there is no way of deriving an idea of such a connection from impressions at all (since the mere diachronic repetition of similar impressions adds nothing more in the way of experiential content). In that case, no representation of a causal connection as anything more than a mere constant conjunction and temporal succession can arise from or be grounded in experience. Hume's writings contained the rudiments of a theory of "habit" or "custom" and of an active "faculty of imagination," which all did heroic service in filling gaps in our conceptual resources.

Yet, it may be argued, Hume's explanation of causality in terms of custom, habit, and repetition does not fare well with the experienced facts. Why, for example, do our eyes blink when a bright light is beamed at them? The physiological explanation, shorn of its technical details, is well known: a spasm of neuromuscular excitement is transmitted along nerves to some nodal center, and a responding nervous impulse causes the contraction of the eyelids. There is no need here to refer to impressions of sensations or ideas. The account can be made wholly in causal terms. Moreover, we are inclined to describe our experience in directly causal terms by saying such things as "the light *made* me blink; I felt it."

Hume would find no impression of *making*; there are just the flash and the blink, and what we actually feel is our *habit* of blinking after flashes. Even granting this, and ignoring cases in which newborn babies, who have not developed the acquired habit, react to a bright light in the same way, there are serious difficulties with Hume's explanation. How can a habit be felt when a cause cannot? Is there any more immediacy in the feeling of a habit than in the feeling of a cause? The feeling of a habit, after all, is not the perception of something that is there as a spatial object; it is not an impression of sensation, as Hume freely admitted. The formation of a habit requires time; and the feeling of a habit requires memory, that is, the feeling of the conformation of the present to the past. How is it different from a cause? Hume would have us confuse a habit of feeling blinks after flashes with something quite different—the *feeling* of the habit of feeling blinks after flashes. But Hume's dogma about the acausal nature of experience was not to be so easily upset by a mere appeal to direct experience.[17]

Hume's major difficulty with cause and effect was that it lies "beyond the immediate impressions of our memory and senses."[18] In other words, this manner of connection is not given in any impression. Thus, the basis of the idea of causation was to be traced to the repetition of impressions. But repetition, too, lies "beyond the immediate impressions of our memory and senses." Even if we allow with Hume mere succession or repetition as the only kind of connective tissue in experience, this, too, requires, on Hume's own terms, some corresponding impression. A repetition of impressions is not the same thing as an impression of a repetition of impressions. Habit, repetition, and cause all appear to be in the same boat: they either sink or swim together.

There is a further objection to Hume's view that causal feelings are produced by the association of well-marked perceptions occurring in certain patterns. If this were the case, inhibitions of clear-cut perceptions should be accompanied by a diminution of causal feelings. But just the opposite occurs in human experience. A blindfolded, sensory-deprived adventure in the forest is apt to leave us fantastically prey to feelings of causal operations around us. And in the dim twilight zone between sleep and wakefulness, we regularly sense a vague and enveloping world of causal influences. Nor are these causal feelings exclusively related to the presence of human consciousness. At the level of submammalian organisms where the clarity and variety of sensory perceptions are lacking, causality is not diminished. A jellyfish advances and withdraws, exhibiting some dim perceptivity of its causal relationships with an environing world. A plant grows downward to water and upward to sunlight.[19]

The criticisms advanced above all serve to suggest that Humean empiricism was not *empirical enough*. From the standpoint of radical empiricism, Hume presented a nonempirical doctrine of experience. John Dewey made the point in a vivid way:

> [T]raditional accounts have not been empirical, but have been deductions, from unnamed premises, of what experience *must* be. Historic empiricism has been empirical in a technical and controversial sense. It has said, Lord, Lord, Experience, Experience; but in practice it has served ideas *forced into* experience, not *gathered from* it.[20]

Dewey went on to delineate the principal differences between classical empiricism and his own conception of experience in an important but frequently overlooked article entitled "The Need for a Recovery of Philosophy." His specific criticisms of the tradition to which Locke and Hume gave rise can serve as a convenient summary description of classical empiricism's theory of experience. In the first place, Dewey charged, experience was identified with *knowledge*, leading to a virtual "industry of epistemology."[21] Second, it was primarily associated with "inner" or psychical or *mental content*, as though infected throughout by "subjectivity." Third, experience was either confined to a "bare present" or enmeshed in a *passive registration* of what has taken place in a spectator-consciousness. Fourth, classical empiricism was committed to a *particularism of sense data* whereby all relations and dynamic continuities were supposed to be foreign to experience, mere by-products of dubious validity. Fifth, according to Dewey, experience and *thought* were considered antithetical terms, such that inference was viewed either as invalid or else as a "measure of desperation by which, using experience as a springboard, we jump out to a world of stable things and other selves."[22]

Radical empiricism, in the hands of Dewey, C. S. Peirce, and William James, will dispute these claims at every point. But if Hume's philosophical premises concerning the nature of experience are not particularly persuasive today, his critique of classical theism continues to offer fresh challenges. We need to turn now to a consideration of the relevance of this critique for empirical philosophy of religion today.

Hume's Critique of the Religious Hypothesis

In the eleventh chapter of the *Enquiry*, Hume considered the use of causal arguments in connection with the "religious hypothesis." Here, and at greater length in his masterpiece *Dialogues Concerning Natural Religion*, Hume launched the most powerful criticisms in history against the only religious argument with a claim to an empirical premise—the argument from design. The compact argument presented in the *Enquiry* is noteworthy. Hume's own attitude was put into the mouth of an "Epicurean friend" who delivered an imaginary speech to the Athenians, observing that

> [t]he chief or sole argument for a divine existence is derived from the order of nature . . . You allow that this is an argument drawn from effects to causes. From the order of the work you infer that there must have been project and forethought in the workman. If you cannot make out this point, you allow that your conclusion fails: and you pretend not to establish the conclusion in a greater latitude than the phenomena of nature will justify. These are your concessions. I desire to mark the consequences.[23]

The consequences were twofold. First, it is not permissible, when inferring a particular cause from an effect, to ascribe to the cause any qualities other than those that are required and sufficient to produce the effect. Second, on Hume's premises, it is not permissible to start with the inferred cause and infer other effects besides those already known. In the case of a human artifact we may validly argue that its author possesses certain attributes other than those immediately displayed in the effect. But we may do so, Hume pointed out, only because we are already acquainted with human beings, their attributes and capacities, and ordinary activities. In the case of God, however, this condition does not obtain. We may think that the world as we know it presupposes an intelligent cause, and that we can infer the existence of such a cause. But Hume insisted that we cannot legitimately infer that the cause possesses other attributes, such as moral qualities, or that it can or will produce other effects than those we already know. While it *may* possess other attributes, we cannot know this. And even though metaphysical conjecture may be allowed, it should be recognized as being no more than conjecture. The inference from the natural order to an intelligent designer is uncertain "because the subject lies entirely beyond the reach of human experience."[24] We can establish a causal relation only when we observe constant conjunction. But we cannot observe God at all, and natural phenomena remain what they are regardless what explanatory hypothesis we adopt. The religious hypothesis is one way of accounting for the visible phenomena of the universe, but it is not, Hume insisted, a hypothesis from which metaphysics can deduce any facts other than those which we already know, nor derive from it principles and maxims of conduct. The religious hypothesis, on Hume's terms, is quite useless to metaphysics.

> It is useless because our knowledge of this cause being derived from the course of nature, we can never, according to the rules of just reasoning, return ... from the cause with any new inference, or making additions to the common and experienced course of nature, establish any new principles of conduct and behavior.[25]

In the *Dialogues*, Hume's litany of difficulties in inferring the properties of a divine being from evidence found in the world multiplied even further. The weakness of the analogy from the world as effect to God as cause was exposed in a deft series of dramatic exchanges between the skeptic Philo, the "anthropomorphite" Cleanthes, and the orthodox Demea. Hume so skillfully orchestrated their dialogues that in the end the careful reader is left with no satisfactory options, not even with Philo's tongue-in-cheek recommendation that "a person, seasoned with a just sense of the imperfections of natural reason, will fly to revealed truth with the greatest avidity."[26] Finding room for God only on the basis of faith, Hume made it clear that the skeptic and the fideist stand together against rational theology. At most, one may perhaps conclude that "the whole of natural theology ... resolves itself into one simple, though somewhat ambiguous, at least undefined proposition, that the cause or causes of order in the universe probably bear some remote analogy to human intelligence."[27] The problem for the theist, in the aftermath of

Hume's brilliant maneuvers, was to show that order and creativity in the world are neither mere effects on the one hand, requiring a dubious argument to an inferred "cause," nor wholly autonomous on the other hand, rendering reference to "God" unnecessary.

But the traditional moves were all greatly hampered, if not completely blocked, by Hume. If we accept his general empirical principle that our ideas reach no further than our experience, how do we characterize that which, being ultimate, is both nonhuman and superhuman? What terms will be used? And on what basis? Cleanthes's anthropomorphic inferences, if consistently followed, lead to the embarrassing consequences that Philo was quick to note. But if we ignore experience altogether, as offering not even a clue as to the divine character, we have only Demea's "arbitrary suppositions" about an infinite and incomprehensible deity. Both Demea's theological agnosticism, with its complacently pessimistic view of the miseries and terrors of life, and Cleanthes's teleological argument for the infinite God of classical theism, with its anthropomorphically proportioned conclusions, play into the hands of Philo's skeptical reading of the limited and ambiguous nature of the evidence.

The valid and permanent contribution of Hume's empiricism is its enduring constraint on idle speculation. Above all, in the *Dialogues* Hume showed, unanswerably, that if we start with this world of experience, there is no way to get to where religious orthodoxy comes out. Specifically, there is no way from human experience to a *Wholly* Other. In fact, Hume might have scored this particular point even more easily; it should be a simple matter of logic to conclude that there cannot possibly be more than one world. If we postulate a Wholly *N. B* Other, or two worlds, they could only be two in virtue of some difference. But a difference already implies a relationship, a connection, and presupposes other connections, so that they make up, after all, one world.

We may therefore safely reject any notion of absolute transcendence. Do we do so on the basis of an empirical principle of any kind? Yes, in the sense that we can exclude any metaphysical conception which does not in some way refer to and characterize what we experience. But no, in the sense that this rejection is not based on an empirically demonstrable principle. For there is no positive way to confirm from within experience that there is nothing that transcends experience absolutely. Anyone who claims that there is *no* reality beyond the world of experience must appeal to a ground other than experience itself.

But rejection of absolute transcendence still leaves much room for theological debate. To the extent that the debate is informed by the contemporary and historical experience of the reality of evil, it will proceed with a clear acknowledgment of the problem forcefully posed by Hume's construction of the following logical trilemma: (1) that God is all-good or omnibenevolent; (2) that God is all-powerful or omnipotent; and (3) that evil of some kind or in some form is real or exists. One may affirm any two of these three assertions consistently with one another, but the addition in any case of the third plunges one immediately into self-contradiction. To avoid self-contradiction, one of the three assertions must be abandoned. By rejecting or redefining the attribute of "omnipotence," for example, a first step could be taken toward a conception of God that is both more coherent and more adequate to experience than either Cleanthes's anthropomorphic deity or Demea's infinite and incomprehensible deity.

This is, in fact, the direction many modern philosophers and theologians have taken in developing the possibility of a finite theism, involving a conception of divinity as only one power among others, not the only power existent. The main support for the hypothesis of finite theism is the possibility of a coherent explanation of the experience of evil. At the same time, it is a hypothesis consistent with the scientific theory of evolution, with the findings of the physical sciences concerning the nature of the material world, and with empirical knowledge of the world in which opposition and struggle, possibility and limitation, are exhibited throughout experience.

Interestingly, Hume allowed Cleanthes to raise the possibility of a nonfinite deity at the beginning of Part XI. For a moment, it appeared that a new and fourth position was about to be introduced in the *Dialogues*. However, it was an option that was never clearly developed or carefully considered. Philo's strenuous objections intervened as soon as Cleanthes invited his opinion "of this new theory." Since Part XI of the *Dialogues* is commonly interpreted as an expression of Hume's opinion that the facts of human misery and suffering and natural disasters count against even the hypothesis of a God finite in power, it may be well to reexamine the objections Philo made. In critically considering them, I find that not only are each of the four points comparatively weak, but they also depend upon smuggling in a presupposition of omnipotence. The hypothesis Philo was rejecting is, in the last analysis, only a small variation on the traditional theme of Almighty Power, First Cause, Architect of Nature.

That this is so is apparent in the first of the four circumstances Philo cited as counting against Cleanthes's modest "new theory." The capacity for pain, Philo complained, has been built into life unnecessarily, when pleasure alone could have sufficed nicely for self-preservation. "Men pursue pleasure as eagerly as they avoid pain; at least, they might have been so constituted," Philo concluded.[28] The implication is that a finite deity is *ex hypothesi* capable of so constituting creatures that the capacity for pain might easily have been eliminated from the "contrivance or economy of the animal creation." But this presupposes an incoherent view of divine power as unilaterally capable of effecting any conceivable state of affairs. The problem with a conception of divine power as unilateral power is that it is in principle impossible, on the very definition of power as a relational concept, for one being to have the unilateral power to completely determine the constitution of a multiplicity of other actual beings. To suppose a deity capable of so acting as to eliminate all pain, Philo must dispense with any supposition of genuine freedom of self-constitution on the part of a multiplicity of creatures distinct from the deity. This would be, frankly, to embrace some form of metaphysical monism, which neither Philo nor Hume intended.

Second, Philo ascribed to a finite deity the power of "conducting of the world by general laws." He asked, "might not the Deity exterminate all ill, wherever it were to be found, and produce all good, without any preparation or long progress of causes and effects?" Again, the very framing of such a question presupposes a version of absolute or nonrelational power which is intrinsic to the standard notion of omnipotence but which is not at all appropriate to finite theism. If, indeed, no "long progress of causes and effects" were required in order to produce good, it could only be on the condition that omnipotent power is the *sole* power there is, a condition that is incompatible with the independent power of the other actual entities which, far from being "effects" of divine omnicausality, could at best be mere "modes" of it. More leniently, Philo went on to say he would even settle for a few less stringently applied regularities of nature. Why, after all, should not even a deity of finite power see to it that ships whose purposes were salutary to society might always meet with fair winds, that good leaders enjoy sound health and long life, that persons of power and authority be favored with good temper and virtuous dispositions—at least a little more often? "A few such events as these," he pointed out, "regularly and wisely conducted, would change the face of the world." No doubt Philo was right. Even such modest requests would be reasonable ones to make of a deity who established the uniform laws of nature in the first place, or one who, as Philo further added, "knows the secret springs of the universe," or one who could be credited with having the "particular volitions" which Philo also presumed, or finally, one whose power was sufficient to "turn all these accidents to the good of mankind and render the whole world happy." But what is this, it may be asked, if not another disguise for a version of omnipotence, omniscience, and unilateral power, and thus not truly an alternative theory of finite theism at all?

Third, Philo complained of the "great frugality with which all powers and faculties are distributed to every particular being." But this point only serves as an objection against theistic finitism on the supposition that deity could, in principle, be so generously distributive of powers and faculties that the failure to do so shows a clear lack of goodness, taste, or thoughtfulness. Here it was Philo's explicit adoption of the notion that "the Author of Nature is inconceivably powerful," which betrayed his failure to consider seriously a genuine form of theistic finitism. Furthermore, in pressing this third objection to the hypothesis of a deity who "is supposed great, if not inexhaustible," Philo's anthropomorphic analogies to "a rigid master" and "an indulgent parent" compare suspiciously with Cleanthes's earlier arguments rather than with any new or alternative hypothesis. If a finite God were still able, in Philo's words, "to have created fewer animals, and to have endowed these with more faculty for their happiness and preservation," then this is a picture quite at odds with the evolutionary, finitistic form of theism which Philo was purportedly considering.

The fourth circumstance that Philo counted against an alternative hypothesis was "the inaccurate workmanship of all the springs and principles of the great machine of nature." Citing instances of excess and defect in the physical order of nature, Philo argued that these facts across the whole range of human experience were perhaps compatible with, but certainly not grounds for inferring, the existence of a finite deity. He caustically suggested that "one would imagine that this grand production has not received the last hand of the maker; so little finished is every part, and so coarse are the strokes with which it is executed." This point is closer to the mark. Indeed, why should we suppose it to be finished, or even finishable? Furthermore, why should we suppose, even on the hypothesis of a finite theism, any "maker" in the sense in which Philo evidently associated it with a first cause and especially with a temporally antecedent act of creation?

Assuming the possibility of a theism modified in light of the facts of experience, the evolutionary character of nature, and the relational conception of power, there is no reason to suppose, as Hume did throughout Part XI, that it would entail the notions of unilateral power, or of creation *ex nihilo*, or of first cause. Each of these notions makes escape from the logical trilemma virtually impossible except by way of denying the genuineness of evil.

Nevertheless, even a modified theism will need to come to terms with the warning which Hume issued in the end of Part XI that: " . . . the bad appearances, notwithstanding all my reasonings, may be compatible with such attributes as you suppose; but surely they can never prove these attributes." Very emphatically, this is still the most effective logical objection to any form of finite theism. A finite deity may possibly be *consistent* with the observed evidence, but mere nonabsurdity gives no grounds for its valid *inference* or acceptance.

Despite Hume's argument in the *Dialogues*, even in Part XI, a modified finite theism may yet be tenable. To show this, however, it would be necessary to add a fourth speaker to the *Dialogues Concerning Natural Religion*. But the missing voice is not to be found among Hume's twentieth century spiritual descendants, the logical positivists.

A.J. Ayer and Logical Positivism

Perhaps the only time in this century when a substantial number of philosophers were able to agree on important issues was during the heyday of the movement of logical positivism, from roughly the 1930s to the mid-1950s. Originating in the famed Vienna Circle and fueled by the emigration to England and America of some of its key figures, logical positivism promised to put philosophy on a truly scientific footing. First among its priorities was the elimination of metaphysics through the logical analysis of language. Statements purporting to deal with some transcendental reality, or being in itself, were to be regarded as cognitively meaningless because they failed to admit, even in principle, of verification.

In 1936, with the first edition of A.J. Ayer's *Language, Truth and Logic*, the creedal formulas of logical positivism were aggressively revealed. Verification was the key to the kingdom of cognitive significance, and it could be unlocked only by two varieties of statements: logical and factual. Logically meaningful assertions were analytic; that is, true under any circumstances by virtue of considerations of language alone. Factually meaningful assertions were synthetic; that is, verified or falsified according to specific empirical procedures. Metaphysical assertions did not seem to fit neatly into either the analytic or the synthetic category. They were banished to the limbo of "expressive" and "emotive" noncognitive meaning. So too was theology, which suffered its "pseudo-synthetic" fate in common with ethics and aesthetics. Ayer was blithely able to report:

> Thus we offer the theist the same comfort as we gave the moralist. His assertions cannot possibly be valid, but they cannot be invalid either. As he says nothing at all about the world, he cannot justly be

accused of saying anything false, or anything for which he has insufficient grounds . . . The point which we wish to establish is that there
cannot be any transcendent truths of religion. For the sentences
which the theist uses to express such 'truths' are not literally significant.[29]

Logical positivism attempted to outlaw and avoid inferences
from the structure of language to the structure of the world. At the
same time, however, it seemed to offer a theory of a world ultimately
composed of "sense-data." In order to account for the logic of expressions about material objects, for example, Ayer thought he had to
embrace phenomenalism, the view that sensations are the stuff from
which we "construct" matter. To the extent that it presupposed Humean sensationalism, logical positivism employed a theory of experience that simply assumed that "perception" or "experience" is adequately defined in terms of "sense-data" and the supposed simple and
clear-cut deliverances of the standard five senses. It was this linking of
empiricism with sensationalism which, more than anything else, made
it implausible to regard religious claims as cognitively meaningful. In
this respect, logical positivism managed to move only a short distance
from the empiricism of Locke and Hume and the insistence that every
word which has cognitive meaning must have a sensible reference.
Whenever the verification principle, in any of its formulations, was
invoked against putatively assertive religious claims, it was a demand
to know what fact or facts there are in the sensible world that would
verify (or falsify, or confirm) the proposition in question. Any statement in which the term "God" occurred could be predictably analyzed
as either (1) factually significant, or (2) vacuous, where the "facts" or
"state of affairs" or "observations" that could be cited as evidence were
defined exclusively in terms of sense experience. Lacking any sense
experience to verify or falsify assertions about "God," theistic claims
could not count as (1) factually significant, and therefore could only
be considered (2) cognitively vacuous.

The difficulties that logical positivism encountered in formulating a satisfactory version of the verification criterion of meaning are
well-known and have been recounted many times.[30] Ayer's preface to
the second edition (1946) of *Language, Truth and Logic* pointed to the
chief problem on which logical positivism foundered, the nature of
verifiability. Ayer distinguished a "strong" verifiability principle, according to which a proposition was meaningless unless it could conclusively establish its truth, and a "weak" principle, which required only
that observation should be "relevant" to the determination of a proposition's truth or falsity. But once having conceded this much, due

largely to inconveniences the original principle posed for scientific theory and practice, Ayer had to acknowledge that the "strong" sense of the verifiability principle ruled out all but "basic" propositions, and yet in its "weak" sense it was not sufficiently restrictive, since experiences were certainly "relevant" to some metaphysical propositions. In short, the problem for logical positivism was how to avoid throwing the scientific baby out with the metaphysical bathwater. Once the plug was pulled on metaphysics, science threatened to leak away too. But if science was not to go down the drain, metaphysical statements of unrestricted generality would not, in principle, be washed up either.

The Verification/Falsification Challenge to Theism

The eventual demise of logical positivism is often cited by philosophers of religion as sufficient reason to regard verificational analysis as dated and not worth taking seriously. On the contrary, it seems to me that empirical philosophy of religion still has important and unfinished business with the verification/falsification challenge to theism.

Despite its well-documented deficiencies, the verificational program for establishing factual, and, more broadly, cognitive meaningfulness, is difficult to dispose of. Any empirical justification of theism, if such be possible, requires an appeal to some version of the verification/falsification principle with which contemporary empiricists have grappled. Although Alvin Plantinga and others may regard verificationism as nothing more than a flash in the old theological pan, I contend that the serious challenge of verificationism yet persists for any philosopher of religion who engages the questions of the meaningfulness and of the truth or falsity of religious language and belief.

The positivists' division of cognitively meaningful statements into those that are either analytic or synthetic may be criticized as dogmatic, restrictive, and dichotomous, but it is by no means yet clear how theists might successfully navigate this new version of Hume's fork and still defend the cognitive significance of religious beliefs. If a statement cannot be said to be either analytic or synthetic, we may wonder just what kind of statement it is. According to the positivists, such statements are "pseudo-synthetic," having no cognitive meaningfulness, *i.e.*, not capable of being either true or false. Omitting the pejorative connotation of "pseudo-synthetic," we are left with a category remarkably close to what theologians have called "symbolic language." But to rest there, or to point to postpositivist developments that recognize the diversity of (nonassertive) functions peformed by religious language, is only to forfeit the cognitive significance of religious language and to retreat into some noncognitivist theory, which itself presumes the legitimacy of the synthetic/analytic distinction. If religious language is held to be irreducibly symbolic, then there is no way of showing any of it to be cognitively significant, and there is an insuperable problem as to how anyone could ever learn such language in the first place. Or, if religious language is held to have some kind of cognitive meaning other than the analytic/synthetic kind, anything spelled out by way of a third category becomes problematic insofar as it is different from the scientific truth claims that are so widely taken to be the paradigms of cognitive meaning. On the issue of *cognitive* meaning, therefore, we indeed seem to be restricted to something like the general categories of the analytic and the synthetic. Furthermore, if our interest centers on a possible *empirical* justification of religious belief, we may bracket consideration of the role of analytic claims in theological or metaphysical statements. We are left, then, firmly impaled on one side of Hume's fork. At *some* point at least *some* of the claims found in any given theistic system must be synthetic or empirical claims.

The fact that earlier versions of the verification principle have gone by the wayside does not, I submit, warrant the conclusion that the use of any or all notions of confirmation as a standard of factual meaningfulness have been subjected to completely crippling criticisms. On the assumption that the verificationists, thought hampered by an inadequate notion of the nature of experience, were on the right track in demanding a statement of the circumstances that would count for or against the cognitive meaningfulness of certain theistic claims, I believe it is possible to show one way in which that challenge can be met within one of the variants of contemporary empiricism, that of radical empiricism to be considered in the next chapter.

Here I want only to begin by noting a purely formal requirement. As long as it is agreed that truth or falsity is at stake in religious belief, certain elementary points of logic apply. The truth or falsity of a theistic proposition, for example, must make a difference in the world. Furthermore, the truth or falsity of a cognitively significant theistic assertion must correspond to a difference in *fact*. The state of affairs in which it is true must be different from a state of affairs in which it is false, or else nothing empirical is really being asserted by a theistic proposition. One cannot escape this purely formal requirement as long as the concept of truth (minimally) has to do with what is actually the case. On the surface, then, there should be nothing very controversial about Antony Flew's falsification challenge to theism: "What would have to occur or to have occurred to constitute a disproof of the . . . existence of God?" Flew's valid point is that "to assert that such and such is the case is necessarily equivalent to denying that such and such is not the case."[31] This is only an analytic truth about statements, and it leaves open what particular kind of verification or falsification will do. Flew wants the truth value of assertions about God to be tied to the occurrence or nonoccurrence of possible events, facts, or states of affairs. An assertion which is subject to this kind of empirical testability will bear factual significance, because its truth or falsity can be known to make a difference, a difference which is discernible in the evidence which is used as a measure of its truth.

But this still tells us nothing about what a "fact" is or what are to be taken as those facts which comprise the domain of the empirical. It also gives us no reason to require that the "facts," "state of affairs," or "possible events" in terms of which any proposition should "make a difference in the world" must be relevant to actual or possible *sense-perception* as proposed by logical positivism.

The basic question concerns establishing a criterion by which factuality or cognitive significance can be measured. All talk of cognitivity in religious language is dependent on the determination of standards of factuality. But this is not ascertainable by purely empirical means. Specification of such standards is a properly philosophical matter, calling for argumentation in philosophical terms, not merely in canons carried over from science or common sense. Otherwise, the proposal of standards of factuality can be little more than an earnest stipulation, an arbitrary convention, or a dogmatic claim. The full justification of any set of criteria for cognitive or factual significance will involve the justification of the standards or norms devised to provide the test of cognitivity or factuality.

The task of coming up with an adequate version of the test of whether a statement has factual meaning has occupied analysts for decades. The falsifiability challenge associated with Karl Popper and Antony Flew and the translatability challenge advanced by logical positivists such as Ayer and Carnap appealed to some version of a confirmability criterion of cognitive significance. Their assumption was that if a sentence is to be cognitively significant (*i.e.*, if it is to function to assert facts, if it is to be capable of being either true or false) then it must stand in certain confirmation relations to certain basic observation sentences. That is, for any cognitively significant statement there will be basic observation sentences that provide evidence either for or against the statement.

Is the confirmability criterion of cognitive significance an acceptable criterion? Many difficulties have been thought to be involved in any attempt to formulate this criterion in a precise fashion.[32] By all acknowledgment, a precisely formulated confirmation criterion of cognitive meaningfulness has not been achieved. Many have rejected the confirmability criterion either because it is too unrestrictive, and admits as cognitively significant sentences that it would be generally agreed do not function to assert anything, or because it is too restrictive, and excludes from the class of cognitively significant utterances sentences that it is generally agreed are cognitive in nature. However, it can be shown that all of the objections directed against various atempts to formulate a confirmability criterion of cognitive significance turn out to be nothing but objections to the particular *ways* of analyzing the concept of empirical verifiability implicitly contained in such formulations to date. The concept of empirical verifiability has not itself been shown inexplicable in principle by any of these objections to specific ways of formulating its criteria. The conclusion to draw from past failures is not that the confirmability criterion is impossible to formulate satisfactorily, but that a satisfactory account of the notion of empirical confirmation has not yet been given.

Following Wesley Salmon's contribution to the discussion in an article entitled "Verification and Logic,"[33] I suggest that the confirmability criterion of cognitive significance can be construed as involving the following series of explications:

1. A statement has factual meaning if and only if it is empirically verifiable or confirmable.
2. A statement has formal meaning if and only if it is either analytic or self-contradictory.
3. A statement has cognitive meaning if and only if it has either formal meaning or factual meaning.
4. A statement is either true or false if and only if it has cognitive meaning.

According to Salmon, these explications identify cognitive meaningfulness with the possibility of being either true or false, and they reduce these properties to empirical verifiability and analyticity (or self-contradiction). He pointed out, however, that "there remain the tasks of explicating empirical verifiability and analyticity."[34] In other words, it is now crucial to distinguish between two issues: first, how the notion of empirical confirmation is itself to be analyzed and, second, whether confirmability in terms of basic observation sentences should be taken as a criterion of cognitive significance. Salmon's able defense of the reasonableness of employing empirical verifiability, properly analyzed, as a criterion of cognitive significance is a strong deterrent against the philosophically premature assumption that the concept of empirical verifiability is inexplicable in principle. He notes correctly that "many philosophers who have had little hesitation in dismissing the possibility of formulating an unobjectionable explication of cognitive meaningfulness in terms of empirical verifiability would be far more hesitant to conclude that the concepts of scientific confirmation and confirmability are inexplicable in principle."[35] Philosophers of religion, I would add, need not be at all hesitant to accept the general idea of a confirmability criterion of cognitive significance.

This still leaves us, however, with the critical task of explicating the nature and role of "basic observation statements" as part of a precisely formulated confirmability criterion of cognitive significance. Here, too, the major controversies that stalled this discussion for many years need not be taken as invalidating the task itself. Two familiar alternatives for the role of basic observation statements have been proposed by philosophers, neither of which has been completely successful. Those who have viewed the nature of verification as a public procedure, an intersubjectively checkable operation, have tended to favor, with Otto Neurath and Rudolf Carnap, the selection of physicalistic sentences as basic observation sentences. These consist either of everyday statements about physical objects or statements formulated in the technical language of physics and the other sciences. The disadvantage of this approach when applied to religious language, however, is that such physicalistic sentences are predictably used to challenge, rather than to confirm, claims to religious knowledge which are typically viewed, by comparison, as private and incurably subjectivistic.

The other alternative has been to select pure first-person phenomenalistic statements about one's own sensations or raw feels. But this second approach has the defect that the raw feels are construed as private inner mental events to which one has logically privileged access and which are described without reference to anything external or public. In the end, phenomenalism was driven toward a behavioristic interpretation of mental acts, and this move has proved inadequate for an analysis of intentional statements.

Needless to say, the selection of the class of basic observation statements presupposes some fundamental philosophical decisions. The prevailing options have tended to generate a rather oversimplified understanding of basic observation statements either according to phenomenalism, as accounts of the sensual experience of a knowing subject, or according to physicalism, as reports concerning the physical states of the universe. With the waning of positivism by the late 1950s, many concluded that traditional empiricism had failed because it depended on the availability of a pure observation language, which had in fact proved unavailable; and that falsification had failed, because it had effectively rendered all theory advance impossible, if strong, or, if weak, had been arbitrary, self-destructive, or ineffectual. From the perspective of postpositivistic empiricism and philosophy of science, earlier philosophical efforts to formulate an acceptable empiricist criterion have depended too heavily upon an epistemologically privileged and narrow choice of the class of sentences that were to be taken as the basic observation sentences. The progressive questioning of the empiricist thesis within successive cycles of analytic philosophy has ended by blurring all the distinctions positivists presupposed—between the analytic and the synthetic, percepts and concepts, theory and observation.

Linguistic Empiricism

When twentieth century empiricism took a sharp linguistic turn, it plunged into a new method of analysis which promised to untie old conceptual knots. The linguistic turn in philosophy found its inspiration and plausibility in the fact that primary intellectual experience is indeed linguistic throughout. Conscious reflection begins with a world already formulated, already sorted out into the categories of our institutionalized linguistic habits. The merit of linguistic empiricism was to have recognized this basic fact. The main trouble was not with its admirable analysis of linguistic data but with its dismissal of extralinguistic data from the domain of philosophical attention. Here I will single out only those features of linguistic empiricism which seem to me to have special, and overlooked, relevance to empirical philosophy of religion and to the notion of justification. I mean to call attention to (1) certain methodological deficiencies of this development, and (2) several inconvenient consequences that arise from collapsing the category of "experience" too far into the category of "interpretation."

By and large, linguistic empiricism advanced no explicit general theory of the nature of experience. Rather, its entire methodological drift was to begin with language and a description of its functions and uses, from which experience was secondarily, if at all, to be understood. Implicitly presupposed in this approach was the primacy of language over perception. Emphasis was centered on understanding linguistic phenomena, not any relation between language and experience which may be condensed in language. On the interpretation of virtually the entire analytic tradition, it makes no sense at all to want to compare linguistic formulations with bits of nonlinguistic experience. Philosophy can only compare the way various linguistic items fit together with other linguistic items. Completely undercut by this method was the notion of any such thing as prelinguistic awareness which can serve as any kind of test for the adequacy of linguistic formulations. One severe consequence of thus assuming the primacy of language over perception was the narrowing within linguistic empiricism of the meaning of "experience" to conceptual knowledge, and the tendency to regard even that form of experience as limited to those concepts and distinctions already enshrined in the intricacies of ordinary language.

In a statement designed to express the central aim and underlying assumption of the linguistic turn in philosophy, P. F. Strawson wrote that "the actual use of linguistic expressions remains the philosopher's sole and essential point of contact with the reality he wishes to understand, conceptual reality; for there is the only point from which the actual mode of operation of concepts can be observed."[36] Far from making an insidious attempt to equate reality with concepts, Strawson and other analysts only claimed to be looking for "facts about our concepts" as these are revealed or concealed in language. Eventually, however, the assumption that the reality the philosopher wants to understand is *conceptual* and not also extralinguistic led some critics to complain of a deplorable constriction of interest into which analytic philosophy had fallen. All but eclipsed, for example, was the kind of method Whitehead had in mind when he contended that "the elucidation of immediate experience is the sole justification for any thought; and the starting point for thought is the analytic observation of components of this experience."[37] On the whole, for linguistic empiricism there was no need to separate language from the phenomena which prompt its use, nor to attribute to the latter an original, prepredicative importance around which language, or the abuse of language, then weaves clarifying distinctions or confusing phantoms. But a method whose aim is only to clarify, by analysis of language, whatever meanings and experiences have already found expression through that language is empirical in only a curious way. It is empirical to the extent that it consists in looking at language as it is, rather than supposing what it must be according to some *a priori* scheme, in seeing language as it is actually used in practice, rather than as deduced from preconceived conditions, or as built up from little atoms. But it is unempirical to the extent that, when one looks at language this way, one has to take for granted the world in which one finds all these linguistic activities, contexts, concrete doings and purposes said to *be* language. An empirical approach to language presupposes an unempirical approach to the world.[38]

In this respect, linguistic empiricism stands more in the tradition of Kant than of Hume and presents an interesting example of how contemporary empiricism has worked its way out of "genetic empiricism" and toward "justificatory empiricism" but only by passing through Kant's critical philosophy, transposed into the twentieth century linguistic key. At this stage, Hume's assumption that what we directly experience is only our own sensations has been abandoned, along with the whole positivist machinery of sense data and the atomism and logical scaffolding that went with it.

Psychological introspectionism, in which so much genetic empiricism became entangled, has also been left behind in the shift from the First Person to the Third Person perspective. Analytic philosophy in most of its linguistic phases thus became a protest against the earlier empiricist quest for a touchstone of knowledge in pure, brute, unmediated, nonconceptual, nonlinguistic encounters with reality. It challenged the Humean idea that all our knowledge is *derived from* experience by taking the Kantian line that perception of reality is impossible except relative to conception. Gradually, as doctrines of the ideal language, the given, and the verification theory of meaning receded, the recognition of the relativity of all meaningful talk about the world to linguistic considerations ushered in a kind of linguistic Kantianism. Language itself came to be regarded as embodying a basic conceptual scheme in terms of which the world and all our experience of it are necessarily understood. Language was now seen to play the very role Kant had assigned to the conceiving mind. Just as for Kant there could be no pure perception of reality unmediated by human conceptualization, linguistic empiricism assumed that there can be no nonlinguistic perception of reality. Whereas Kant had located the organizing conceptual manifold through which all experience is filtered in the structure of the human mind, linguistic empiricism saw it as embodied in the very structures of language. Any knowledge of the world was necessarily, not just contingently, relative to some linguistic scheme, and the idea of any direct apprehension of reality was rejected as an impossibility.

Those linguistic philosophers who broke with the earlier positivist practices and beliefs concerning the systematic uniformity of language and who adopted the view that language uses are inseparable from our everyday forms of life, took a partial step toward the data of lived experience. But as long as language was still accorded privileged status as the first order of business, linguistic empiricism promoted the danger of allowing what is valuable only as a means to come to be valued as part of the end. In this respect, the work of John L. Austin is particularly illustrative. According to Austin, "ordinary language is *not* the last word: in principle it can everywhere be supplemented and improved upon and superseded. Only remember, it is the *first* word."[39] Austin himself, however, rarely got beyond the first-word stage. Experience, which was never directly considered in its relation to linguistic expression, was assumed to be structured via language. Increased sensitivity to the logic and complexities of grammar would presumably yield a better understanding of experience. Austin told us:

> When we examine what we should say when, what words we should use in what situations, we are looking again not *merely* at words . . . but also at the realities we use words to talk about: we are using a sharpened awareness of words to sharpen our perception of, though not as a final arbiter of, the phenomena.[40]

Austin claimed that examining "what we should say when" has value as a means of sharpening our perception of the things we talk about. Of course, no one would deny that one's perception may be sharpened and become more discriminating through learning or inventing some *new* way of seeing and describing one's experience, but the method by which Austin sought to sharpen our perception of "the phenomena" was through reminders of the familiar ways in which we *do*, normally, describe them, in the everyday uses of English which have "stood up to the long test of the survival of the fittest."[41] This seems to be one of the least promising ways of sharpening, or indeed altering, our perception of anything. Even the new descriptions Austin himself introduced, such as "performative utterances," "stipulative if," and "illocutionary forces," were descriptions of *word*-uses and *not* of "the realities we use words to talk about." In the final analysis, what Austin sharpened our perception of was grammar. This may be the inevitable result of philosophical fixation upon ordinary language, evident also in Wittgenstein's determination that philosophy "leaves everything as it is."

Linguistic empiricism as it touches upon the study of religious language and belief has been seriously deficient in at least two respects. First, the model of theism invariably selected has been that of traditional theism, with all its attendant metaphysical difficulties. Critics of religious language have been singularly sensitive to the problems and pitfalls involved in metaphysical and theological assertions about "God" and the divine attributes as these are conceived in traditional ontologies. But here they have hardly advanced much beyond the critiques levelled by Hume and Kant two hundred years ago. To say that the entire discussion has proceeded as though the

only conception of "God" currently available is that offered by traditional theism is no exaggeration.[42] In focusing primarily on the picture of God as a being who is beyond the world we experience somewhat as the gardener is beyond his garden (a debasement, incidentally,
of classical theism), analytic philosophers of religion paid no heed to
theistic models that have been developed by schools of process theology or, with a few exceptions, by existentialist theologies. This was
especially ironic in a time when revisionist theologies were appearing
as a direct response to a new historical situation in which the classical
language of faith was widely regarded as either discredited or superseded.

Second, the sensationalist doctine of perception, as reinforced
by logical positivism, continued to be widely adopted, either explicitly
or implicitly, by many philosophers working in the area of the analytic
philosophy of religion. By now, of course, postpositivistic analytic
philosophy has repudiated the central theses of logical positivism.
Quine, for example, has convinced many that there is no way to tell
the difference between a platitude grounded in "experience" and a
"linguistic convention" and thus no point to the analytic/synthetic
distinction. And Wittgenstein, Sellars, Kuhn, and others have so thoroughly challenged the idea that attaching meaning to a sentence requires knowing what sensations would confirm or disconfirm it that
by now the abusive use of "meaningless" should itself be philosophically meaningless. Even so, several generations of analysts were still
able to take for granted something like the verifiability theory of
meaningfulness and nowhere more so than in regard to the treatment
of religious language. As John Passmore pointed out, "'Positivism is
dead,' so they say. Rightly, too, [save] where it touches religion."[43] The
residues of logical positivism, and its dependence upon Humean sensationalism, can still be found lurking in linguistic empiricism's challenges to the cognitive meaningfulness of religious language.

Religious Language and Justification

With the advent of the linguistic turn in philosophy, and as the
puzzlement over the cognitive significance of religious language was
found to have few resolutions, many philosophers of religion turned
to a study of the diversity of functions performed by religious language. Primarily it was Wittgenstein's theory of meaning as use, designed to counteract positivistic restrictiveness, which was most helpful in enabling philosophers of religion to recognize important
noncognitive uses of religious language. Under the slogans "don't ask

for the meaning, ask for the use," and "every statement has its own logic," investigators succeeded in delineating a host of descriptive, prescriptive, performatory, and expressive contexts in which religious language is used. Religious language was variously described as evoking and expressing self-commitment, or declaring an intention to act in a particular manner, or endorsing a set of moral principles, or proposing a distinctive self-understanding and engendering characteristic attitudes toward human existence. These strictly noncognitive interpretations of religious language, insofar as they purported to cover the entire class of religious assertions, including theistic ones, ran the obvious risk of being reductionistic. If theistic assertions were thus "justified" on the basis of their noncognitive significance, they were nonetheless justified at the expense of having anything to do with stating the truth and expressing facts.

One particular development appeared to unite many diverse proponents of noncognitive theories of justification. In one manner or another, it was commonly agreed that religious assertions functioned characteristically as expressions of a vision of life and that their primary function was to present a way of interpreting life taken as a whole. Rather than beginning in religion with brute facts and concluding to an interpretation of such data, it was generally understood that we begin instead with an interpretation, a way of looking at life and human experience, and any way of moving closer to "the facts" is always through the avenue of interpretation. Thus, with respect to religious attitudes, John Hick developed an account of "experiencing-as," Donald Evans of "looking-on," and Ian Barbour of "interpreting-as."[44] All acknowledged that there was no sharp line between experience and interpretation. We cannot isolate uninterpreted experience either in the scriptural accounts of particular religions or in the contemporary life of believers. Despite the surface plausibility of this claim, I find it in serious need of supplementation. There has been something altogether too facile about the way in which experience and interpretation have been muddled together by analytic philosophers of religion.

The theory that a primary function of religious language is to present a way of interpreting life is to some extent a development of ideas implicit in Part II of Wittgenstein's *Philosophical Investigations* which was devoted to exploring the phenomenon of visual recognition or "seeing-as . . ." Using the illustration of the duck-rabbit, Wittgenstein pointed out that in either case "we intepret it, and *see it as we interpret it.*"[45] Seeing an object according to an interpretation involves in part noticing a new way of organizing the unchanged material that had not previously been noticed.

> I suddenly see the solution of a picture puzzle. Before, there were branches there; now there is a human shape. My visual impression has changed and now I recognize that it has not only shape and color but also a quite particular 'organization.'

> I meet someone whom I have not seen for years; I see him clearly, but fail to recognize him. I see the old face in the altered one. I believe that I should do a different portrait of him now, if I could paint.[46]

Wittgenstein suggested that "recognition" "seems half visual experience and half thought." "Is it a special sort of seeing? Is it a case of both seeing and thinking? or an amalgam of the two, as I should almost like to say."[47]

Wittgenstein reached no clear or notable conclusions in this analysis. He stated, but did not explain, the opinion that "What I perceive in the dawning of an aspect is not a property of the object, but an internal relation between it and other objects." He also suggested, again without elaboration, that the concept of "experience" is different, though related, in "seeing" and "seeing-as. . . ."[48]

Perhaps the most suggestive contribution of Wittgenstein's discussion was his conclusion that the phenomenon of "seeing-as" is an art that is acquired not by the application of rules but by a kind of inexpressible experience through which one receives a feeling for doing something. It is, in fact, a form of knowledge.

> Can one learn this knowledge? Yes; some can. Not, however, by taking a course in it, but through 'experience.' Can someone else be a man's teacher in this? Certainly. From time to time he gives him the right *tip*.—This is what learning and teaching are like here.—What one acquires here is not a technique; one learns correct judgments.[49]

One application of these insights as they bear upon the problem of religious language was sketched many years ago by John Wisdom. In his influential essay "Gods," Wisdom interpreted belief and nonbelief in divinities as different ways of seeing the world. "What is so isn't merely a matter of the facts."[50] There may be agreement as to "the facts" and yet very different interpretations of them. This was the point of Wisdom's now classic parable of the garden, in which he compared the theist and atheist to two men who, after examining a garden for a long time and agreeing on all "the facts" it contains, nevertheless disagreed as to whether it was being looked after by a gardener.

> The difference as to whether a God exists is more like a difference as to whether there is beauty in a thing . . . Suppose two people are looking at a picture or natural scene. One says 'Excellent' or 'Beautiful' or 'Divine'; the other says 'I don't see it.' He means he doesn't see the beauty. And this reminds us of how we felt the theist accused the atheist of blindness and the atheist accused the theist of seeing what isn't there. And yet surely each sees what the other sees.[51]

Wisdom treated the matter primarily as a difference of attitude, an interpretation which focuses a particular way of "seeing-as." He was concerned to stress the important insight that the patterns in which facts are arranged and the connections that are drawn between them have as much to do with meaningfulness as does the narrower question of establishing the facts.

Wisdom's discussion was elusive, enigmatic, and finally equivocal between a factual or a nonfactual account of religious belief. Other writers associated with the "attitude to life" view took a clearer (and perhaps less nuanced) position in favor of religious faith as a mode of "experiencing-as" or "total interpretation." John Hick, for instance, arrived at the conclusion that things or events can be experienced in a religious way, yet the same things or events can also be experienced in a nonreligious way. Starting from Wittgenstein's discussion of puzzle-pictures, such as the drawing of a cube viewed from below and from above, Hick compared the two "aspects" of such a drawing with the experience of a religious and of a nonreligious person. After extending the *visual* ambiguity of the pictures to *all* the senses for this purpose, Hick then applied this "experiencing-as" not only to drawings but to real life.

> And the analogy to be explored is with two contrasting ways of experiencing the events of our lives and of human history, on the one hand as purely natural events and on the other hand as mediating the presence and activity of God.[52]

The effect of this move, whether or not Hick intended it, seems to be that religion is emptied of any particular content. The difference between a religious and nonreligious person lies in identical facts being experienced differently, like cube-pops.

Hick noticed the difficulty this created. If an event can be "experienced-as" a natural event *or* as an act of God, we need to know how to recognize natural events and acts of God. We also need to know what is the difference between them, for otherwise there is no use in talking in terms of "acts of God" at all. (Or, for that matter, there would be no use in talking in terms of "natural events" either.) Just as to experience the ambiguous cube drawing *as* a cube from above, we need first to have had acquaintance with cubes seen from below, so too, on Hick's analogy, to experience an event *as* an act of God requires *prior* acquaintance with acts of God. But when we try to scrutinize an act of God, we see only an event which *can* be experienced-as an act of God.

Hick's reply to this difficulty seems to me inadequate. He claimed first that there is no such thing as raw experiencing. All experiencing is experiencing-as *something.* If we see a fork we recognize it *as* a fork, or, if we are mistaken, we see it *as* something else. The ability to successfully recognize forks depends upon our having learned to recognize forks at some time. Second, according to Hick, we can analogously "learn to use the concept 'act of God', as we have learned to use other concepts, and acquire the capacity to recognize exemplifying instances."[53]

But the analogy breaks down in ways Hick failed to resolve. "Exemplifying instances" of forks present no difficulty; they can be pointed out straightforwardly. But to see an "act of God" is, in Hick's view, to see "an event experienced-as an act of God." It is impossible to point unambiguously to an "act of God" even after one may have learned "exemplifying instances" of them. There is always the alternative way of experiencing events experienceable-as acts of God, and that is to experience them as natural events. Unlike the case of experiencing an object as a fork, which involves separating it out from its nonfork surroundings, the case of acts of God involves talking of experiencing *everything* as an act of God, again raising the problem about prior understanding. And unlike the case of recognizing a natural event by having our attention drawn to certain regularities and patterns in the events of the world, there is no comparable way of recognizing an act of God as such. Hick's explanation in terms of "experiencing-as" did not in itself get us anywhere. The person who might hope to learn "exemplifying instances" of an act of God is caught in the ironic predicament of those zealous students who underline *every* word in the textbook and are left with nothing in particular to study for the exam.

The analysis of the function of "seeing-as" and the role of interpretation in the religious dimension of experience remains seriously incomplete at this stage. "Experience" cannot so easily be collapsed into forms of "interpretation" and "seeing-as" in philosophy of religion any more than in courts of law. But those who have recommended a theory of religious language along the lines of interpretive activity have made little or no attempt to analyze why it is that one might ever "adopt theistic attitudes," "construe" life religiously, or "interpret" historical events in accordance with a particular religious framework. While it may be the case that a theistic interpretation of life enables one to discern patterns amid the flux, it is clear that one cannot induce oneself to adopt such an interpretation simply in order to possess a more intellectually coherent and emotionally satisfying perspective on the flux of experience and the ambiguities of history. Advocates of the indistinguishable interweaving of experience and interpretation in religion have failed to explain the exact nature of "interpretation" or to spell out more fully what is involved in the phenomenon of "seeing-as," "looking-on," "construing-as," and so forth.

A critical issue in this discussion is whether and to what extent the data of experience exercise any influence on the interpretations. If there is no self-evident, uninterpreted datum of any sort of experience, is there, nevertheless, a distinctive otherness or objectivity to the data? Is interpretation *derived* from experience as much as it is *added* to it? How far can we assume that human interpretations provide reliable evidence of the actual nature of things? Is interpretation sometimes antithetical to objectivity or is it the necessary condition of any experience whatsoever? Are our theories constructed only to satisfy our intellectual and emotional demands or do they in some sense, however problematically, "fit" the nature of the reality they claim to render intelligible? In religion, are we talking equally about concrete immediacies of experience or merely about abstract "picture preferences" and changing *Gestalten?*

These are of course formidable questions. They seem to me to be ones which can no more be readily resolved than they can be easily evaded. At issue, finally, is not simply the question of the relativity of worlds to words, a harmless assumption, generally granted, but the question *how far are we to take this assumption?* Assuming a dialectical relation between experience and interpretation, the problem becomes one of critically incorporating *both* as a paired phenomenon in a theory that does not displace either by the other. No existing models in the study of religion, however, seem capable of giving equal weighting to both extralinguistic and linguistic considerations at the same time. In the past, studies on the subject of religious experience, for instance, and especially of mysticism, tended to minimize the role of the interpretive theory in terms of which certain experiences were judged to be significant, as well as to overlook the conditioning imposed by the particular cultural context in which certain experiences had religious value. This seems no longer to be a clear and present danger.[54] Currently, many scholars are favoring an inverse weighting of the experience-interpretation pairing, coming down so heavily on a recognition of the interpretive element that any delineation of the category of "experience" can only appear arbitrary and contentless. On these terms, it seems virtually impossible to state whether the theology is vindicated by the experience, or the experience by the theology.

From the perspective of radical empiricism, the near collapse of experience into its interpretations is as unempirical as was an earlier disabling antithesis between experience and interpretation. Once experience and interpretation come to be regarded as indistinguishable within the hermeneutical circle, any testing of the one in terms of the other is rendered either very unlikely or extremely precarious. Experience, in the radically empirical sense, can no longer serve as a mute standard for its own description. Either it is relegated to a secondary, derivative status, or it falls out altogether, as an echoing source of acoustical illusion.

The dialectical turns recently traveled within American analytic philosophy, to which I turn now, introduce another, more complicated, chapter in the history of empiricism's attenuation of the category of experience.

Neopragmatic American Empiricism

The story of philosophical empiricism since the seventeenth century can be told in terms of four successive cycles, each representing a wider scope of semantic focus. From preoccupation with ideas, there was a shift to concern with words; from words, there was a shift to sentences and propositions as the primary epistemological unit for grounding empirical knowledge; and from that, semantic attention has lately shifted to consideration of whole conceptual schemes or interpretive frameworks. The fourth cycle of development within the empirical tradition may be termed "neopragmatic" in the sense that it has shed any narrow "empiricist" criteria in favor of broadly defined pragmatic warrants. Long-standing problems with the thesis of "genetic empiricism" about the causal origins of knowledge have been superceded by versions of "justificational empiricism" or theses about the proper criteria for appraising knowledge claims. The only live issues in debates about empiricism now concern the nature, scope, presuppositions, and relative power of the relevant empirical criteria. Increasingly, with the waning of foundationalist epistemology, these have been seen as pragmatic criteria.

In related developments in the philosophy of science, traditional empiricist views have become almost universally discredited under the growing recognition of the "theory-ladenness" of observations. As summarized by Mary Hesse, five points stand out in the new account of natural science being offered by philosophers of science: (1) data are not detachable from theory, for what count as data are determined in the light of some theoretical interpretation, and the facts themselves have to be reconstructed in the light of interpretation; (2) theories are not models externally compared to nature in a hypothetico-deductive schema, they are the way facts themselves are seen; (3) the law-like relations asserted of experience are internal, because what counts as facts are constituted by what the theory says about their interrelations with one another; (4) the language of natural science is irreducibly metaphorical and inexact, and formalizable only at the cost of distortion of the historical dynamics of scientific development and of the imaginative constructions in terms of which nature is interpreted by science; and (5) meanings are determined by theory; they are understood by theoretical coherence rather than by correspondence with facts.[55] Literally, this has meant a shaking of the foundations in philosophy of science.

Within American philosophy during the last twenty-five years or so, a similar shaking down has been going on due to the work of Wilfrid Sellars, W. V. Quine, Donald Davidson, Richard Rorty, and others. The basic stance these authors take with respect to questions of epistemic justification has been characterized as holistic, contextualistic, and historicist. It is, in any case, an introduction of pragmatism into the theory of empirical justification at just the point of most controversy: the consideration of whole conceptual schemes or frameworks as the unit of empirical inquiry. As might be expected, implications here lead in the direction of shaking the foundations in philosophy of religion, too.

In particular, I want to consider three moves which appear in postempiricist American philosophy and which can be traced, respectively, to the work of Sellars, Quine, and Davidson. The first move is toward demythologizing the Myth of the Given, the second dissolves the "two dogmas of empiricism" in the interests of a thoroughgoing holism, and the third discards the dualism of "scheme and content" of knowledge. In tracing out each of these features of recent American philosophy, I am less concerned to present the full story in its painstaking detail than to show the moral that Richard Rorty has recently drawn from his (sometimes) controversial reading of the same sources.

Sellars's Critique of the Myth of the Given

Antifoundationalism in epistemology, which I spoke of in the first chapter, owes much of its inspiration and impetus to Wilfrid Sellars's critique of the notion of the "given" in experience. After his milestone "Empiricism and the Philosophy of Mind,"[56] it has been hard to find many able defenses of the claim that epistemic justification must, or ever can, terminate in some self-authenticating, intrinsically credible, theory-neutral, incorrigible element. Sellars characterized traditional empiricist philosophy as subscribing to the view that there is a structure of particular matter of fact "such that (a) each fact can not only be noninferentially known to be the case, but presupposes no other knowledge either of particular matter of fact, or of general truths; and (b) such that the noninferential knowledge of facts belonging to this structure constitutes the ultimate court of appeals for all factual claims—particular and general—about the world." The trouble with this view, as Sellars showed, was that one could not have observational knowledge of any one fact unless one knew many other things as well.

Any expression of observational knowledge needs to be backed by some assessment of the reliability of the perception itself. But this introduces a whole conceptual network, involving problems such as "standard conditions" of perception, concepts of the objects reported perceived, etc. Observational knowledge carries no privileged status of its own. Specifically, the point Sellars was making was that observational knowledge of any particular fact—for example, that this is green—presupposes that one knows general facts of the form "x is a *reliable symptom* of y." And to admit this means that the traditional empiricist idea that knowledge "stands on its own feet" must be abandoned. Above all, Sellars judged the notion of the "given" to be a misleading myth because of its static character. It rests on a false picture:

> One seems forced to choose between the picture of an elephant which rests on a tortoise (What supports the tortoise?) and the picture of a great Hegelian serpent of knowledge with its tail in its mouth (Where does it begin?). Neither will do. For empirical knowledge, like its sophisticated extension, science, is rational, not because it has a *foundation* but because it is a self-correcting enterprise which can put any claim in jeopardy, though not *all* at once.

In rejecting this picture, Sellars distinguished explicitly between the acquisition of knowledge and the justification of knowledge. He wanted to avoid the confusion between empirical causal accounts of how one comes to have a belief and the separate question of how one justifies a belief one has. Causal antecedents, on Sellars's view, are noncognitive; all awareness is a linguistic affair. This means that there is no such thing as "prelinguistic awareness." Sellars's attack on prelinguistic awareness and the whole notion of intuition was a persuasive attempt to show that "knowledge," that most honorific of terms in the arsenal of epistemology, begins with the capacity to use words and that "not even the awareness of such sorts, resemblances, and facts as pertain to so-called immediate experience is presupposed by the process of acquiring the use of a language." Rather, knowledge of particulars or of concepts is an abstraction from knowledge of propositions, not something temporally prior to it. If knowledge is a relation to propositions, as Sellars urged, rather than a privileged relation to the objects propositions are supposed to be about, then justification of belief is a public and intersubjective matter. "The essential point," Sellars concluded, "is that in characterizing an episode or a state as that of *knowing*, we are not giving an empirical description of that episode or state; we are placing it in the logical space of reasons, of justifying and being able to justify what one says." Justification is, therefore, a public and intersubjective matter. That it is also a holistic and pragmatic affair is most clearly seen in Quine's critique.

Quine and the Two Dogmas of Empiricism

The essay "Two Dogmas of Empiricism"[57] became famous for the way in which it called into question the distinction between synthetic truths and analytic truths, enshrined in the verification theory of meaning. Quine exposed the reductionism that survived in the supposition that individual statements, taken in isolation, could admit of confirmation or infirmation at all. In proposing the countersuggestion that "our statements about the external world face the tribunal of sense experience not individually but only as a corporate body," Quine was shifting the notion of empirical testability away from attention to individual statements and toward whole contexts. Indeed, it seemed that nothing less than "the whole of science" could constitute the basic "unit of empirical significance."

More drastically, Quine extended his critique to the other bulwark of analytic philosophy, the self-evident and necessary character of logic. Here his challenge consisted of denying that any categorical distinction can be drawn between matters of definition and matters of fact. In the case of an alien culture, for instance, how could we possibly tell whether its native speakers assent to propositions of the form "no bachelor is married" because they feel compelled by their language, or simply because they can think of no counterexamples and have encountered no exceptions in their experience? Acording to Quine, allegedly "analytic" truths may merely be those for which no one has yet given us any interesting alternatives that might lead us to call them into question. Assaulting the "folly" of seeking a boundary between synthetic statements, which hold contingently on experience, and analytic statements, which hold come what may, Quine concluded that:

> Any statement can be held true come what may if we make drastic enough adjustments elsewhere in the system. Even a statement very close to the periphery can be held true in the face of recalcitrant experience by pleading hallucination or by amending certain statements of the kind called logical laws. Conversely, by the same token, no statement is immune to revision.

The totality of our so-called knowledge or beliefs is a human fabric which "impinges on experience only along the edges." In Quine's metaphor, total science is a "field of force whose boundary conditions are experience." But the total field is underdetermined by its boundary conditions, experience. This leaves much room for choice as to what statements are going to be reevaluated in the light of any single contrary experience. And it means that "no particular experiences are linked with any particular statements in the interior of the field, except indirectly through considerations of equilibrium affecting the field as a whole."

If Quine is right, the ultimate justification of our beliefs and the ultimate purpose of the total enterprise of science is a pragmatic one: "Each man is given a scientific heritage plus a continuing barrage of sensory stimulation; and the considerations which guide him in warping his scientific heritage to fit his sensory promptings are, where rational, pragmatic." Nowhere is Quine's pragmatic appeal more evident than in the following famous passage which is worth quoting at length:

> As an empiricist I continue to think of the conceptual scheme of science as a tool, ultimately, for predicting future experience in the light of past experience. Physical objects are conceptually imported into the situation as convenient intermediaries—not by definition in terms of experience, but simply as irreducible posits comparable, epistemologically, to the gods of Homer. For my part I do, *qua* lay physicist, believe in physical objects and not in Homer's Gods; and I consider it a scientific error to believe otherwise. But in point of

epistemological footing the physical objects and the gods differ only in degree and not in kind. Both sorts of entities enter our conception only as cultural posits. The myth of physical objects is epistemologically superior to most in that it has proved more efficacious than other myths as a device for working a manageable structure into the flux of experience.

The point is that epistemologically the "myths" (if we choose to call them that) of physical objects and of gods are on the same logical footing. How does the philosopher of science justify such language? How does the scholar of religion justify language about the gods? No *a priori* norms or principles come to the aid here. In neither case can we expect to find justificatory procedures that are anything other than historically evolved conventions. We choose among them according to our various interests and purposes.

Davidson and the Dualism of Scheme/Content

Quine and Sellars suggested reasons for believing that there is no need that there be a single observation language common to all alternative theories. Thomas Kuhn and Paul Feyerabend, from a different direction, gave further reasons for supposing that notions of "truth" and "reference" are relative to a "conceptual scheme." It remained for Donald Davidson to discard what he called "the third dogma" of empiricism, namely, the "dualism of scheme and content, of organizing system and something waiting to be organized." As we have seen, this Kantian legacy survived in linguistic empiricism's assumption that a conceptual scheme is an inherent feature of a linguistic system that determines, at least in part, how we see and describe reality.

Davidson's criticisms, "On the Very Idea of a Conceptual Scheme,"[58] are directed against the suppositions that there can be such a thing as massive, global conceptual disparity, and, less massively, that there can be a preponderance of disagreement among languages. First, we have no good evidence to suppose that alternative, alien conceptual schemes even exist. The notion of an alternative conceptual scheme, utterly alien to ours, is the notion of a language that is true but not translatable, and we cannot recognize something to be a language without at the same time knowing a lot about how to translate it. In the second case, instances of disagreement between cultures and speakers, however extensive the disagreement, are intelligible *as* disagreement only holistically, against a background of substantial agreement and shared beliefs. A necessary condition for successful interpretation is the existence of *some* fund of massive agreement between any two language users, though not any *invariant* set of beliefs and principles.

Davidson's reflections on the methodological constraints on translation and interpretation show us how we can make do without having to invoke either of the traditional Kantian distinctions of scheme and content. After his sustained criticism of several variations on the notion of a division of labor between conceptual "schemes" and uninterpreted "content," no such distinction appears plausible. Whenever the scheme is thought to stand in a certain relation (predicting, organizing, facing, or fitting) to experience (nature, reality, sensory promptings), we simply discover variations on the dualistic problem of accurately fitting a scheme or representations to something that supplies a content for that scheme. The trouble with this, according to Davidson, is that

> the notion of fitting the totality of experience, like the notions of fitting the facts, or being true to the facts, adds nothing intelligible to the simple concept of being true. To speak of sensory experience rather than the evidence, or just the facts, expresses a view about the source or nature of evidence, but it does not add a new entity to the universe against which to test conceptual schemes.

Davidson's conclusions cut in the same direction as those we have seen from Sellars and Quine, with the added benefit of showing the incoherence of conceptual relativism. In the end, he tells us to give up dependence on the concept of an uninterpreted reality, something outside all schemes and science. Is this to relinquish the notion of objective truth? Quite to the contrary, according to Davidson. Indeed, it is precisely the dogma of a dualism of scheme and reality which he says leads to conceptual relativity, the notion of truth relative to a scheme. "Without the dogma," Davidson says, "this kind of relativity goes by the board." He allows that truth of sentences remains relative to language, "but that is as objective as can be." In summary, then, "in giving up the dualism of scheme and world, we do not give up the world, but reestablish unmediated touch with the familiar objects whose antics make our sentences and opinions true or false."

What, then, is left of empiricism, indeed of modern philosophy, shorn of its three dogmas? If empirical inquiry has the holistic character that Sellars, Quine, and Davidson claimed, where does it go from here? One provocative answer has been offered by Richard Rorty who draws the moral that what remains of empiricism once its dogmas have fallen away is just this: pragmatism.

Rorty's Radical Holism and Historicism

Surveying the philosophical scene from Descartes to Sellars, Quine, and Davidson, Richard Rorty has fashioned a dramatic narrative about *Philosophy and the Mirror of Nature*[59] in which he describes the dominance of the ocular metaphor in the history of philosophy and its deconstruction in our time. Rorty also offers his own "epistemological behaviorism" which has a short way with theories of the justification of our beliefs. On his account, epistemic justification takes a pragmatic turn, theoretical reason collapses into practical reason, and epistemology empties into hermeneutics.

Sellars may have destroyed "the myth of the given," but he still held (mistakenly, Rorty thinks) to analytic propositions. Quine destroyed the analytic, and thus the distinction between the conceptual and the factual, while still holding (mistakenly, Rorty thinks) to a version of the given. By extending and combining the work of Sellars and Quine, Rorty arrives at a more radical holism than either. His contention is that their arguments are

> . . . complementary expressions of a single claim: that no "account of the nature of knowledge" can rely on a theory of representations which stand in privileged relations to reality. The work of these two philosophers enables us . . . to make clear why an "account of the nature of knowledge" can be, at most, a description of human behavior.

Basically, Rorty's account of empirical inquiry is Sellars without the picturing, and Quine without the scientism. What this amounts to, I believe, is that the unit of empirical inquiry, which Quine had seen as "the whole of science," becomes for Rorty virtually *an entire culture*. Epistemic authority is to be explained by reference to "what society lets us say" rather than by appeal to inner privileged representations or to privileged discourses, whether of the natural sciences or of the social sciences.

Sellars's and Quine's holistic accounts of empirical inquiry stressed that systematically interrelated wholes constitute the units of empirical inquiry and epistemic appraisal in such a way that it becomes pointless to try to distinguish what is prior conceptual scheme on the one hand and what is currently accepted theory and observation on the other. Rorty carries this to the conclusion that the entire epistemological project of specifying the prior conceptual framework and ground of cognitive knowledge in general and of empirical inquiry in particular, is futile. Without the standard distinctions of logical empiricism, there is simply no way of singling out one set of warrantedly assertible propositions as alone representing a repository of empirical truths or observable facts of the matter. And in the absence of privileged matters of fact, there is no point to the requirement that all putative factual assertions be tied by logical or epistemic rules to certain privileged ones in order to acquire or certify their own factual significance. This is conversational democracy *par excellence*.

The "epistemological behaviorism" Rorty advocates comes down to "explaining rationality and epistemic authority by reference to what society lets us say, rather than the latter by the former." This sort of behaviorism, Rorty tells us, "can best be seen as a species of holism—but one that requires no idealist metaphysical underpinnings. It claims that if we understand the rules of a language-game, we understand all there is to understand about why moves in that language-game are made." This is merely to say that "nothing counts as justification unless by reference to what we already accept, and that there is no way to get outside our beliefs and our language so as to find some test other than coherence." And *that* is merely to point out, as Rorty does repeatedly, that there is no other way to justify knowledge claims or truth-claims than by appealing to specific social practices that have been hammered out in the course of history and that are the forms of inquiry within which we distinguish what is rational and irrational, objective and idiosyncratic, "normal" discourse and "abnormal" discourse.

This does *not* mean that "anything goes." There is, it is true, a disturbing aspect to Rorty's remarks that "the True and Right are matters of social practice," "justification is a matter of social practice" and "objectivity should be seen as conformity to norms of justification (for assertions and for actions) we find about us," but his historicism is not, he insists, relativism of the sort which denies that there is any truth, objectivity, or standards for judging better and worse arguments or actions. Against the Kantian claim that knowledge and morals have foundations, Rorty is only advancing the Hegelian argument that we do not have and can not get ahistorical standards of rationality and objectivity; there are no permanent standards, criteria, or decision procedures to which all disputants could univocally appeal for adjudicating arguments, and thus no ultimate support to which we can appeal in trying to "ground" the decisions which confront human freedom and responsibility. We should just give up the philosophical hope of having anything *general* to say about our epistemic appraisals, and accept that all that is available to cope intellectually are the continuing pragmatic appraisals made within existing social practices. Here we will find framework-dependent contexts of empirical inquiry

that are indistinguishable from social practices and the latest reper-
toire of warrantedly assertible propositions. No longer vainly trying to
put the mirror to Nature, seeking accurate representations under
images of constraint and compulsion, we will be able, Rorty hopes, to
envision a new metaphor for understanding philosophy as "a voice in
the conversation of mankind."[60]

Of course, the real questions begin here, where Dewey, one of
Rorty's heroes, struggled. To *which* social practices are we to appeal?
How do we discriminate the better from the worse? Which ones need
to be discarded, criticized, and reconstructed? Rorty's critics have
been right to zero in on his unexplained references, indeed deference,
to "social practice." To avoid mystification we need to know much
more about social practices than Rorty has yet supplied. For example,
in what does a social practice consist? What are the differences and
similarities between scientific practices and literary, political, or religious ones? Granted the absence of any transhistorical criteria, are
there nevertheless *some* criteria for criticizing, evaluating, and improv-
ing or abandoning our practices?[61]

The Voice of Religion in Contemporary Culture

After Sellars, Quine, Davidson, Kuhn and their interlocutors, we
now have good reasons to resist the foundational concerns that define
the post-Cartesian legacy in epistemology, philosophy of mind, and
philosophy of science. Thanks to Richard Rorty, we are beginning also
to have at least a hazy idea of what philosophy might look like after it
shakes off the vestiges of the old empiricism and continues with the
new business of neopragmatism. What we do not yet have is a clear
idea of the way the insights and methods in this most recent cycle of
empiricism might apply to the philosophy of religion. One admirable
beginning has been made by Jeffery Stout, whose book *The Flight from
Authority: Religion, Morality, and the Quest for Autonomy*,[62] makes an
important application of holism, historicism, and antifoundationalism to the study of religious belief in modern Western intellectual
culture. Two features deserve mention here. The first is the account
Stout gives of what justification looks like in religious studies when we
relax the concerns that defined the Cartesian period, and the second
is his much too simple verdict on the fate of theism in the modern
period. In the first case, Stout argues persuasively in favor of setting
aside the Cartesian either/or dilemma that would have us imagine that
either there is some foundational justification of basic beliefs *or* we are

doomed to skepticism, fideism, or relativism. But in his treatment of theism Stout succumbs to another numbing either/or—either classical theism (judged to be a lost cause)—or none at all.

On the issue of justification, Stout is splendidly lucid and presents a convincing sketch of the kind of holism and historicism which can make the task of justification of beliefs something less stringent than Cartesian philosophy demanded. By "holism" Stout means no more than the view that language cannot be divided in the way envisioned by proponents of the distinctions between the analytic and the synthetic, theory and observation, or fact and value. The historicism he espouses involves, among other things, the belief that thought is historically conditioned and therefore that genuine "self-understanding" must be informed by historical insight. Historical analysis of, for example, the quest for Cartesian certainties or Kantian transcendental groundings and epistemic foundations, displays the culturally specific problems and discursive practices that marked those particular historical settings, which are no longer ours. Consequently, Stout writes, having "placed" the Father (Descartes), we can "displace" him now as well. These methodological commitments lead Stout away from epistemologically oriented philosophy, as expressed in the notion that there is a *general* problem of justification to be solved (in connection with religious belief or ethics or anything else). It leads him toward historically oriented philosophy, "as expressed in the view that all problems of justification are radically situated in specific historical contexts."[63]

Stout's argument against foundationalism in the justification of beliefs partakes of familiar antifoundationalist moves. First, he rejects any version of "strong" foundationalism which requires foundational beliefs that enjoy incorrigibility, infallibility, indubitability, self-justification, and logical independence. Second, he displays the "minimal foundationalism" defended by William Alston and James Cornman as "indistinguishable from their opponents" and suggests that there is nothing even in minimal foundationalism that the opponents of foundationalist philosophy need have any stake in denying. Next, he meets the issue of infinite regress or circularity by calling up the image of Neurath's boat and suggesting that, since we always need some planks in place to stay afloat, and since the hope for reconstruction in dry dock is utopian, then "which planks will be keeping us afloat at any given moment depends on the course of our voyage, what we are up to, and why." In a similar fashion, Stout disposes of radical skepticism, the attempt to call into question all of our beliefs at once, by making the Davidsonian point that belief in the truth of a range of sentences is a condition of the very possibility of doubt; in order to doubt any one sentence one must interpret it, and to interpret it "one must establish its relation to a content of generally accepted and deeply entrenched sentences in the same domain."[64]

The rejection of foundationalism leads Stout toward a Rortyian view of justification as "the social practice of giving reasons for belief and plans within some highly specific context." This makes justification *relative* to epistemic context, and here Stout faces up squarely to the difficulty of fending off the unpalatable premises of conceptual relativism without relinquishing the historicism which he thinks is the only alternative to the demise of foundationalism. The burden of most of Stout's work, in fact, succeeds in showing that historicism neither presupposes nor entails the conclusion that rational appraisal and justification is itself inherently relative to one or another conceptual scheme, or that we lack a good reason for preferring one conceptual scheme, such as scientific rationality, with its standards of judgment, to another, such as Christianity.

On the fate of theism, Stout is less convincing. His historical thesis, that the situation in contemporary epistemology, theology, and ethics is the product of an authority breakdown whose roots go back to the religious conflicts of sixteenth- and seventeenth-century Europe, tells a plausible story only by omitting from its genealogy various chapters and episodes, especially of American religious thought, that cannot be squeezed so conveniently into the too-neat dichotomies which Stout favors.

Post-Humean reconstructions of theism follow only two avenues in Stout's story. Both are viewed as dead ends. There is, on the one hand, the option of a Kierkegaardian abandonment of any hope of making theistic belief rationally credible. But the category of paradox is no refuge today, Stout argues, and a theology which stresses belief as an offense to the modern consciousness winds up isolating itself into irrelevance. On the other hand, forms of liberal Protestantism, which have attempted to salvage rationality by reinterpreting traditional theism in modern discourse, forfeit anything distinctively Christian and wind up offering "less and less in which to disbelieve." Stout dismisses Rudolf Bultmann's reinterpretation of Christian theism as "hard to distinguish from Heidegger's existentialism" and Paul Tillich's theism as "suspiciously close to Feuerbach's atheism."[65] He seems to think relevance can only be purchased at the price of redundancy and that distinctiveness can only be acquired with the risk of irrelevance.

Lurking in the background of this is Stout's uncritical consent to the sweeping assessment which Alastair MacIntyre made of "The Fate of Theism" in his Bampton lectures in Columbia University in 1966.

In MacIntyre's view, "any presentation of theism which is able to secure a hearing from a secular audience has undergone a transformation that has evacuated it of its theistic content. Conversely, any presentation which retains such theistic content will be unable to secure the place in contemporary culture which those theologians desire for it."[66] MacIntyre's disjunctive alternatives [either "evacuated of theistic content" or "unable to secure a place in contemporary culture"] are scarcely exhaustive, but Stout endorses this cavalier reading as "deeply attractive." He also adds his own artificial dichotomy in the following statement:

> Reformulations of traditional theism like Deism and liberal Protestantism have tended to shade off into atheism, unable to retain enough distinctiveness to justify the use of traditional vocabulary or sustain the interest of the host culture. Less thoroughgoing reformulations maintain distinctiveness, but only by holding onto features that seem indefensible or unintelligible in modern terms. The horns of this dilemma constitute the dialectical situation that is the fate of modern theism . . . neither thinly disguised atheism nor Kierkegaardian unwillingness to argue makes a vital and interesting opponent in debate.[67]

One might suppose that this is a perfect example of the fallacy of the excluded middle. Why are there no possibilities other than the extremes of either "thinly disguised atheism" or "Kierkegaardian unwillingness to argue"? Stout is right that neither makes an interesting debating partner and so it is no wonder that the cultured despisers, of whom Schleiermacher was so conscious, no longer waste their time even despising such options today. But why should the fate of modern theism be read entirely out of continental sources and the history of liberal Protestantism with its heavy Kantian baggage? Stout's artful historical narrative remains somewhat parochial and even artificial as a story of "modern theism." Kierkegaard, Schleiermacher, Barth, Bultmann, and Tillich figure in it, but no mention is made of distinctive American contributions to the development of an empirical or pragmatic theism. This seems especially puzzling when in fact the philosophical sources Stout appeals to (Richard Rorty, Thomas Kuhn, Ian Hacking, W. V. Quine, Wilfrid Sellars, Donald Davidson) all support an anti-foundationalist, pragmatic account of epistemic justification which is consistent with the tradition of American religious empiricism.

Part of the answer to this may be traced to Stout's own restrictive assumptions about the nature of "experience." Consider, for example, one of the difficulties he believes has haunted the liberal theological tradition from the beginning. Speaking of Schleiermacher's use of apparently epistemic categories for characterizing piety, Stout poses the following either/or dilemma: "Now either explanatory claims are being made here," he says,

> or not. If not, we remain in the realm of heartburn and tickles. But if such claims are being made, the Kantian criticisms can be brought to bear. If religious experience is immediate or intuitive, in the sense of 'not mediated by the concepts of the understanding,' then it must surely be blind by Kantian standards. If it is blind, it is unclear how one theological utterance could be judged better than another as an expression of religious experience except perhaps with respect to emotive tone.[68]

The tip-off here is the reference to the realm of heartburn and tickles and to emotive tone.

Another reason for Stout's inability to find a voice for religion in contemporary culture may be related to his tendency to assume that any alternatives to deism or traditional theism do not seem, as he says, "religiously satisfying."[69] This odd expression turns up several times and is nowhere subjected to historicizing analysis. Does Stout think there is any one meaning or constant content to what is "religiously satisfying?" How would we ever discover it? It would make more sense to suppose that "religiously satisfying" is a matter of social contexts and changing emphases, just as Stout says "good reasons" are. But he does not examine the possibility that what is "religiously satisfying" in our theisms as much as in our moralities may vary from one historical period and culture to another. For this could in turn permit the emergence of qualitatively new revisionary theisms, capable of gaining a hearing in an intellectual culture very much like the one Stout depicts us in now. "Historicism" should mean never having to say you're satisfied.

If we are not bound by the norms of past satisfactions, the verdict we can draw from Stout's own historicist method is not the sealed one he delivers. The fate of a new form of theism is still open. Having learned from the history of philosophy and of science to be wary of dichotomies between analytic and synthetic statements, between theories and observations, and between schemes and contents, we might now learn to be just as dubious about dualisms between nature and supernature or theism and atheism in contemporary religious inquiry. These distinctions no more exhaust our intellectual and practical options in the realm of religion than Ptolemaic astronomy exhausts our present cosmological models. The issue then is not the dyadic one of *either* theism (traditionally defined in Western thought) *or* atheism.

In between the horns of this artificial dilemma it is possible to locate an archaeological layer Stout failed to excavate, in the work of American religious empiricists from William James to the present.

In this chapter, I have tried to trace some of the principal forms which philosophical empiricism has taken in its long history, and to suggest some of the responses which philosophers of religion have made to each stage. But the story is still seriously incomplete. When the history of empiricism is read only in terms of its progression from British empiricism straight up to its transmutations in the analytic tradition, something is lost. Just as surely, when the history of modern religious thought is read primarily out of continental sources, from Schleiermacher and Ritschl to Barth and Bultmann, an important development in American religious thought is overlooked. In the first case, what is lost is the epistemological alternative called radical empiricism, as proposed by William James. In the second case, what is overlooked is the work of American religious empiricists, such as Henry Nelson Wieman and others, who articulated a religious perspective consonant with radical empiricism.

Chapter Three

Radical Empiricism in Religious Perspective

When contemporary philosophers argue that the false hope of a firm foundation is gone, that the world is displaced by worlds that are but versions, that substance is dissolved into function, and the given must be acknowledged as taken,[1] they are echoing themes already present in the work of the classical American pragmatic-empiricists Charles Sanders Peirce, William James, and John Dewey. In this sense, Richard Rorty may be right to say that "James and Dewey were not only waiting at the end of the dialectical road which analytic philosophy traveled, but are waiting at the end of the road which, for example, Foucault and Deleuze are currently traveling."[2] At the same time, however, the authors of the Golden Age of American philosophy did not hesitate to offer fresh theories of experience. In that sense they took the road now less traveled by recent analytic philosophers—and that has made all the difference.

The difference shows itself principally in the fact that Peirce, James, and Dewey evinced much more of a theoretical interest in the role of experience, broadly conceived, in knowledge, including religious knowledge. Their pragmatism, in which there is currently a renewed interest, was only one deployment of that broader interest, as an answer to the question of how to justify knowledge-claims—in the evaluation of consequences, not in the search for origins. What distinguishes Peirce, James, and Dewey most strikingly from more recent American philosophers is the prominent attention they gave to the role of the aesthetic or qualitative dimension of experience. Thus they offered, in my view, an account of the nature of experience that is more empirical and adequate to actual experience than any of those considered thus far. For Peirce, it involved an analysis of experience in terms of three categories: an immediate qualitative dimension; a brute dyadic compulsiveness; and an element of generality or law-likeness ingredient in all experience. For James, radical empiricism

83

consisted of an analysis of experience that dissolved traditional dualisms between subjectivity and objectivity, mental and physical, thought and thing thought of, knower and that which is known—dualisms he thought had vitiated too many descriptions of experience. For Dewey, the biological notion of organic interaction or transaction between an organism and its environment yielded a richer understanding that, he argued, rescued the concept of experience from subjective, atomistic, and narrowly epistemological approaches. For all three thinkers, each with different emphases, radical empiricism is defined by the understanding that sense-perception is neither the only nor the primary mode of experience, but is rather derived from a still more elemental and organic togetherness of the experiencing subject and the experienced environment. In the language of Dewey, experience designates *all* transactions between organism and environment, both of which are co-constitutive of one another. On this view, before ever undertaking the comparatively high-level discriminations of the world by means of the senses or linguistic forms, the subject is aware of itself and others as causally efficacious powers mutually interacting with a world of qualitative values where memories of the past and anticipations of the future are felt as given.

Thus, at every point radical empiricism challenges the assumptions of classical, logical and linguistic empiricism. In a useful summary of this alternative philosophy, John Smith finds radical empiricism distinctive for holding that: (1) the organism sustains relations with the environment other than knowing and these equally belong to experience, so that knowledge is not identical with either sense experience or consciousness; (2) experience has a public origin and is not exhausted by what is immediately present to an individual or private mind; (3) experience includes tendency and direction and is not a discrete, instantaneous occurrence; (4) connections and transitions are likewise given in experience as felt, not as inferred; and (5) thought and reason, though not experientially primitive, are higher phases *of* experience and not a contrasting domain *to* experience.[3]

These contentions will become clearer when understood against the interpretation offered in this chapter of (1) William James's description of radical empiricism, and (2) John Dewey's analysis of the quality of the "religious" in experience.

William James and Radical Empiricism

Empiricism, when it becomes radical, thickens the thin empiricisms canvassed in the last chapter. It becomes an empiricism in which perception, understood as inclusive of transitions and activity, is accorded a deeper meaning than sensation. It becomes an empiricism that sees "knowledge of acquaintance" as having a vital function in interaction with conceptual "knowledge about." Preeminently, it becomes an empiricism that stresses the temporal, processive, anticipatory, and intentional modes of experience, where the "given" is experienced relationally. More than anything else, the doctrine of the givenness of relations is what distinguishes James's radical empiricism from classical empiricisms and reveals radical empiricism to be less a continuation of traditional empiricism than a protest against it. If James's radicalization of the concept of experience is to be understood historically as a criticism of earlier British empiricism, it must also be distinguished from later critiques of the "Myth of the Given." James was no friend of the sense-datum theory, and the doctrine of the givenness of *relations*, so crucial to his philosophy, was no myth in the sense described by Sellars.

Radical empiricism can be summarily presented as involving just what James described it as in the Preface he wrote in 1909 to *The Meaning of Truth*: It consists first of a postulate, next of a statement of fact, and finally of a generalized conclusion. The postulate is that "the only things that shall be debatable among philosophers shall be definable in terms drawn from experience."[4] This postulate is a methodological, not a metaphysical one, and it is one James consistently invoked throughout his later writings. But James was not asserting here that the only things that exist are those that are experienced, for he added: "Things of an unexperienced nature may exist *ad libitum*, but they form no part of the material for philosophical debate."[5] Just as James's pragmatic method started from the postulate that there is no difference of truth which does not make a difference of fact somewhere, and that all asserted differences must be experienceable as factual differences, the empirical postulate says that all facts must be experienceable, and that all assertions must be experienced as facts. Both postulates begin with an epistemological assertion and both trace their verification to experienceable facts.

Next, radical empiricism asserts as a statement of fact that "the relations between things, conjunctive as well as disjunctive, are just as much matters of direct particular experience, neither more so nor less so, than the things themselves."[6] With this assertion that relations are experienced as given, radical empiricism signals its most important departure from classical empiricism's picture of experience as pulverized into discrete data devoid of conjunctive relations. In terms of James's formulation, Hume's clear and disconnected impressions are abstractions from a stream of experience, which is essentially continuous and inclusive of relations from next to next. Conjunctions and prepositions, according to James, are not empty of sensory content. They arouse definite feelings of motion, of anticipation, of proximity, and so on. Therefore, they function as transitive states between more stable perceptions. From his earliest writings to his last, James labored to show that relations are as real as the terms they relate, and moreover, that they are felt as immediately as anything else. His theory of relations, conjunctive as well as disjunctive, is the crux of radical empiricism.

Third, the generalized conclusion to which radical empiricism leads becomes a naturalized metaphysical position. On the basis of the postulate and of the statement of fact, James could assert: "The parts of experience hold together next by next by relations that are themselves parts of experience. The directly apprehended universe needs, in short, no extraneous transempirical connective support, but possesses in its own right a concatenated or continuous structure."[7] Experience, in other words, already contains within itself the conjunctions requisite to whatever unity and continuity obtains. There is therefore no need to presuppose transcendent entities, activities, or principles as cosmic glue. Any moment of experience flows beyond itself to connect in relations. James thought that an indefinite variety of conjunctive relations were available. In contrast to the ancient world that hypothesized a finite universe, and in contrast to modern science that hypothesizes an infinite universe, James's radical empiricism offered another hypothesis: reality is simply indefinite. It flows. We are unable to say whether it flows in a single direction or even whether it is always and everywhere the same flow. Human experience too is continuously in flux, exhibiting tendencies and resistances, and giving rise to specific things and relations only insofar as it enters into particular, reticulated contexts. Relations and objects that are perspectivally selected out of the flux are really given, but so are many more that human attention ignores.

Summarily expressed, radical empiricism meant by "experience" a network of concatenatedly related objects or things, selected out by human perceptual activity, consonant with the possibilities and limitations provided by nature, and historically structured by antecedent purposes and activities. Conscious human experience is an aspect of the flux within the processes of nature, itself also in process, unfinished, giving rise to novelties relative to inherited structures. The focus of much human attention occurs within the familiar, habitually accepted perceptual field. But the focus opens outward, inclusive of a fringe of further possibilities, often vague and indistinct, but quite continuous and relationally rich.

James called experience a "double-barreled" term, an experiencing *of* an experienced world. Not only sensation, but also personal activities of will, belief, interest, feeling, and need were essential to James's analysis. In thus broadening the notion of experience from that of classical empiricism, James gave to human volition, rather than simply to cognition, an actual role in creating what we experience. He also succeeded in dragging experience back on the philosophic stage "reeking and dripping with the rawness of actual life." Lived exper- ience, as James was concerned with it, unfolds much like Beckett's *Waiting for Godot:* the scenes are not clear-cut; there is no beginning, middle, and end; a confusing number of lines go on at once; superflu- ous gestures occur; acts overlap; there is no fully satisfying conclu- sion; and no absolutely determinative action. But experience is not for that reason absurd or incoherent. There are relationships among things and connections among facts. These relations are experienced as being as real as the things and facts themselves. But the things are fluid and the relations fluctuate. Experience is not the tidy drama constructed by some philosophers.

Radical Empiricism and the Religious Dimension of Experience

James's disparate writings on the subject of religion are not easily reconciled with each other, nor do they all readily relate to religious inquiry in the present. In the notorious essay "The Will to Believe," James claimed that belief in God was a live, momentous, and forced option, a presumption less likely to be favored today. It did not help much that he later explained he was arguing for "the *right* to believe." Elsewhere, he suggested that belief in God cashes out as the adoption of a certain moral attitude. Sometimes he seemed to sidestep fideism by appealing to the perfectly natural experience of "spirit," where "spirit" described a quality perceived as other than physical or strictly intellectual. At other times, he eschewed appeals to perceived qualities of experience and treated the physical-spiritual distinction as a misleadingly metaphysical way of expressing a difference between lifestyles. In the end, James was very wary to asert the fact of a cosmic consciousness. There was too little in experience to directly support the notion. Indirectly, there was only the evidence of pathology and psychical research, as well as some evidence from mysticism and reli- gious experience, but it was difficult to turn testimony into evidence in these areas. All that James's researches along these lines produced was a recognition of the ambiguous uses of such evidence and the tantalizing possibility that "we may be in the universe as dogs and cats are in our libraries, seeing the books and hearing the conversation, but having no inkling of the meaning of it all."[8]

I am not interested here in following James into his tentative statement of "over-beliefs," but rather in examining aspects of his radical empiricism for their religious import. James himself did not explicitly connect his doctrine of radical empiricism to his earlier religious investigations. Little effort has been made by his commentators to do so either.[9] Far more scholarly attention (much of it critical) has been devoted to James's pragmatic method and to the ambiguous results of its application to questions of religious truth. But pragmatism without radical empiricism is like a menu without food: appetizing but not digestible. Even the very terms in which James presented the method of pragmatism presupposed the fuller understanding of "experience" as supplied in radical empiricism, as when, for example, he stated:

> Pragmatism . . . asks its usual question, 'Grant an idea or belief to be true,' it says, 'what concrete difference will its being true make in any one's actual life? How will the truth be realized? What experiences will be different from those which would obtain if the belief were false? What, in short, is the truth's cash-value in experiential terms?'[10]

The similarity between the pragmatic principle and the falsification challenge of Antony Flew is evident. Both hold that all meaningful distinctions depend on discernible differences in fact, but James's radical empiricism not only denies the definition of experience as sense-perception, it also calls into question the standard empiricist way of posing the problem.

The significance of James's work for empirical inquiry in religion seems to me to turn most fully on an appreciation of those texts in which he worked out his philosophy of radical empiricism, rather than on his explicitly religious investigations. His radical empiricism is *epistemologically* significant for (1) its elimination of those problems associated with correspondence views in the theory of knowledge, and (2) its broadening of the understanding of experience from a mere modality of cognition to an inclusion of experienced relations, felt transitions, and qualitative feelings. It is *religiously* significant because it (1) not only permits but demands a nonreductive way to overcome dualisms between "God" and "world," and (2) flatly opposes the subject-object view of experience that historically has perpetuated the assumption that the religious dimension of experience has to do with a subject experiencing a religious object as an object among others, much as a person experiences a chair or a table.

These remarks can be developed with reference to three texts I want to consider not in their entirety, nor even in their historical context, but in their potential for contributing to an empirical philosophy of religion. In the first, *Principles of Psychology* (1890), James made no mention of religion at all, but he did advance three notions that I will treat as suggestive for developing a theory of the religious dimension of experience: the "fringe" of the perceptual field, the nature of "knowledge of acquaintance," and the cognitive function of feeling. In the second work, *The Varieties of Religious Experience* (1902), James was directly concerned with displaying testimonies of religious phenomena and developing a defense of what he called a "full fact." Rather than concerning myself with the special interest James had here in varieties of individualized mysticism, I will consider only the incipient views on the subject of the "divine" that his empirical method permitted at this stage in his thought. In the third work, a series of essays published posthumously in 1912 under the title *Essays in Radical Empiricism*, James again made no explicit mention of any religious topics. Although the book is primarily a record of James's last wrestlings with philosophical problems distinctive of his period and a continuation of efforts begun in *Principles of Psychology*, I believe it also can be read as a sustained, if not systematic, attempt to work out certain philosophical problems occasioned by the religious hypotheses he had already presented in 1902.

Perceptual Experience and the Reinstatement of the Vague

Three features of radical empiricism which are foreshadowed in James's *Principles of Psychology* are his discussion of the "fringe" of perception, the nature of "knowledge by acquaintance," and the cognitive function of feelings. These themes are interesting not only because they serve to upend the entire program of logical and linguistic empiricism, but because they suggest features of experience that figure crucially in a radically empirical account of the religious dimension of experience.

Rather than taking as normative the noncontroversial way in which the properly programmed speaker cannot help believing that the patch, for example, is red, and then applying this stripped-down analogy for the larger and more controversial beliefs in religion, James's method would have us begin instead with values, interests, and feelings. For radical empiricism, there is no interesting metaphysical difference between facts and values, and no epistemological one between feelings and cognitions. That is, values do not get *mixed with* facts by a process of *fusion* on the part of a separated mind. Rather, "facts" get sorted out from other facts and values by a supplemental process of *discrimination* within the life-world. Perceptual experience for James was not the chaotic manifold supposed by the rationalism of his day. Perception in the mode of what James called "knowledge of acquaintance" already contains relations, fringes, patterns which are ready to be discriminated, clarified, and spelled out in our "knowledge about." There is no infallibility or certainty about this knowledge by acquaintance, of course. Its discrimination always involves uncertainty and the risk of error.

The "fringe" is James's term for relations and objects which are but dimly perceived, the halo of relations, references, and pointings of which we have only an inarticulate and vague awareness. By this term he meant to designate "part of the *object cognized*—substantive *qualities* and *things* appearing to the mind in a *fringe of relations*."[11] Those parts of experience which cognize relations, rather than substantives, James called "the transitive parts." Transitive states belong with the fringe in general. The fringe conveys a "sense of affinity" and a "feeling of tendency."[12] Overtones in music provide a striking example of the fringe in experience. Different instruments give the "same note," but each in a different voice. There is something "more" than the note. There are the various upper harmonics of it which differ from one instrument to another. James considered that "they are not separately heard by the ear; they blend with the fundamental note, and suffuse it, and alter it; and even so do the waxing and waning brain processes at every moment blend with and suffuse and alter the psychic effect of the processes which are at their culminating point."[13]

When epistemologists habitually focus on substantives or culminating points of perception, they overlook the subtle feelings of tendency, affinity, and feelings of transition structuring the fringe of awareness. James knew that for purposes of logic, precision, and clear thinking, sharpened forms of attention must inevitably screen out the accompanying vague fringe, but he showed also how indifference to the fringe of relations leads to a falsification and mechanization of our conception of the intellect. What he contended for, and accumulated examples to show, was that "tendencies are not only descriptions from without, but that they are among the *objects* of the stream, which is thus aware of them from within, and must be described as in very large measure constituted by *feelings of tendency*, often so vague that we are unable to name them at all. It is, in short, the reinstatement of the vague to its proper place in our mental life which I am so anxious to press on the attention."[14]

Implicit in James's discussion of the fringe of perception is a critique of any attempt to restrict empirical testability solely to what is publicly observable, clear, and precise. Classical empiricists, logical empiricists, and linguistic empiricists, all in various ways, have considered the clear and distinct aspects of experience the foundation for knowledge. James would counter that the vague and the fringed, the dimly discerned relational data of experience, are more primitive. These could not be made foundational in any usual sense of the term, but their presence or absence was what served to make the difference between the two kinds of knowledge James distinguished in the *Psychology*: knowledge of acquaintance and knowledge-about.

The distinction between knowledge of acquaintance and knowledge-about, introduced by James before it was made famous by Bertrand Russell, has proved to be a most troublesome feature of other forms of empiricism. The best interpretation of James's use of this distinction in *The Principles of Psychology* is to see knowledge of acquaintance as the more primitive mode, concerned with the vaguely given, overabundant relations of the fringe, where resistances and tendencies in the stream of experience are immediately apprehended. Knowledge-about, as a complementary mode of awareness, concerns the focal region wherein the vague relations are discriminated according to some selective interest and purpose.

But it would be mistaken to view James's distinction between knowledge of acquaintance and knowledge-about as falling within any dichotomy between percepts and concepts, as though either one occurs independently of the other. Knowledge of acquaintance does not represent a misguided desire to "get outside language." Indeed, one of the interesting features of James's discussion of this point is the linguistic evidence he cites in support of his conclusion that knowledge-about depends upon and presupposes knowledge of acquaintance. Interjections, such as *Lo!, there!, ecco!,* and *voilà!,* or articles and demonstrative pronouns introducing sentences, such as *the, it,* and *that,* simply point to something that is directly perceived or felt, together with its fringes.[15] We ought to say, according to James, that there is "a feeling of *and,* and a feeling of *if,* a feeling of *but,* and a feeling of *by,* quite as readily as we say a feeling of *blue* or a feeling of *cold.*"[16] Without this knowledge of acquaintance, our words would be empty and meaningless. But, at the same time, James was able to acknowledge that "in minds able to speak at all, there is, it is true, *some* knowledge about everything. Things can at least be classed and the times of their appearance told . . . The two kinds of knowledge are, therefore, as the human mind practically exerts them, relative terms."[17] So although the distinction cannot be pressed too far, it is useful, James found, for affirming an indispensable aspect of the process of experience, one which may always in principle *eventuate* in linguistic expression, but which never in fact is *exhaustively* expressed.

Whether knowledge of acquaintance should also receive the honorific stamp of "knowledge" is a question that divides radical empiricists and many analytic philosophers in this century. The ubiquity of language in human experience has been a central theme of linguistic philosophy, to the point of identifying knowledge, strictly speaking, with conceptual knowledge or the end result of conscious processes, propositionally expressed. The issue has to do with the kind of data that radical empiricism has located at the fringe, but not at the foundations, of the web of experience. These data include quality as well as quantity, relations as well as relata, valuations as well as so-called facts. With respect to these data, two kinds of empirical approaches are currently available. One attempts to reduce all that is to count as "knowledge" to the mathematical-deductive model; the other attempts to resurrect the meanings contained in human symbols, feeling-tones, and valuations. The problematic delimited by these two approaches is fundamental; it provides the background for contemporary discussions and barriers between the natural sciences, behavioral sciences, linguistic philosophy, and psychoanalysis, phenomenology, hermeneutics, and theology. The underlying dilemma not only confronts us with a choice between clear, distinct, and manageable data or dim, vague, and unmanageable data in conducting inquiry, but also with the question, which modes of understanding are to be rewarded with the title "knowledge." Due to the impressive ascendency of modern science and the mathematical-deductive model as paradigmatic of knowledge in our culture, it is not surprising that religious, moral, and aesthetic claims have had an uphill battle in establishing their cognitive value.

One of the contibutions James's radical empiricism can make in this situation consists in his demonstration first in the *Psychology* and later in the *Essays* of the many ways in which cognition is a function of feeling. It is through feeling, James showed, that we *cognize relations*, particularly by the cognitive feelings of tendency and transition. "Feeling" thus signifies a discriminatory sense in radically empirical discussions and is not to be confused with purely private dispositions or with whooshy wooly-headed findings. It is therefore a complete mistake to diagnose and dismiss James's radical empiricism as Richard Rorty does, calling it merely "a weakened version of idealism," and to read it, quoting Hans Reichenbach, as an attempt to answer "unscientifically" formulated epistemological questions about the "relation of subject and object" by "naive generalizations and analogies" which emphasize "feeling" rather than "cognition."[18] James was arguing precisely *against* any such presumed bifurcation between feeling and cognition. His point, carefully and consistently applied, was that feeling *is* cognitive. And as evidence for this claim, James cited a wealth of examples drawn from his psychological studies. The use of experimental psychological data did not entail that his method was one of psycholog*ism* or the perverse introspectionism despised by later empiricists. Rather it had much more in common with the descriptive method prized by later phenomenologists. In common with the phenomenological tradition that was soon to regard him as something of a pioneer, James found that the aesthetic and valuational elements involved in the cognitive act are themselves composed of objective qualities and active intentions to which observational science, in the strict sense, has no access by the nature of its methods. It is these data which are most prominent in radically empirical discussions of the religious dimension of experience. However, even if it be granted that cognitive claims to knowledge properly pertain to this domain of lived experience, it is a further question whether any "truth" or "justification" can be derived from them. This is the problem which appears in *The Varieties of Religious Experience.*

Religious Experience and the "More"

Consistent with its emphasis on the flux of experience, the givenness of relations, and the fringe of awareness, radical empiricism marks an important shift in the locus of justificatory criteria for belief. In *The Varieties of Religious Experience,* his major work dealing with religion, James explicitly rejected versions of genetic empiricism in favor of a pragmatic mode of justificatory empiricism. It was clear to James that religion could not be dogmatically justified by pointing to its privileged origin in some kind of revelation, nor could it be summarily discredited by pointing to its disreputable origins in pathological instances. Instead, it must run the gauntlet of confrontation with the total context of experience. In radical empiricism, the process of the empirical justification of beliefs of any kind is prospective and consequential, not antecedent or foundational. Justification is finally a matter of *felt* differences which *make* a difference. Lived experience, with all its contingency and fallibility, either does or does not provoke its own verifiability in the lives of individuals, even when it carries no authority for observers. But it discloses no foundations, no self-certifying grounds in any area of human conduct. James listed and rejected the following traditional specification of grounds that strikingly resemble those of much of the empiricist philosophy of this century: "(1) definitely statable abstract principles: (2) definite facts of sensation; (3) definite hypotheses based on such facts; and (4) definite inferences logically drawn."[19] No justification of religious beliefs (or of any other beliefs) existed on any of these grounds for James. Nor was he fooled into thinking that any "logic-chopping rationalistic talk, however clever" could justify human projects and practices.

As James saw it, the whole history of architectonic metaphors used in philosophy in a search for grounds of belief systematically distorts the shape of mental life. We do not in actual practice build our beliefs from firm foundations up or from abstract principles down. We are born, James might say with Quine, into "webs of belief." But James would also add, we are born into a web of life as well, and it is the priority of the natural life-world that guides, judges, and—in the long run—transforms our social and linguistic conventions.

Rationalism, no less than empiricism, gives only a "relatively superficial" account of what James thought was our "whole mental life as it exists." Regardless what epistemology may demonstrate by way of justification, James concluded that "it will fail to convince or convert you all the same, if your dumb intuitions are opposed to its conclusions." With this, James was by no means licensing a feckless orgy of inarticulate intuitionism. But he was most definitely dismissing the kind of epistemology that, in the history of philosophy, has prompted a search for origins, foundations, and grounds as warrants for belief. He was also dismissing the kind of philosophical theology that is wedded to rationalist forms of religious reflection and that prompts a concern for divine "proofs." "Our generation," James declared in 1902, "has ceased to believe in the kind of God it argued for."[20]

James concluded his Gifford Lectures with a theory of religion and a tentative statement of the empirical-pragmatic method he was to work out more fully over the next eight years before his death. Every religion, he claimed, consists of two parts: (1) an uneasiness; and (2) its solution. The uneasiness, reduced to its simplest terms, he said, was "a sense that there is *something wrong about us* as we naturally stand." The solution was "a sense that *we are saved from the wrongness* by making proper connection with the higher powers."[21] The mass of religious testimony that he had gathered together for these lectures all involved cases of self-transformation. Leaving to each religion the articulation of its own exact "uneasiness", and its own "solution," James described the process of self-transformation in the barest possible language, couching his summary, typically, in terms of "the individual." Insofar as the individual suffers from a sense of wrongness and criticizes it, James said, he is to that extent consciously beyond it, and "in at least possible touch with something higher, if anything higher exist." Little else is obvious to the individual at this state. But when the stage of "solution or salvation" arrives, the individual

> *becomes conscious that this higher part is conterminous and continuous with a MORE of the same quality, which is operative in the universe outside of him, and which he can keep in working touch with, and in a fashion get on board of and save himself when all his lower being has gone to pieces in the wreck. (James's italics)*[22]

As far as this analysis goes, however, James could be describing only psychological phenomena. The critical questions, as he knew, all concerned the objective "truth" of these experiences. "Is such a 'more' merely our own notion, or does it really exist? If so, in what shape does it exist? Does it act, as well as exist? And in what form should we conceive of that 'union' with it of which religious geniuses are so convinced?" Having bravely broached these questions, James's theory needed some way of answering them. But it had to be a theory that was impartial enough, he thought, not to get bogged down in the "speculative differences" over which pantheism and theism, nature and second birth, works and grace and karma, immortality and reincarnation, rationalism and mysticism, carried on their "inveterate disputes." The question of truth was one which had to be raised in the context of "other sciences and general philosophy."[23]

Casting around for a way to offer a "definite description" of "the More" which would mediate between psychology, on the one hand, and theology, on the other, James settled on the term "the *subconscious self.*" He then proposed the hypothesis that "whatever it may be on its farther side, the 'more' with which in religious experience we feel ourselves connected is on its *hither* side the subconscious continuation of our conscious life."[24] Admitting that this hypothesis was only a "doorway" into the subject, James recognized the difficulties that presented themselves as soon as we step through it "and ask how far our transmarginal consciousness carries us if we follow it on its remoter side." Over-beliefs, as he called them, present themselves at once. Here the prophets of all the different religions come with their visions, voices, raptures, and other openings, "supposed by each to authenticate his own peculiar faith." Since specific revelations corroborate incompatible theological doctrines, James supposed that they "neutralize one another and leave no fixed results." Confining himself to what he found to be "common and generic," James concluded only to "*the fact that the conscious person is continuous with a wider self through which saving experiences come."* This was the one positive content of religious experience which to James seemed *"literally and objectively true as far as it goes."*(James' italics)[25]

But had he succeeded in establishing any such truth "literally and objectively"? Indeed, had he even presented a method, theory, or additional set of hypotheses that could show in what a truth that is literal and objective would consist? Rather than answering this question, James proceeded to offer his own over-belief, with only the barest hint as to how this might be pragmatically justified. First, he speculated that "the unseen region in question is not merely ideal, for it produces effects in this world." James's reasoning here was that "that which produces effects within another reality must be termed a reality itself." But in saying this, he left completely unspecified the question of the *ontological* mode of that reality. Was it an actual or an ideal reality? Could not an ideal reality produce the same set of effects as a real existent? At this point, James seemed content with the ambiguous formulation that "God is real since he produces real effects." Did this then mean that divinity is simply whatever it is that enters into the religious sense of union? Taken this way, James thought it would fall short of the condition for being a "real hypothesis," that is, one which has "other properties than those of the phenomenon it is immediately invoked to explain, otherwise it is not prolific enough." If the god hypothesis were true, it would mean that religion is something more than "a mere illumination of facts already elsewhere given, not a mere passion, like love, which views things in a rosier light." In marked contrast to the line later taken by John Hick and other proponents of religious faith as a way of seeing or interpreting-as, James thought that "the world interpreted religiously is not the materialistic world over again, with an altered expression; it must have, over and above the altered expression, *a natural constitution* different at some point from that which a materialistic world would have." The world "must be such that different events can be expected in it, different conduct must be required." Beyond this "thoroughly 'pragmatic' view of religion" James was unprepared to go. He did not know, he said, what the more characteristically divine facts were, aside from "the actual inflow of energy."[26]

The Postscript which James appended to *The Varieties of Religious Experience* made only a little plainer the position James promised to state more amply "in a later work." Here he tried to distinguish his position from that of transcendental idealism and romantic pantheism, confessing, too, his own inability to accept either "popular Christianity" or "scholastic theism." The whole interest in the question of God's existence, James stressed, seemed to lie in "the consequences for particulars which that existence may be expected to entail." Both instinctively and logically he found it "hard to believe that principles can exist which make no difference in facts." That no concrete particular of experience should alter its complexion as a consequence of the putative existence of God, was for James "an incredible proposition." But just where do the differences in fact that are due to the existence of God come in? In answer to this, James again restated his hypothesis, suggested by "certain incursions from the subconscious region," of a union with something which "actually exerts an influence, raises our centre of personal energy, and produces regenerative effects unattainable in any other ways." The cautious, almost hypothetical, way in which James expressed this conclusion is significant. "If, then," he said, "there be a wider world of being than that of our everyday consciousness, if in it there be forces whose effects on us are intermittent, if one facilitating condition of the effects be the openness of the 'subliminal' door, we have the elements of a theory to which the phenomena of religious life lend plausibility." In these places at least, it was "as though transmundane energies, God, if you will, produced immediate effects within the natural world to which the rest of our experience belongs."[27]

On the subject of immortality or the metaphysical attributes of God, James was equally cautious. Consistent with his empirical respect for facts, and his pragmatic concern for effects, he refused to "pass to the limit" as he called it, with those philosophers and mystics whose "passion for unity" or "monoidealistic bent" permitted much bolder speculation. Immortality was a question that was "eminently a case for facts to testify," and in the absence of these, James did not know how to decide. Similarly, the notion of God as "infinite" or "one and only" found no unequivocal support in religious experience. All that the facts required, according to James, was that the power should be both "other and larger than our conscious selves." This could even mean a sort of polytheism, a topic James did not propose to pursue on that occasion. But in reply to those who might object that only an all-inclusive or an absolute God could offer a "guarantee of security" or "divine protection" or "religious consolation," James closed his Postscript with the perfectly empirical point that, for all we know, there may be irretrievable loss, only partial and conditional salvation, at any rate, simply the *chance* of salvation. This was already quite enough for William James.

Nevertheless, other questions were not disposed of so easily. As the history of the reception of James's Gifford Lectures makes clear, beginning in his own time and continuing in ours, critics have heaped scorn on James for his claim that "the conscious person is continuous with a wider self through which saving experiences come," or for his blunt belief that "God is real since he produces real effects." The psychologist James Henry Leuba was quick to point out that James's discussion of religious experiences concerned *feelings,* and feelings, being mental and subjective, could not in themselves guarantee any objective referent.[28] Recent philosophers of religion have been no less unsympathetic to James's treatment of religious experience. Anthony O'Hear, for instance, complains that "such a direct appeal to experience is, in this context, entirely question-begging, once we realize that no experience in itself can ever guarantee the truth of any statement beyond that asserting that the subject of the experience has had such and such an experience." O'Hear accuses James of having glossed over an important distinction when he claimed that "God is real because he produces real effects." While O'Hear agrees it is true that our only direct evidence for electrons, for example, is the observable effects they are taken to have, he argues that "the force of the move from effect to postulated reality is entirely vitiated" when, as he believes is the case for James, "the effect depends on the psychological state of a human agent and the postulated reality is taken to be something nonpsychological."[29]

The pattern of these and of other objections to James's conclusions in his Gifford Lectures opens the whole subject of what "truth" means. James had raised this question himself when he asked of the psychological phenomena he had assembled, "What is the objective 'truth' of their content?" But he had relegated to a footnote the remark that "the word 'truth' is here taken to mean something additional to bare value for life."[30] At the conclusion of *The Varieties of Religious Experience* the problem of religious truth was left unresolved.

Pure Experience and Affectional Facts

My next concern is with the implicit but largely overlooked contribution James's *Essays in Radical Empiricism* can make to a theory of the religious dimension of experience. It is a text full of serpentine surprises. First among these is the introduction of what James called "pure experience," something which is neither physical nor mental, nor nonphysical nor nonmental. Pure experience, James explained, is simply a "that" in "the instant field of the present."[31] The crude term "stuff of pure experience" was James's expression for the fact that the flux of reality cannot be described appropriately either in objective language or in subjective language. Beginning with the supposition that "there is only one primal stuff or material in the world, a stuff of which everything is composed," and which he called pure experience, James concluded that "then knowing can easily be explained as a particular sort of relation towards one another into which portions of pure experience may enter."[32] This thesis was not to be taken as positing an essence or any universal element out of which all things are made, for James cautioned that there is no general stuff out of which experience at large is made. If one asks what any one bit of pure experience is made of, the answer, James said, is always the same: "It is made of that, of just what appears, of space, of intensity, of flatness, brownness, heaviness, or whatnot."[33]

No feature of James's philosophy has generated more diverse interpretation than the doctrine of pure experience. A. J. Ayer interprets James's radical empiricism as a reconstruction of what is phenomenally given.[34] D. C. Mathur interprets James as reconstructing the life-world or the phenomenologically given world.[35] Bruce Wilshire claims that James was on the way toward positing a transcendental reduction of phenomenological "originals," while John Wild considers James to have rejected just such a transcendental reduction.[36] Others see a fundamental tension between the doctrine of pure experience and the pragmatic program which has sometimes been charged with "oscillating between two contrary notions: the one, that experience is 'through and through malleable to our purpose,' the other, that facts are 'hard' and uncreated by the mind."[37] In questioning the status of pure experience, R. B. Perry asks, "Is it a neutral stream of 'pure' experience, or is it the mental series, which constitutes the metaphysical reality?"[38] Charlene Haddock Seigfried answers that pure experience is "a limit concept, an explanatory hypothesis which can be postulated but not experienced as such. . . . "[39] But how is this to be reconciled with James's own characterization of empiricism as radical only insofar as it refuses to "admit into its construction any element that is not directly experienced"?[40]

What few interpreters notice is the implicit reconcilability between James's interpretations of experience as both malleable and as already structured. The thesis of pure experience can be consistently maintained by showing how relations are really given in experience, and yet need the specification of a context to differentiate them.[41] The inconsistencies into which James sometimes lapsed on this point can be avoided by joining his thesis of immediately experienced conjunctive relations, "actual in their immediacy but not in their specific construction," with his realization of what Seigfried calls the "context-dependency of all relations which have been explicitly grasped in their intellectualized form."[42] Rather than being completely malleable or an absolute chaos, pure experience is best characterized as only a "quasi-chaos" in which the continuity of the flux is real, with its own resistances, tendencies, and relations, but the relations have not yet emerged as fully constituted. James emphasized that "thoughts and things are absolutely homogeneous as to their material, and . . . their opposition is only one of relation and of function."[43] And as Seigfried explains, "pure experience is not a composition of thought and thing, but an identical experience which can stand either for a fact of consciousness or for a physical reality depending on which context is taken."[44] Thus "the given" for James, far from being single discrete bits of sense data, is a "much-at-onceness" of dynamic felt transitions which become fully constituted relations according to the selective interests and purposes reticulated by the individual. Out of the literally hundreds of "observation statements" I *could* give at any moment of "blooming, buzzing confusion," the ones I *will* give depend in part upon my interests, desires, and purposes.

On my reading, the single most important contribution of James's radical empiricism to an understanding of experience is its provision for a unified bridge between the onesidedness of two extremes: either of asserting the priority of selective "subjective" interests (thus making relations an arbitrary imposition) or of asserting the priority of implacable "objective" facts which the mind only mirrors (thus making relations immutable). With one stroke, the thesis of pure experience initiates a fundamental revision of the traditional concepts of object and subject, of thought and thing, and of percept and concept. James's argument that pure experience precedes and calls into question these distinctions serves to undercut any supposed irreducible dualisms in experience and also has tremendous significance for developing a radically empirical account of religious experience, the main outlines of which we can now begin to trace.

The first major consequence to be derived from James's account of radical empiricism is that the contrasting terms of subject and object, thought and thing, perception and conception, are secondary intervening categorizations which we build into our experiences depending upon functional contexts. That they are complementary distinctions is explicit in James's claim that "subjectivity and objectivity are functional attributes solely, realized only when the experience is 'taken,' *i.e.*, *talked-of*, twice, considered along with its two differing contexts respectively, by a new retrospective experience, of which that whole past complication now forms the fresh content."[45] As John E. Smith justly points out, "James's proposal is not, as has sometimes been thought, to eliminate the distinction between thought and thing by returning to an undifferentiated experience or feeling, but to reinterpret the traditional subject/object distinction in terms of contexts and functions."[46]

The discovery that subjectivity and objectivity are only contextual and functional distinctions has far-reaching consequences for breaking one of the deadlocks surrounding discussions of the religious dimension of experience. For instance, in *The Varieties of Religious Experience* James himself concluded that the "full personal facts" of religious experience vindicate the hypothesis that "the conscious person is continuous with a wider self through which saving experiences come."[47] Critics charged then, as they do now, that "saving experiences" are subjective, not objective, that they pertain to feelings, not to cognitions, and that they cannot themselves play any validating role in cognitive questions. On the assumption of the traditional, dualistic distinction between objectivity as applicable to extended material stuff out there and subjectivity as applicable to unextended spiritual stuff nowhere, critics easily challenge the right to ground "objective" claims on "subjective" experience. But James's doctrine of radical empiricism subverts the very dualism behind this objection. Thoughts and things do in fact share attributes. Both may be "beautiful, happy, intense, interesting, wise, idiotic, focal, marginal, insipid, confused, vague, precise, rational, casual, general, particular, and many things besides."[48] Moreover, distinguishing clearly between the contributions that both sensations and thought make to experience becomes impossible. "Sensations and apperceptive ideas fuse so intimately," James claimed, "that you can no more tell where one begins and the other ends, than you can tell, in those cunning circular panoramas that have lately been exhibited, where the real foreground and the painted canvas join together."[49]

As James construed it, the distinction between subjective and objective experiences serves most usefully to separate the energetic from the inert. Objective experiences are those that "act." Subjective experiences are those "whose members, having identically the same natures, fail to manifest themselves in any 'energetic' way." Subjective fire never burns real sticks; mental water may or may not put out a mental fire, whereas with objective experiences, "consequences always accrue."[50]

Implicit in this discussion is an answer to the question that dogged James in the *Varieties* and that still appears to vitiate discussions of religious experiences. The question whether religious experiences are merely "subjective" or "objective" may be answered, on radically empirical grounds, by observing the connections between religious experiences and other, subsequent experiences that persons have. Those experiences which are shown to be demonstrably inactive over the long haul may turn out to be classified as "subjective." But this is established not by showing their lack of reference to material objects, but their ineffectiveness in entering into relations of continuous transition with other experiences. Indeed, reference plays no general role in the subjective/objective distinction at all, since "objectivity" is analyzed in terms of "activity" rather than objective reference or picturability or representation, and so forth.

Not only does radical empiricism dissolve the standard subjectivist objections to religious experiences, it also provides a key to understanding the place of the religious dimension in experience. There are certain experiences, James showed, which are neither subjective nor objective but "affectional." Feelings, particularly appreciations, "form an ambiguous sphere of being, belonging with emotion on the one hand, and having objective 'value' on the other, yet seeming not quite inner nor quite outer . . . ." For instance, experiences of painful objects are usually also painful experiences. "The adjective wanders as if uncertain where to fix itself." Shall we speak, James asked, of wicked desires or of wickedness? Of healthy thoughts or of thoughts of healthy objects? Of good impulses, or of impulses toward the good? James said of these and other affectional facts and appreciations:

> Both in the mind and in the thing these natures modify their context, exclude certain associates and determine others, have their mates and incompatibles. Yet not as stubbornly as in the case of physical qualities, for beauty and ugliness, love and hatred, pleasant and painful can, in certain complex experiences, coexist.[51]

In working out "The Place of Affectional Facts in a World of Pure Experience," James advanced two important arguments. First, if we were to rigidly classify feelings, affections, or appreciations as subjective or objective, "language would lose most of its esthetic and rhetorical value . . . . The man is really hateful; the actions really mean; the situation really tragic—all in themselves and quite apart from our opinion."[52] Second, experimental evidence points to the discovery that there is "a primitive stage of perception in which discriminations afterwards needful have not yet been made" and in the affectional facts James was considering this is precisely the condition which lasts.[53] There is no urgent need to treat affectional facts as rigorously mental or as rigorously physical facts. Even when subjected to later discriminations, they cannot be unambiguously classified as either objective or subjective. How do we tell whether they denote activity or inertness? James reasoned that

> although they are inert as regards the rest of physical nature, they are not inert as regards that part of physical nature which our skin

covers. It is those very appreciative attributes of things, their danger-
ousness, rarity, utility, etc., that primarily appeal to our attention
. . . . The 'interesting' aspects of things are thus not wholly inert
physically, though they be active only in these small corners of nature
which our bodies occupy. That, however, is enough to save them
from being classed as absolutely nonobjective.[54]

Although James himself did not do so, this argument may be
directly applied to the analysis of religious facts. Once religious experiences are classified as affectional facts, neither subjective nor objective in any dualistic sense, they may be appraised as *active* in specifi-
able ways, *inactive* in others. The peculiarity of religious experiences,
gliding as they seem to between subjectivity and objectivity, is then no
more exceptional than the larger class of experiences which share this
same status. The religious experiences considered by James in *Varieties*
are objective in the sense that they are encounters of something there.
When persons encounter divinity this way, their experiences are thus
actual. Little else may be indicated, however. But at least any charge of
granting privileged treatment or exceptional status to religious experiences is dispelled, along with the dualistic impugning of such experiences as "merely subjective."

Furthermore, the affectional facts and appreciative perceptions
which comprise the religious dimension of experience are distinguished by their orientation to the experienced relations, the felt
transitions, the qualitative feelings James described in the *Varieties* as
the sense of the "More" in experience that is lived. These are *active*
experiences of conjunctive relations and, as such, are objectively giv-
en. Hence the "piecemeal supernaturalism" which James subscribed
to in the *Varieties* and his postulate of an "unseen world" should not be
misunderstood. Against the background of the scientific materialism
of his day, "naturalism" was mechanistic, not yet organic, and not then
a suitable category for expressing James's vision. But once the vague,
dimly given "More" manifested in religious experiences is seen in the
light of James's later essays on radical empiricism, the "More" can be
explicated as a penumbral region of *relations*.

To draw out the implications of this statement, we need to develop the *religiously* significant shift involved in James's argument that
"while common sense and what I call radical empiricism stand for
[relations] being objective, both rationalism and the usual empiricism
claim that they are exclusively the 'work of the mind'—the finite mind
or the absolute mind, as the case may be."[55] By counting conjunctive,
no less than disjunctive, relations as *given* in experience and felt *as
given*, James corrected classical empiricism's disjointed world and at
the same time obviated the need for rationalism's postulation of a

transempirical agent of unification. He thereby affected a stunning shift of emphasis with respect to the locus of religious attention and interest: away from absolutes and toward relativities; away from the focus of sense perception and toward the background fringe experiences. Not *another* world, but a *wider* world is the locus of religious interest.

Among other things James advocated radical empiricism for its "matchless intellectual economy." He was able to eliminate numerous outdated metaphysical mysteries and paradoxes simply by making the argument that "though one part of our experience may lean upon another part to make it what it is in any one of several aspects in which it may be considered, experience as a whole is self-containing and leans on nothing."[56] By refusing to entertain the hypothesis of transempirical reality, for instance, James side-stepped the whole agnostic controversy of his time. By insisting that the conjunctive relations found within experience are "faultlessly real," he removed any need for an absolute of the Bradleyan type. And by his pragmatic treatment of the problem of knowledge, he eliminated the need for an absolute of the Roycean type.

Above all, James claimed that radical empiricism saves us from the great pitfall of an artificial conception of the relation between knower and known. Whenever in the history of philosophy the subject and its object have been seen as absolutely discontinuous entities, James found that "all sorts of theories had to be invented to overcome" the paradoxical character of an object's "presence" to a subject or of a subject's "apprehension" of an object. James singled out three for particular criticism: representative theories, which put a mental representation, image, or content into the gap, as a sort of intermediary between subject and object; commonsense theories, which left the gap untouched, declaring the human mind able to clear it by a self-transcending leap; and transcendentalist theories, which left the gap impossible to traverse by finite knowers, so that an Absolute had to be brought in to perform the saltatory act.[57] In contrast to these, radical empiricism found that at the very heart of finite experience, "every conjunction required to make the relation intelligible is given in full."[58]

What James criticized in these philosophical theories finds a ready point of comparison in theological constructs as well. If radical empiricism is therapeutic for the philosophical ills James diagnosed, it should also have importance for some of the theological devices that have been invented to explain the relation between "the divine" and the self. In place of the representational theories, the commonsense theories, and the transcendentalist theories, we could trace the appearance in the history of theology of revelational theories which put a divine *logos*, or sacred scripture, or incarnational figure into the gap, as a kind of intermediary between "God" and "world"; fideistic or kerygmatic theologies which leave the divine-human gap untouched, declaring the individual able to clear it only by a grace-full leap of faith; and ontological theories which traverse the gap by appealing to "the power of Being-Itself," which manages to perform the saltatory act in every shudder against "nonbeing."

Radical empiricism in the philosophy of religion needs no recourse to the strategies of these theologies. If it is radical, it will "neither admit into its constructions any element that is not directly experienced, nor exclude from them any element that is directly experienced." What bearing does this have on developing a radically empirical philosophy of religion? We may say, first, that by the principle of pure experience—the principle that everything real must be experienceable and everything experienced must be real—what "God" means will be found in some concrete kind of experience. There is at least a minimal sense in which we can say "God is real since he [sic] produces real effects" and in which we can also acknowledge with James that "the divine can mean no single quality, it must mean a group of qualities."[59] But more particularly, two other aspects of James' radical empiricism bear on the question of the justification of theism. First, as we have already noticed, James's widening of sensation to include relations, his closure of any presumed gap between facts and valuations, and his assimilation of cognition to modes of feeling, all accommodate a view of "matters of fact" and the domain of the "empirical," which not only supplements but upends that of traditional empiricism and logico-linguistic empiricism. Additionally, this calls attention to the possibility of reviving the controversy over the factual meaningfulness of theistic statements on a new basis. It suggests, in terms of empiricial testability as a criterion of cognitive significance, that there are more modes of perception than meet the eye, and more to observation-statements than the physicalistic or phenomenalistic terms displayed in Chapter Two.

Against the background of the kind of empiricism which came to prevail in Anglo-American philosophy only a few decades later, James's radical empiricism should be read as a constructive corrective to empiricism's traditional concern with "facts." The collection of *Essays in Radical Empiricism* is designed as a defense of James's notion of a "full fact," which he first concluded to in *The Varieties of Religious Experience*. There James defined a full fact as "a conscious field *plus* its object as felt or thought of *plus* an attitude towards the object *plus* the sense of a self to whom the attitude belongs."[60] In this statement

James was straining for a formulation to fit four features into one: perception of whole "fields" which are irreducible in their wholeness, not discrete or atomistic sensa; an intentional aspect; a valuational attitude; and a bodily locus. As he explained:

> Such a concrete bit of personal experience may be a small bit, but it is a solid bit as long as it lasts; not hollow, not a mere abstract element of experience, such as the 'object' is when taken all alone. It is a *full* fact, even though it be an insignificant fact; it is of the *kind* to which all realities whatsoever must belong; the motor currents of the world run through the like of it . . .[61]

Precisely here is where radical empiricism locates its own resolution of the confirmability criterion debates which have formed the background of so much twentieth century empiricism. If the task of empirical justification cannot be adequately defined with reference to classical empiricism's narrow preoccupation with sense-data, nor with reference to logico-linguistic empiricism's inconclusive search for a basic observation language, it may be explored instead with reference to felt qualities of lived experience, on the basis of a radical empiricism that recognizes the givenness of relations and connections within nonsensuous modes of perception. The particular class of observation statements to which radical empiricism appeals to confirm statements of fact in the religious dimension of experience is akin to James's "affectional facts in a world of pure experience." Just such a class of observation statements will be seen to be amplified (in the next section) by Dewey's delineation of consummatory aesthetic experiences, to be attested to also in the writings of American religious empiricists (Chapter Four), and finally to be generalized metaphysically by Whiteheadian and Buddhist process philosophy (Chapter Five). On this basis, theistic and other religious statements are factually meaningful if and only if they stand in confirmation relationships to, and hence are expressible in terms of, felt qualities of experience.

John Dewey and the Religious Dimension of Experience

A remarkable feature of the academic study of religion in the latter half of this century is that no satisfactory definition of religion is agreed on by scholars. In such a situation, certain proposals made by John Dewey in the second quarter of this century may have fresh significance. Dewey regarded the quest for a satisfactory definition of religion as impossible. There is no such thing as religion in general, he said, any more than there is one kind of experience that is religious. Dewey wanted to speak instead of a religious quality of experience, a quality that could belong to all experiences. He argued against any appeal to the category of the supernatural, on the grounds that it was an unwarranted belief that introduced an ontological dualism between the realms of the natural and the supernatural. And he resisted any equation between the "religious" and "religious experience" understood as some special kind of experience that provides some individuals with a privileged access to truth not available to others.

In place of supernaturalism and *sui generis* religious experiences, Dewey offered in *A Common Faith* a naturalistic faith liberated from what he called "the load of current beliefs and institutional practices that are irrelevant" to the religious quality he wanted to preserve and express.[62] The religious as adjectival denoted for Dewey attitudes that may be taken toward every object and every proposed end or ideal. As a quality of experience, the religious signifies something that may belong to all kinds of experiences—aesthetic, scientific, moral, political—not something marked off from other experiences. What, then, is the distinguishing feature of the "religious?" Three proposals appear in *A Common Faith*. First, the religious quality of experience points to some complex of conditions that operate to effect a significant adjustment in life, a reorientation that is transformative and integrative in effect. Various interpretations may be given to this complex of conditions but for Dewey these are not inherent in the experience itself. In the same way that he regarded the doctrinal and institutional aspects of religions as largely adventitious, Dewey thought that any particular religious interpretations were to be viewed as "derived from the culture with which a particular person has been imbued." It may be argued that this view involves many more complexities than Dewey himself acknowledged, but his basic point was clear: "The actual religious quality in the experience described is the *effect* produced, the better adjustment in life and its conditions, not the manner and cause of its production."[63] This was an explicit connection of the religious in experience with the problem of integrating the self as a whole.

Second, Dewey linked the religious quality with the key role imagination plays in the unification of the self in harmony with its surroundings. The creative process of integration depends on an ideal of the *whole* self, held as an imaginative projection. So, too, "the idea of a thoroughgoing and deepseated harmonizing of the self with the Universe (as a name for the totality of conditions with which the self is connected) operates only through imagination."[64] But the integration of the self cannot be effected solely by acts of the will. The will itself is dependent upon "an influx from sources beyond conscious deliberation and purpose."[65] In Dewey's view, there was no need for recourse to the category of the supernatural here, for the process could be understood as entirely natural, in so far as "the self is always directed toward something beyond itself and so its own unification depends upon the idea of the integration of the shifting scenes of the world into that imaginative totality we call the Universe."[66] This ideal functions as a unification of an imaginatively projected totality of conditions and possibilities. Because the unification embraces a totality far more inclusive than that envisioned in cases where ideals are projected as solutions to specific problems, Dewey designated it as religious, and he considered religious faith to be the appropriate response in the presence of such an ideal. Religious faith was the unification of the self through allegiance to inclusive ideal ends, which imagination presents to us and to which human will responds as worthy of controlling our desires and choices.[67]

On this basis, the third feature of Dewey's discussion in *A Common Faith* becomes intelligible. He proposed that the object of faith and of the term "God" designated "the active relation between the ideal and the actual." With this formula, Dewey intended to straddle two quite different conceptions of the "object" of religious faith, neither of which did justice, in his view, to the fact of human experience as it is situated against the background of a natural environment. Supernaturalism, on the one hand, stood for an antecedent Being, fully existent, while "aggressive atheism" could only view the divine as a product of utter hypostatization, a mere fantasy. But Dewey countered each of these extremes by insisting that "we are in the presence neither of ideals completely embodied in existence nor yet of ideals that are mere rootless ideals, fantasies, utopias."[68] For there are forces in nature and society that generate and support the ideals. The ideal possibilities that are unified in imagination have roots in existence. Far from being made out of "imaginary stuff," they are "made out of the hard stuff of the world of physical and social experience."[69] But there is tension here, too. In order for ideals to have the force of operative purposes, they need to be brought into *active union* with actual conditions of human life that support their realization. Dewey was willing to use the term "God" to denote the function this active union of ideal and actual performs in human experience.

The constructive import of Dewey's discussion in *A Common Faith* was limited to the points I have just mentioned. Santayana could sardonically describe this as "a very common faith indeed!" but that was to miss the point of Dewey's explicit desire to put the religious quality of experience on a naturalistic footing, freed from specific sectarian absurdities. And yet, if this were all that Dewey had to offer, it would not take us even as far as James in articulating the radically empirical locus of the religious dimension of experience. There is, however, another side to Dewey's thought, one which Santayana with his aesthetic interests should have appreciated, and it is this side, I am suggesting now, which holds the most importance for radical empiricism today. I believe the best way to follow up on Dewey's suggestive statements in *A Common Faith* is to turn to his discussion of quality in *Art as Experience,* a book he was completing concomitantly with the writing of *A Common Faith* in 1934. Here the close connection between the aesthetic and the religious is made explicit and the status of "wholes" in experience is further clarified. Dewey's understanding of aesthetic experience is susceptible to a positive and richly suggestive interpretation of the religious in experience. The quality of experience with Dewey called "religious" in *A Common Faith,* where he advocated its liberation from institutional religions, is remarkably close to the aesthetic quality of experience described in *Art as Experience.*[70]

Basic to the radically empirical interpretation of the religious dimension of experience is the kind of meaning Dewey described as "qualitative." It is James's "blooming, buzzing confusion" once having buzzed to some effect, bloomed to some fruitage. The effect or fruitage is what Dewey termed qualitative meaning.[71] *Art as Experience* presents several important claims that shed light on James's earlier notion of a fringe of relations, a horizon, a "More." According to Dewey, quality is located in every experience, event, or situation as its pervasive texture, functioning as the background to everything in the focus of consciousness. It is directly experienced ordinarily through the meditation of acting and thinking. Quality, as basic and objective to any human experience, is what renders a situation or experience just what it is and not another. A situation is a whole, in Dewey's sense, by virtue of its immediately pervasive quality. The pervasively qualitative, Dewey explained, is not only that which binds all constituents into a whole, "but it is unique; it constitutes in each situation an *individual* situation, indivisible and unduplicable."[72] In the interaction between human beings and the environment, quality is experienced as the goal and point of human effort. In instrumental experience, qualitative meaning is accompanying and directing; in what Dewey called "consummatory" experience, it is primary, direct, and focal.

Qualitative meaning is most directly and focally met in aesthetic experience. The aesthetic dimension of experience can be a feature of ethical, religious, and all other forms of experience. In *Art as Experience,* Dewey analyzed the consummatory phase of experience as dominated by "esthetic quality that rounds out an experience into completeness and unity."[73] According to this analysis, "in a distinctively esthetic experience, characteristics that are subordinate are controlling—namely the characteristics in virtue of which the experience is an integrated complete experience in its own account."[74] Aesthetic experience is "consummatory," that is, it is whole, wholly had, and enjoyed. Consummatory experiences are marked by their completeness and integrity; they are pervaded by a heightened aesthetic quality. Consummatory experiences involve "an adjustment of our whole being with the conditions of existence," precisely the language Dewey also used in *A Common Faith* to describe the religious in experience.

The particular quality that links aesthetic experience, ordinary experience, and religious experience is the quality of "wholeness." Dewey advanced, but did not develop, several important claims about this quality. The whole, he said, is what calls forth the mystical in us, in any intensely experienced work of art. Ordinary experience, too, possesses a unifying qualitative background. Every experience, whether aesthetic or ordinary, possesses a peculiar "dim and vague" quality, of "margins" or "bounding horizon." It is a sense of "an enveloping undefined whole." Any work of art itself may be described as a *whole* which elicits and accentuates a sense of "belonging to the larger, all-inclusive whole which is the universe in which we live." This fact, Dewey thought, is the explanation of that feeling of "exquisite intelligibility and clarity we have in the presence of an object that is experienced with esthetic intensity." He added that it also explains "the religious feeling that accompanies intense esthetic perception." It is as though we are "introduced into a world beyond this world which is nevertheless the deeper reality of the world in which we live in our ordinary experiences. We are carried out beyond ourselves to find ourselves."[75]

The explicit connection Dewey made between art and religion, between aesthetic and religious experience, opens up radical empiricism's conception of the religious, indeed of the divine, to something more than Dewey himself allowed in *A Common Faith* as the "Ideal." Drawing together the various strands which have emerged in this chapter as ingredients in a radically empirical account of the religious dimension of experience, we can now summarize briefly two principal methodological conclusions.

In the first place, the reconstruction of the religious as an accentuation or intensification of the aesthetic permits us to explicate the radically empirical *content* of the religious dimension of experience in terms of aesthetic qualities of experience, involving the criteria of harmony, intensity, contrast, and complexity. The quality of the religious dimension of experience, like that of art, is a matter of maximizing complexity and intensity in harmony. The more contrast in the harmony, the richer and more complex the experience. But whereas art represents a movement from complexity to simplicity within the limits of a canvas, or a musical score, or poem, novel, or play, religious experiencing seeks an unrestricted field of value whose harmony involves an ever-enlarging integration of complexity and intensity of relational data.

Second, Dewey's suggestive language about "an enveloping undefined whole" and the "larger, all-inclusive, whole which is the universe in which we live" designates the naturalistic equivalent of the traditional theistic *referent* of the religious in experience. This is precisely the language currently favored by a wide variety of contemporary religious thinkers who seek to interpret the ontological referent of the religious in experience. But to raise the question of the theistic or ontological appropriation of "the whole" is to raise explicitly the very issue which is at the heart of contemporary religious and theological disputes.

Just here is where radical empiricism, as a distinctive philosophical position on the overall character of experiencing *per se*, presents a sharp alternative to theological conceptions of "the whole" generated by strictly metaphysical or transcendental methods of analysis. For radical empiricists, contemporary attempts to state metaphysically the abstract, general, universal, and necessary features of the reality of the whole merit the suspicion of falling prey to Kant's transcendental illusions and of hypostasizing metaphors about "limits," "grounds," and "horizons." In their own more modest and tentative approach to language about the whole, radical empiricists stand closer to Wittgensteinians and most phenomenologists than to Heideggerians, Tillicheans, Neo-Thomists, and Hartshornians. Following James and Dewey, radical empiricists have not presumed, as do many contemporary theologians, that the pattern of human logic reproduces the structure of nature or that the whole possesses a rational structure readily accessible to the human mind. Having no reason to suppose that ontology recapitulates philology, radical empiricism therefore sees no reason to ascribe strictly literal meaning to metaphysical language about the whole.

What radical empiricism does see reason to stress, and what the American religious empiricists of the next chapter emphasized above all, is the reality of relations. For to stress relations is to emphasize the social conception of the self, to characterize the "religious" as constituted by the greatest complexity, deepest intensity, and widest range of experienced contrasts, and finally to conceive the whole primarily as an aesthetic matrix rather than as a rational structure.

Chapter Four

Radical Empiricism: A Theistic Interpretation

Theisms, like empiricisms, come in many varieties. Those who are theologically accustomed to identifying theism only with its transcendental or supernatural forms are apt to take a rather blinkered and unhistorical view of the matter, failing to see the variants and mutations in the concept of God that have been thrown up in the ongoing historical debate in the West. Even many scholars of religion, who may have moved beyond the quest for certainty (with Rorty) and beyond the flight from authority (with Stout), still tend to take their philosophy of religion at a gallop, overlooking as full partners in the "conversation" an important group of American religious thinkers who were never seriously tempted by that quest or traumatized by that flight.

In this chapter, I want to single out three principal figures in the history of American religious empiricism: Henry Nelson Wieman (1884–1975), Bernard E. Meland (1899–   ), and Bernard M. Loomer (1912–1985). By bringing their versions of religious empiricism to attention now, when the philosophy of religion may be at the point of according new sympathy to antifoundationalist, neopragmatic, and historicist themes, I intend a double retrieval: first, of the primacy of the category of experience in their religious inquiries, and second, of the possibility of a theism emergent from a radically empirical perspective.

Henry Nelson Wieman: Empirical Theism and Naturalism

More than any other philosopher of religion or theologian of his generation, Henry Nelson Wieman kept alive William James's hope

113

for a new "association of religion with empiricism." Hailed as "the most comprehensive and most distinctively *American* theologian of our century,"[1] Wieman developed a uniquely empirical method of religious inquiry. In a career covering a sixty-year period until his death in 1975, Wieman's work spanned several distinct phases of American religious thought. In most of these he was moving against the stream. In contrast to his predecessors Edward Scribner Ames, Shailer Mathews, and Gerald Birney Smith of the early "Chicago school" in the 1920s and 1930s, Wieman protested the modernist move to make "God" just an imaginative construct or a symbol for human ideals. He wanted instead to capture the sense of "God" as a living power, concretely experienced. In contrast to John Dewey in the 1930s and 1940s, Wieman argued for a theistic rather than a humanistic naturalism, all the while using the language of Dewey's instrumentalism and James's radical empiricism. Against Barth, Brunner, and the post-World War II development of neoorthodox theology in America, Wieman protested the notion of a faith which burns all philosophical and cultural bridges in a retreat to a "Wholly Other" God. At a time when neosupernaturalism and "revelational positivism" appeared to be winning the day, Wieman repeatedly raised the question of God in the context of religious empiricism. Later, against Tillich's depiction of the importance of noncognitive symbols in religious life, Wieman called for even greater attention to the importance of the cognitive relation. Against Whiteheadian philosophy, with which he had at one time sympathized, Wieman issued sharp criticisms of the metaphysical approach to religious problems. And against the "death of God" theologians, whose criticisms he had in many ways foreshadowed, Wieman carried the conviction that the only "God" worth talking about was one that could be found in the actual processes of human life, however drastically different this might be from traditional conceptions of God.

If only for its singlemindedness, Wieman's work represents the most tenacious effort in the history of American religious thought to find and to analyze the empirical meaning of "God." Like Hume, he assumed that human knowledge is vitally dependent on what affects the senses and what operates in human life. Unlike Hume, however, Wieman's empiricism did not *derive* knowledge from immediate experience as such, but stressed also the role of knowledge as *interpretation* of sense experience. Like the logical positivists, Wieman at times took the stand that "observation and experiment alone can inform us." Unlike them, however, he held that values are manifest in the stream of experience and have more than merely emotive or expressive significance. Like analytic philosophers in general, Wieman recognized the futility of talking about "nonlinguistic knowledge," but unlike most of those who have used the analytic approach to interpret problems of religious belief, Wieman did not assume that the idea of God must mean only what it meant in the orthodox theological or ontological traditions.

In evaluating the questions Wieman's work raises for empirical philosophy of religion today, it is necessary to appreciate the way in which he posed and answered the religious question, related it to radical empiricism, and pressed its conclusions in the context of certain naturalistic assumptions.

The Human Predicament and The Religious Question

Wieman's basic quest was to describe that empirical process upon which human "salvation" or transformation depends. The soteriological concern was evident throughout his work. The religious question for him was finally a soteriological one, but it was posed in humanistic terms. How can we be transformed so as to save ourselves from the depths of evil and to attain the greatest good? How should we live so as to realize our potentialities, to move beyond our present powers of appreciation, valuation, and judgment, to effect new growth? What ultimate commitment can release human life from the predicaments of superficiality, meaninglessness, and destruction? The recurring direction of Wieman's whole inquiry was the question, Is there a process which *operates in human life* to which we can and should give ultimate commitment so as to be transformed by it? In this respect, his work can be read as one prolonged amplification of William James's succinct conclusion that religion has to do, in one way or another, with (1) an uneasiness, and (2) its solution. Of course, humanists, secularists, existentialists, and a host of other voices have agreed with Wieman's assessment of the human predicament. There is something wrong with us as we naturally stand, and there is something to be done about it. Wieman located religion squarely in the context of questions which concern soteriological matters and the nature of ultimate human commitment. But he sought answers to these questions just as firmly in the actual practice of human life, in a way which was not strictly dependent upon the forms of any particular religious tradition.

As Wieman analyzed the human predicament, he was struck by the fact of human incapacity to transform itself simply by pursuing proper ideals or desired goals. Conscious volition alone, social programs, scientific advance, were not enough to effect the kind of creative transformation Wieman thought was needed. The problem with all humanly projected values and ideals was their very controllability, their susceptibility to manipulation, their restriction to human experience as presently structured. The transformation that is needed, Wieman decided, is a fundamental one, beyond the level of any present human appreciations, valuations, and ideals. But this is precisely what Wieman considered human beings most unable to accomplish. The tendency to rest content with achieved levels of satisfaction, to cherish the present good rather than to risk the better, to identify created goods as the key to value, means that human life is blocked at the very point where the new and greater good requires a transformation even of everything that human life already is, has, and cherishes. The answer to the human predicament then can only be found, according to Wieman, in the kind of creative transformation that reorganizes the total personality, fusing conflicting oppositions, delivering us from the fears and inhibitions that hinder a spontaneous and free life. Creative transformation is what liberates us to see what we did not see before, to appreciate what was previously unappreciated, to integrate the flow of our life through past, present, and future experiences. Creative transformation calls for the development of new structures of perception, new meanings, ideas, habits, attitudes, institutions, and practices.

Wieman was emphatic that theism, if it was to be relevant to the human predicament at all, had to be related to the religious question of creative transformation. Summing up his own intellectual life, Wieman wrote in 1963: "The problem which has engaged me for the past fifty years can be put in the form of a question: What operates in human life with such character and power that it will transform man as he cannot transform himself, saving from evil and leading him to the best that human life can ever reach, provided he meet the required conditions?"[2] But creative transformation can occur only in the form of events, and the empirical method, Wieman believed, was the only possible way to distinguish events and to have any knowledge of what transformation results from them. "Nothing can transform man," Wieman claimed, "unless it actually operates in human life. Therefore, in human life, in the actual processes of human existence, must be found the saving and transforming power which religious inquiry seeks and which faith must apprehend."[3]

Convinced that the question "is there a God?" could lead only to idle philosophical speculation or else to reaffirmation or denial of a traditional belief, Wieman hoped "so to formulate the idea of God that the question of God's existence becomes a dead issue."[4] By posing the religious question in soteriological form and by exploring the theistic problem in the context of a naturalistic evolutionary worldview, a radically empirical epistemology, and a contextualist theory of value, he argued for the importance of observation, experimental testing, and rational inference in determining what is that "existing reality" upon which human life is most dependent for an *increase* in value of any kind.

Throughout his writings, Wieman employed various formulas to designate the meaning of "God" in naturalistic and empirical terms. In an early forthright statement, he declared:

> Whatever else the word God may mean, it is a term used to designate that Something upon which human life is most dependent for its security, welfare and increasing abundance. That there is such a Something cannot be doubted. The mere fact that human life happens, and continues to happen proves that this Something, however unknown, does certainly exist.[5]

This sufficed for a minimal definition of God, so as to focus inquiry away from supernatural postulates or authoritarian appeals, but by itself it offered no more than a self-confirming proposition. Later, he was to use other, roughly synonymous terms: Growth, Creative Synthesis, Creativity, Creative Event, and Creative Interchange. From Wieman's earlier writings to his later writings, we find a shift of emphasis from terms such as "ultimate cause" and "growth," which indicated a process operative throughout the whole of nature, to terms such as "creative event" and "creative transformation," which Wieman defined as referring to the more limited sphere of human life. As he explained this shift:

> Increasingly, I am convinced that religious inquiry is misdirected when some presence pervading the total cosmos is sought to solve the religious problem. It is even more futile to search infinite being which transcends the totality of all existence. It is impossible to gain knowledge of the total cosmos or to have any understanding of the infinity transcending the cosmos. Consequently, beliefs about these matters are illusions, cherished for their utility in producing desired states of mind . . .[6]

The polemical nature of this argument was characteristic of Wieman's strict adherence to radical empiricism. All conceptions of God, of mind, of forms, and of possibility had to be shown to refer to experienceable events and their structures and qualities. This was a protest against the appeal to transcendental grounds, orders, causes, or purposes beyond time and beyond nature. Beyond the structure of natural events, their qualities and relations, there was—Wieman bluntly stated—nothing.

Religious Experience and Scientific Method

Wieman's initial effort to examine the empirical meaning of God led him to the topic of religious experience, an interest prevalent among American religious thinkers in the 1920s and 1930s. The conclusions he reached in his 1926 study of *Religious Experience and Scientific Method,* and the criticisms he himself later made of it, are noteworthy for what they reveal about the hesitations religious empiricism has had in dealing with the topic of religious experience.

Wieman began by laying down three directives which were required for a more adequate and, in his sense, a more "scientific" knowledge of God: (1) a clarification of that type of experience which can be called distinctively religious; (2) an analysis or elucidation of that datum in this experience which signifies the object being experienced (God); and (3) inference concerning the nature of this object.[7] Even on a sympathetic reading, Wieman's conclusions regarding the second and the third points must ultimately be judged to fail, largely due to the difficulties attending his description of the first.

The difficulty appears immediately in Wieman's very general description of religious (or mystical) experience as "a certain way of experiencing the world of empirical fact, and nothing more."[8] In context, Wieman clearly offered this as a statement of naturalism and as a way of qualifying even James's "piecemeal supernaturalism." But it soon became clear that by "the world of empirical fact" Wieman meant nothing less than the whole passage of nature. He went on to describe religious experience as an immediate experience of "that undefined awareness of total passage of nature, the undiscriminated event" where one becomes aware of "a far larger portion of that totality of immediate experience which constantly flows over one."[9] Further, this was said to involve a "state of diffusive awareness, where habitual systems of response are resolved into an undirected, unselective aliveness of the total organism to the total event then ensuing."[10]

Bordering on what James had called "the threshold of consciousness," the occurrence of religious experience could be provoked by anything that broke up routinized habits of attention and response, whether it was bewilderment in the face of crisis, experience of intense sorrow, beauty or grandeur, intimate personal encounter, or deep reflection. Unlike everyday consciousness, it was, Wieman said, "experience caught in that intervening period when old meanings have faded out and new meanings have not yet been born."[11] Some might wonder whether this is not in fact a rather precise definition of meaninglessness. Wieman, however, considered it "experience *pregnant* with meaning . . . a quivering mass of sensitivity to the total undiscriminated situation."[12]

It appears then, that to Wieman at this stage in his thinking, the distinctive feature of religious experience, in contrast to aesthetic experience with which it is frequently compared, is its receptivity to "some more inclusive event, ultimately to that totality which is the 'operative present . . . urging nature forward,' including 'the whole, in the remotest past as well as in the narrowest breadth of any present duration.' "[13] But if this is the distinction of religious experience as Wieman defines it, we may worry that this is also its extinction from the point of view of conscious discriminations. Responsiveness to "the concrete fullness of immediate experience which is constantly pouring over us and through us, but which we ordinarily ignore"[14] is a hard thing to translate into *knowledge*, especially of the sort for which Wieman was searching. The difficulty, as he later recognized, is that consciousness, which is always selective, cannot deal with the total fullness of immediate experience. Furthermore, if critical intelligence is to be applied to an understanding of religious experience, it is necessary as Wieman himself acknowledged that "the event which is being experienced must be distinguished from the process of undergoing the experience."[15]

On this analysis, what distinguishes religious experience from other forms of experience is its orientation to a mass of merged data, so merged as to be a single unanalyzed and unsifted datum. By contrast, ordinary consciousness gives awareness of only a very few data that have been selected from out of this flood. Religious experience thus involves a form of consciousness in which one is aware of the same world in which one constantly lives, but that awareness is more diffusive, and less selective or analytic.[16]

Such an expanded state of awareness raises serious problems for empirical method in religious inquiry. Its very complexity appears resistant to analysis and, to make matter worse, Wieman's depiction of it as noncognitive would appear to make it completely recalcitrant to cognition. This hardly allows him to proceed to isolate a datum of concrete experience which can be called "God" and for obvious reasons. First, "immediate awareness of the total passage of nature," even assuming such a possibility, does not in itself offer any cognitive significance, nor does "the undiscriminated event" afford much basis for inference. In addition to this, if there is no filtering or selectivity of stimuli in this mode of experience, then there is no organizing or interpretive structure in the experience. *There is also no object.* The experience may be perfectly objective, but that is not to say that is is *of* an object. Wieman's procedure for isolating the "datum" of concrete experience which can be called "God" breaks down precisely at the point of his claim that "only the total undiscriminated event can involve God,"[17] where the total event is apprehended "as the single unanalyzed passage of nature."

Dropping Wieman's more problematic language, we can summarize his early notion of religious experience as that which begins in "open awareness" and ends in an "appreciable world" of much wider and deeper meaning than ordinary experience offers. Ordinary experience may, in fact, continuously offer the possibility of larger and fuller meanings, but the human organism is rarely responsive to this underlying richness. Religious experience, as an element in the creative transformation of the self, frees the self, even if momentarily, from its normal awareness and enables the development of new habits of attention. Old patterns of response, conventional modes of interpretation, loosen their hold. Open awareness of the immense range of possibilities of new experience beyond the reach of normal awareness expands the self. By suspending the habitual structuring of experience, religious experience leaves the person subsequently responsive to a wider, deeper, and richer range of experience. It provides a freedom to transcend established assumptions and unexamined habits of thought.

But this immediate experience, significant as it is, has no truth value in and of itself, and yields no knowledge of the nature of "God." Wieman could conclude at this stage only that "God" is "that object, whatsoever its nature might be, which will yield maximum security and abundance to all human living, when right adjustment is made."[18] It is little wonder that Wieman closed his first book with the wonderfully understated remark that "the exact nature of God is still problematical and may be for many years to come."[19]

Wieman's Radical Empiricism

The distinctiveness of Wieman's radical theism came together in the unique blend of naturalism, neomaterialism, and radical empiricism, which he defended most fully in *The Source of Human Good*. In that work, the basic metaphysical categories Wieman employed were *events,* made up of their *quality* and their *relations.* The ultimate actualities of the world were conceived as events, happenings, specific instances of energy. There is no substance or reality underlying this world of happenings. There are only relations, that is, structures, among these units of energy, at various levels of complexity. In human experience, events or energy-processes are apprehended immediately as the "flow of felt quality." The metaphysical doctrine in Wieman's radical empiricism was implicit in his claim that "quality then is the ultimate substance of the world out of which all else is made."[20]

The place of quality in Wieman's radical empiricism is exactly parallel to what James called "conjunctive relations." Wieman explained that:

> The quality is not in the organism or in the mind or in the table or in any one of the several components necessary to *yield* the quality. They do not merely yield the quality—this complex, structured together-ness *is* the quality. The quality is these components in their total togetherness as one single inclusive event with its components immediately experienced; and beyond such experience we cannot go.[21]

It was Wieman's view that every event accessible to human experience is a quality or a complex of quality and every event is an instance of energy. He argued on this basis that whenever energy is experienced by the human organism, it is quality or a complex of qualities. Therefore, relative to human experience, all energy is "inexhaustible" to analysis and "infinite" in its complexity. Wieman noted that we have names to discriminate only relatively few qualities. The name "structure" is given to the demarcations and interrelations of events whereby events are experienced as different and yet as related. Whereas concrete events as qualities are immediately apprehended by feeling, they are known cognitively only through the discrimination of their structure or character or form. The discrimination is always an abstraction from concrete reality.

Wieman's analysis of quality has obvious affinities with that stream of American philosophy that has repeatedly emphasized the dimension of qualitative immediacy in any comprehensive view of experience and nature. The theme was present in James's attention to the immediate perceptual flow from which concepts are carved out and to which concepts are applied in novel ways. It was represented in Peirce's Firstness, the category of immediacy. It appeared in the work of Santayana as a concern with aesthetic and tertiary qualities. And it was at the heart of Dewey's theory of experience and nature. Like Dewey, Wieman carefully disentangled his appreciation of the qualitative immediacy of life from the troublesome claim that there is such a thing as immediate knowledge.

The importance of the claim that experience is not in itself knowledge, echoing Dewey's distinction between "having" and "knowing," cannot be overestimated in Wieman's work. Qualitative experience is a necessary, though not a sufficient, condition for acquiring knowledge. Knowledge, Wieman always insisted, comes only through the discrimination of structures whereby concepts pertaining to the concreteness of experience can be distinguished, related, and organized. The human mind, he frequently repeated, is not adequate for apprehending the concrete events directly experienced, felt, or had, "but it is fitted to apprehend structures of possibility which may approximate to various degrees the demarcations and interrelations of actual events."[22] Since qualities cannot be described in their immediacy, they can be known only by the structures pertaining to them. Description of those structures is cognitive. Awareness of the immediacy of quality is noncognitive, Wieman maintained.

Given the metaphysics and epistemology of his radical empiricism, two questions must be answered in the affirmative if Wieman's method is to yield knowledge of God. The first is the question whether God is an actual, observable process in nature that is accessible to concrete experience. The second is whether inquiry can discern a structure exhibited by this process which distinguishes God from what is not God. It may be argued that Wieman's contribution to an empirical philosophy of religion stands or falls with his success in answering these two questions.

Functionalist Fallacy of the Creative Event

The religious naturalism Wieman defended led him to insist that a transcendent God has no religious availability unless we can point to events in human life in which God functions. And if we can do that, then it is these events in human life that take on religious meaning and command religious commitment. To say that God is a process, an event, a pattern of qualitative meaning, or creative interchange, is not simply to describe what God *does*. Rather, given Wieman's radical empiricism, it is to describe God's very *being*.

Wieman's attempt to specify the essential structure of that which is God was most fully developed in *The Source of Human Good*. His argument was set in the context of competing value theories and alternative interpretations of the locus of value. Without siding with any particular theory—whether subjective, transcendental, contextual, or instrumental—Wieman's bold objective was to demonstrate that value, however it is defined or wherever it is located, *increases* in just one way. This was a remarkable claim and Wieman clearly intended to establish it empirically. In fact there is human good. Values do get promoted. There must be sources of that good. Is there, he wanted to know, that which is *invariably* at work whenever there is an increase of human good?

Wieman first identified something common to all good, which he termed "qualitative meaning." By this he meant "that connection between events whereby present happenings enable one to feel not only the quality intrinsic to the events now occurring but also the qualities of many other events that are related to them."[23] The richness of qualitative meaning is a function of the connections particular events have to other events.

Yet even qualitative meaning as a created good can become demonic. Wieman's question as to how the *growth* of qualitative meaning occurs was answered by pointing to the creative event as the activity within nature which *increases* qualitative meaning. In what he called the creative event, as distinct from created goods, Wieman found "something which retains its identity and its unity through all change in itself and through all change in other things."[24]

Creativity and the creative event are inseparable in Wieman's discussion, but the two words carry an important distinction in meaning. Creativity is the structure, the character, or form which an event must have to be creative. It is an abstraction from the concrete reality which is the creative event. Whatever unity the creative event has is the unity of the structure which it exhibits. The problem of the one and the many in connection with a naturalistic conception of God thus entails a dialectic between the concrete and the abstract. The creative event in every concrete instance displays multiplicity (as well as change and temporality). Its unity is an identity of structure which pertains to the abstract character of the event.

As a further specification of the character of the creative event, Wieman lifted up for analysis four subevents, all of which call attention to the processive and relational character of the creative event. These are: (1) emerging awareness of qualitative meaning derived from other persons through communication, (2) integrating these new meanings with others previously acquired, (3) expanding the richness of quality in the appreciable world by enlarging its meaning, and (4) deepening the community among those who participate in this total creative event of intercommunication.[25] The creative event, he stressed, is constituted by the simultaneous happening of all four subevents working together and not by any of them alone.

This then was the character of the creative event or what Wieman later called creative interchange. This was what he considered worthy of ultimate human commitment. This was what he discerned as capable of the deepest human transformation. To whatever extent one can speak of God working in human experience, this fourfold process is exemplified empirically. Anything else one may mean by salvation or by God, if it is to be experienced, is experienced concretely as this natural process. If we accept the view that processes are the ultimate and only concrete reality, then Wieman's theism follows empirically. This was *not* the argument that wherever God is manifest, there is creative transformation, but precisely the opposite—wherever one finds creative transformation, *there* one finds what has been meant by "God."

Wieman's conviction that the creative event functions to transform us as we cannot transform ourselves suggests the presence of a strong functional analysis in his method. Even while disclaiming any source of human good that is "metaphysically transcendent," Wieman explicitly claimed that such a source is "functionally transcendent."[26] Furthermore, his identification of "God" with "the creative event" assumed that God is known and described only in terms of certain functions found within human life. The very title *The Source of Human Good* suggests an interest in uncovering antecedents in terms of which creative transformation is possible.

The question must be asked whether any explanatory import can be claimed for Wieman's analysis. Does the fourfold creative event as so described furnish the necessary and sufficient conditions of transformation toward the greater good? It must be shown to be a sufficient condition in order to be certain that the required transformation will actually follow from the creative event. And it must be shown to be a necessary condition in order to guarantee that whenever the required transformation occurs the creative event occurs. If Wieman's argument cannot be shown to satisfy both of these conditions, then his theory of the creative event is, in Quine's words, "a cog which turns no explanatory wheels."

If we examine closely the logic of Wieman's argument concerning the creative event, we discover that it follows the form of functional analysis. And if we compare the logic of Wieman's argument to several well-known critiques of functionalism,[27] it appears to suffer the same fate as other functionalist theories. In particular, the work of Carl Hempel in appraising "The Logic of Functional Analysis" calls into question the logic of Wieman's procedure.

According to Hempel's schematic characterization, a functional analysis takes the following form:

(a) At t, s functions adequately in a setting of kind c (characterized by specific internal and external conditions).

(b) s functions adequately in a setting of kind c only if a certain necessary condition, n, is satisfied.

(c) If trait i were present in s then, as an effect, condition n would be satisfied.

(d) Hence, at t, trait i is present in s.[28]

The problem with the logic of such an argument is that it commits the fallacy of affirming the consequent with regard to conditional premise (c). The fallacy of affirming the consequent can be simply illustrated. For example, I might assert the factual case that I was late for the meeting, and then argue for the following explanation. If I get caught in a slow elevator, I will be late for the meeting. I was late for the meeting; therefore, I was caught in a slow elevator. The conclusion is obviously invalid. I may have overslept, or taken the stairs, or lost my way. As Hempel notes, "it might well be that the occurrence of any one of a number of alternative items would suffice no less than the occurrence of i to satisfy requirement n, in which case the account provided by the premises of [the argument] simply fails to explain why the trait i rather than one of its alternatives is present in s at t."[29]

In order to validly infer (d), (c) would have to assert that *only* the presence of trait i could effect satisfaction of condition n. Otherwise, the reasoning really amounts to no more than saying: if I am late then something must have happened. But it is extremely doubtful that conditional premise (c) could ever be shown to be a *necessary* condition in any such argument.

Transposed to the terms of Wieman's discussion, Hempel's schema yields the following internal structure of Wieman's argument:

(a) At a given time, value increases, s, in a certain setting of kind c.

(b) Value increases, s, in a certain setting only if a certain necessary condition of transformation towards the greater good, n, is satisfied.

(c) If the fourfold creative event is present in s, then as an effect transformation towards the greater good occurs.

(d) Hence, at t the fourfold creative event is present in s.

The problem with Wieman's analysis is, as above, that completely different events might also suffice to produce the same consequences. As an argument, it commits the fallacy of affirming the consequent.

Two revisions can be made in Wieman's argument which would make it formally valid, but neither is very welcome. Briefly, Wieman could rule out the possibility of functional equivalents to the creative event by definitional fiat. That is, he could treat the creative event as the necessary condition that is functionally indispensable to the transformation towards the greater good, thus amending (c) above to read: *Only* if i were present in s then as an effect condition n would be satisfied. This would safeguard the postulate against any conceivable disconfirmation, but at the price of abandoning it as an empirical hypothesis and conceding that it is a covert tautology.

A second alternative is available. Let us suppose that Wieman could replace the troublesome premise (c) by the following statement supplied by Hempel:

(c') i is the class of all empirically sufficient conditions for the fulfillment of requirement n in the context determined by system s in setting c; and i is not empty.[30]

Here, however, the best that one is able to infer from the premises (a), (b), and (c') is the weak conclusion that some one of the items included in class i is present in system s at time t. This conclusion still offers no grounds for expecting the occurrence of any particular item from i rather than one of its functional alternatives. Moreover, as Hempel shows, this kind of inference is trivial.

Both of these moves, which Hempel believes render the argument logically valid,[31] reduce it either to a tautology or to a triviality, neither of which is very helpful to the claims of an empirical theism. My conclusion is that Wieman's theory of the creative event, when mapped against Hempel's model of empirical explanation, is unable to meet the criteria for successful explanation.

At most, Wieman's functionalist method explains only the function (creative transformation) by reference to the phenomenon by which it is achieved (the creative event). This still leaves us with no explanation for the creative event itself and no theory of an empirical sort. It gives us an explanation of transformation, perhaps, but not of God as the creative event. It makes Wieman's model, as far as theism is concerned, heuristic, but not empirical.

As an extension of this argument, I think it must be recognized that the creative event, as Wieman himself depicts its structure, lacks sufficient unity to achieve what is claimed for it. Specifically, this means that Wieman's additional theistic claims, that the creative event is "absolute," in the sense that it is good under all conditions and circumstances, that it is "unlimited," "infinite in value," "unqualified in its goodness," and "entirely trustworthy," are claims that do not appear to be derived from empirical observation of any sort nor verifiable by it.[32] It is doubtful that an *invariant* structure could ever be discerned empirically at all. Upon further investigation, then, the theism in question may turn out to be much more of a *poly*theism, as in fact it is coming to resemble in Charles Hartshorne's recent speculations.[33]

Heuristic Value of the Creative Event

If the preceding criticism is correct, as I believe it to be, then it lends some substance to the appraisal Langdon Gilkey offered some years ago of Wieman's empirical philosophy of religion. What concerned him was the difficulty of the method from the side of contemporary philosophy. "For while many contemporary theologians may ask 'Is this *theology?*,'" Gilkey wrote, "almost all present-day philosophers will apodictically assert, 'This is not *empirical.*'"[34]

There are, however, various ways to be empirical, in philosophy as well as in the study of religion. Wieman's functionalist theory of the creative event fails as a theory, but the *distinction* he made between created goods and the creative event has another, heuristic, function to perform. By means of this distinction Wieman was able to view all created goods (*e.g.*, our present structures of knowledge, achieved values, and highest ideals) as subject to testing, revision, and correction. None is necessary; all may and should be criticized. In this respect, the overall spirit of Wieman's philosophy of religion is very much in line with the important perspective of Karl Popper's falsifiability/criticizability criterion. Popperian empiricism allows us to see that "what characterizes the empirical method is its manner of exposing to falsification, in every conceivable way, the system to be tested. Its aim is not to save the lives of untenable systems but, on the contrary, to select the one which is by comparison the fittest, by exposing them all to the fiercest struggle for survival."[35]

Despite his announced dissociations, Popper was still close to the positivist tradition in his delineation of the *kinds* of available falsification which he saw as falling into the familiar bifurcation of conflict with hard fact and logical contradiction. Later, when he stressed the criterion of criticizability, *i.e.*, willingness to make our claims vulnerable, to innovate, and to treat nothing as exempt from revision, he introduced something far more important, something already central to Wieman's understanding of religious inquiry. When Popper extended his method to apply to political institutions as well as to empirical science, he was advocating a method which Wieman was extending to religious beliefs. Just as Popper argued that the question is not the traditional one about the source of knowledge but rather the question, how can we hope to detect and eliminate error? Wieman articulated a view of all religious knowledge and belief as conjectural, tentative, provisional—unremittingly fallibilistic.

Both projects, Wieman's and Popper's, are engaged in criticism and the growth of knowledge, which is arguably the one feature of empiricism to survive the various assaults against "empiricist" philosophy in this century. Popper's aim was to construct a philosophical program for fostering creativity and counteracting intellectual error, instead of positing authorities in terms of which to guarantee or secure beliefs and opinions. Wieman's aim was to construct a mode of religious inquiry into whatever does empirically operate in human life to create and transform human existence, regardless how drastically different it may be from received beliefs in any area. Within both programs, the question is not how do you know? for we do *not* know. A different question becomes paramount: "How can our lives and institutions be arranged so as to expose our positions, actions, opinions, beliefs, aims, conjectures, decisions, standards, frameworks, ways of life, policies, traditional practice, etc., . . . to optimum examination" and ultimate transformation for the better?[36] Popper wanted commitment to the process of criticism to produce growth of knowledge. Wieman wanted commitment to the creative event to produce growth of value and qualitative meaning.

I am trying to suggest not just that an interesting parallel exists between Popperian and Wiemanian empiricism, but something more: I think that Wieman's writings address a dimension of the problem not seen by Popper. Wieman's is an argument about concrete relations between *people*, not about semantic properties of *statements*. To Wieman, a "ruling commitment," as he called it, clearly should be directed only to the creativity operating in human existence to create, sustain, and transform all structures of life, doing for us what we are unable to do for ourselves. But what are we to make of Wieman's notion that a ruling commitment of a religious sort is to be given to the creative event? Is this no more than his naturalistic version of the old theological idea that human sinfulness and despair puts us in need of a power not our own that makes for creativity? Is the distinction between the creat*ive* event and creat*ed* good simply Wieman's version of what Tillich called the "Protestant principle," an injunction not to absolutize the relative? Perhaps so, but I think it is susceptible to more than this. Disregarding the spirit of high Calvinism which sometimes colors Wieman's rhetoric about commitment to the creative event, I suggest that we can see it as a self-relativizing rule that has both epistemological and existential implications for an empirical philosophy of religion. Epistemologically, it represents a release from the trilemma of dogmatisms, fideisms, and relativisms, the three most common standpoints assumed by philosophers of religion in answer to meta-level justification-questions. Existentially, it leads to felt qualities of experience very much like those associated with Buddhist concepts of "letting go" and of existing without attachment to cravings and desires, even in the realm of belief and opinion. In this way, Wieman's formulation of the creative event is like the Buddha's raft, which is for crossing over, and not for getting hold of.

One may, with Popper and a host of other Western thinkers, simply submit to fallibilism as inherent in all empirical truth-claims and commitments, assenting to this as an ineluctable feature of modern rationality. And one may, with Hartshorne and other rationalist philosophers, press rationality to the point of postulating certain necessary truths for which we have no conceivable alternatives. Or, like Buddhist thinkers of many periods—and like Wieman, too—one may find in the very conditions of contingency a religious significance that informs the whole quality of life as lived. Contingency embraced without any nostalgia or yearning for necessary truths yields a different quality of life than contingency assented to as necessarily so in the absence of any conceivable alternative.

No one knew this better than Bernard Meland whose "elementalism" and method of "empirical realism" involved a constant stress on the experience of creaturehood.

Bernard Meland: Empirical Realism and Lived Experience

One of the singular merits of Bernard Meland's method of empirical realism in religious inquiry is that it offers a version of empiricism which does *not* represent, in John Stuart Mill's telling phrase for Jeremy Bentham's work, "the empiricism of one who has had little experience." Indeed, Bernard Meland could hardly be counted among the academic philosophers and professors of whom Flannery O'Connor complained "I think you folks sometimes strain the soup too thin." Insofar as Meland's empirical realism is a distinct advance upon various forms of classical empiricism, linguistic empiricism, and logical empiricism, it participates in the spirit of William James's radical empiricism and moves in the same general orbit as Wieman's work. But Meland cast an even wider net than Wieman.

By distinguishing his own particular orientation as one of "empirical realism"[37] in religious inquiry Meland meant to distill the resources of the emergent evolutionary perspective and to do justice to the directives within Whitehead's philosophy of organism as much as within radical empiricism. The greatest single impact on Meland's thought, as he himself has recounted it, was the import of relativity physics.[38] He saw the new developments in modern physics, leading to an organic view of nature, as countering the mechanistic view that had been dominant since the time of Newton. The organic imagery, associated with space-time, relativity, and the behavior of wave particles, invoked a new kind of realism among scientists and theologians alike. Meland fully exploited the possibilities this offered for moving beyond the imagery of idealism which liberal theology had leaned on as an exaggerated reaction to scientific mechanism. Breaking completely with the imagery of idealism, Meland was able to attend in his religious inquiry to more holistic, organic, and "elemental" concerns than were to be found in the literature of existentialism and phenomenology. For five decades he hammered away at the holistic point that "ultimacies and immediacies traffic together," conveying the empirical presence of God in the Creative Passage of nature.

Meland's broad definition of empirical realism as "a process orientation of inquiry looking to the lived experiences"[39] should be comprehended in connection with his focus on lived experience as inclusive of real relations, transitions, and tendencies, and the organismic imagery he steadily employed. Empirical realism is undeniably a metaphysical interpretation of human existence, consisting of a certain understanding of the role of creativity, internal relations, emergent events, and the social nature of reality, themes which were systematically elaborated in Alfred North Whitehead's philosophy. If it has been Charles Hartshorne who has most conspicuously pursued Whitehead's recommended "flight in the thin air of imaginative generalization," it was Bernard Meland who again and again landed the airplane on the rich soil of lived experience.

Meland's Appeals to Lived Experience

In order to distinguish various strata of that rather large topography of lived experience, I would propose that "lived experience" is principally used by Meland to mean at least four different things: (1) the emergent act of individuated experiencing as a concrete, holistic perceptual event which discloses a depth of experienced dynamic relations; (2) the disciplined reflexive act of "appreciative awareness" as an aesthetic, valuational, and noetic mode of cognition bringing to dominance the relations dimly discerned in (1); (3) the living nexus of common human activities and relationships, embracing "the full range of immediacy as it applies to individual life spans, families, or communities of people, of whatever scope";[40] and (4) the patterned distillations of past events and valuations persisting within culture and cultus and comprising a "structure of experience" that conditions (1), (2), and (3).

Only experience in the first sense refers to actual experiencing as an activity or perceptual event, akin to James's "perceptual flux" and Whitehead's "causal efficacy." The second, third, and fourth senses correspond to Meland's effort to articulate the first sense in ways that present the primal flux of immediacy "as something more compelling than an ambiguous, preconscious flux, awaiting conceptualization."[41] For the first sense of lived experience is neither self-interpreting nor available to reflection while experience is happening. Therefore, experience in the first sense cannot be simply described. Any effort to render such a description turns out to be a reconstruction. In Meland's case, the reconstruction proceeds along the lines of radical empiricism and process philosophy wherein "the primacy of perception" is acknowledged as "the cardinal doctrine of process thought."[42] Within that framework, Meland was able to assert that "perception, while it carries the risk of illusion, bodies forth the actuality of the occasion as well; and it does so in a way that makes it the final court of appeal."[43]

Yet it would be mistaken to read Meland's appeal to the primacy of perception as referring either to naive experience or to what he called the early empiricists' "priority only in the sense of an elemental antecedent."[44] The first sense of lived experience, even with the features Meland discerns, has only as much primacy as the presupposed philosophical analysis or organismic imagery which renders those features epistemically accessible. This recognition means that the realist appeal to perception as the final court of appeal must admit of some circularity. We cannot fully isolate lived experience from interpretations about the nature of experience, and then compare those assumptions with a theory-free or presuppositionless experience. If we cannot compare interpretations with anything that is not itself a product of another interpretative framework, any appeal to lived experience is relative to the theory available. But this is not vicious circularity as much as it is an astute hermeneutical procedure, on the assumption that the data of experience can be better understood given this presuppositional framework rather than some other. Whitehead, in a rash moment, once wrote: "I hold that the ultimate appeal is to naive experience," "to the general consciousness of what in practice we experience."[45] More carefully, however, Whitehead knew that "the first point to remember is that the observational order is invariably interpreted in terms of the concepts supplied by the conceptual order."[46] There is thus no such thing as uninterpreted experience, and no possibility of a simple consultation of experience. In short, even "the relevance of evidence is dictated by theory."[47] At the same time, it must be stressed, as both Meland and Whitehead do, that experience affects theory and that observations modify the conceptual order as well.

With this in mind, I suggest that Meland's theological treatment of the realities of faith as empirical events most consistently proceeds through an appeal to experience in the third and fourth senses as an invitation to reflexive experience in the second sense for the sake of illumination and expansion of experience in the first sense. In these various appeals to lived experience, the development of Meland's method of empirical realism can be discerned. The explication of lived experience as tied to radical empiricism and the factical, but as an activity, that of the world as given in our grasping of it, is evident as early as *Modern Man's Worship* (1934). By the time of *Fallible Forms and Symbols* (1976), Meland bluntly stated that the scope of lived experience is "as inclusive as the datum that would designate all that is."[48] In the same work, he unified the dominant themes of radical empiricism and process philosophy to formulate his most complete and complex phenomenological expression of lived experience as:

> simultaneously a patterned occurrence exemplifying and bodying forth the stream of ever recurring concretions as a communal event and an intensified channeling of that stream into individuated life-spans, each with its own legacy of inherited possibilities as given in the structure of experience and with its unique fund of possibilities as an emerging event.[49]

It is this "thick" experience of the world, not the thin given of immediacy of traditional empiricism, nor the text-world of current hermeneutics, that constitutes for Meland the primary datum for religious reflection. The realities of faith transpire within (1) lived experience as perceptual events, are known consciously in (2) "appreciative awareness," are lived intermittently in (3) common social events, and are mediated, sustained, and altered by virtue of (4) particular "structures of experiences."

It might seem that any methodological stance which takes as its "most immediate empirical datum" something as inclusive and ill-defined as "the sheer event of existing"[50] would run the risk of losing touch altogether with any recognizable meaning of "empirical" and becoming wholly absorbed in vague appeals to "mystery." It is important to note, therefore, that Meland's recurrent appeals to "the mystery of existing and of becoming" actually function to evoke attention to the insistent particularities which are embodied in experience as lived in all four senses. The inexhaustible allusiveness of these insistent particularities which constitute lived experience gives rise to a sense of mystery, but for Meland it is a mystery which inheres more in the myriad *qualities of the known* than in the mere quantity of the unknown. One result of this orientation is that Meland was able to discern a religious significance in the causal efficacy of life, an emphasis not shared by other leading process theologians whose sensibilities are stirred more profoundly by the open future, the lure of ideals, and the relevance of possibilities. It is no oversight that Meland's writings do not reveal any recourse to the rather desperate White-headian strategy of requiring God to provide an "initial aim" to guide every process of becoming. The conjoint operations of "depth" and "ultimacy," as Meland employed these notions, and their contribution to a "structure of experience," allows the value in past facts to supply incentive for novel concrescence. Novelty is thus always a function of the predominance of some organized qualitative meaning in the structure of experience which gives initial direction to new centers of emergent creativity.

On the naturalistic assumption that it is the insistent particularity of concrete events which comprises the whole of actuality within the Creative Passage of nature, Meland demystified the notions of "depth" and "ultimacy." Both are shown to be given within the immediacies of experience as lived. The depth dimension of lived experience consists in there being a nexus of many more relations than we are explicitly and articulately conscious of, giving a fringe or penumbral background quality to what is immediately in the foreground of experience. The dimension of ultimacy is similarly recast as an aspect of immediacy, connoting an efficacy inherent within "a continuous thrust of the Creative Passage" or relational ground of every existent event.[51] What is ultimate is therefore experienceable now. It is experienced as "simultaneously the present, inclusive of the legacy of the past inherent in its structure of experience, together with what is prescient of its future range."[52] Likewise, all the theological themes of faith, salvation, revelation, creation, grace, and judgment refer to experienceable realities as events now—or they are nothing. "Grace," according to Meland," is not an intrusion from without the plenum of concrete events that are becoming, but a resource . . . emanating from relationships within the context of the lived experience."[53]

As Meland's attention shifted constantly between culture and cultus the realities of faith were found always to refer, in both their derivation and their verification, to the felt qualities, particular events, and dynamic relations of lived experience. Even the experience of "Ultimate Efficacy attending all existence,"[54] Meland's empirical circumlocution for "God," refers to a datum within this world here and now, in which we actually exist. What is at stake then in religious inquiry is the clarification of a nexus of relational events which is a perpetually opening ground of emergent meaning, but never an axiomatically sure source of deductively certain knowledge about the world.

Meland's Empirical Theism

As an empirical theist, Meland recoiled from bold speculations concerning the nature of God and cautioned against any assumption that a metaphysical system, however intelligible it may be, can ever be definitive or adequate. Over the course of his career, Meland employed a fascinating series of circumlocutions to adumbrate the empirical import of "God" as "creative matrix," "matrix of sensitivity," "sensitive nature within nature," and "Ultimate Efficacy within relationships." All bear the stamp of the relational thinking with which he attended to the textured complexities of lived experience. In his last book he explained:

> I have recoiled from trying to envisage or to define God in any complete, metaphysical or ontological sense, preferring instead to confine attention to such empirical notions as the creative act of God and the redemptive work of God in history. Much of the meaning we appear to find in life, we bring to it, as Kant observed, through our own forms of sensibility and understanding. But, as James and Bergson were later to remark, countering the stance of Kant and Hume in one basic respect, the nexus of relationships that forms our existence is not projected, it is given. We do not create these relationships; we experience them, being given with existence. And from this matrix come resources of grace that can carry us beyond the meanings of our own making, and alert us to goodness that is not of our own willing or defining. This goodness in existence which we do not create, but which creates us and saves us, is the datum to which I mean to attend. It is literally a work of judgment and grace, a primordial and provident goodness, the efficacy of which may be discerned in every empirical event of creativity, sensitivity, and negotiability. Thus I am led empirically to speak of God as the Ultimate Efficacy within relationships.[55]

Meland could speak of the creative act of God or the redemptive work of God in history precisely because he could understand these theological concepts as having terminations in experience. Their content could be explicated nonmythologically in terms of the emergence of "creative" and "redemptive" qualities arising out of the interrelatedness of concrete processes entirely within the natural order.

The very terms of his empirical theism allowed Meland to propose a subtle bypass operation on a question which has been a perennial problem for any theism: is the nature of God one or many, or, dialectically expressed, can the nature of God be understood as somehow both one and many? This is the underlying issue that surfaced in the 1930s between Dewey's naturalistic humanism and Wieman's naturalistic theism.[56] Transposed into naturalistic terms, the issue can be posed in the form of the question: which is to be affirmed, the power of corporate human intelligence to draw the world of nature and the projected ideals of the imagination together in a plan of directed activity, or the existence of some more-than-human principle of progressive integration which is operative in human life and possibly in the cosmos? Dewey's position was that there is no single process that works for good. "God" is a symbol for the sum of all processes involved in the union of the actual with the ideal. Wieman, however, held as an empirical claim that there is a unity, an organic connectedness, of the conditions which constitute the good, and that it is not strictly determined by the human imagination. For Meland, who adopted a mediating position on this issue, it was not a particularly pressing problem whether God be conceived as primarily a oneness or a manyness, as long as the *actuality* of that complex reality could be affirmed realistically.

Meland's own solution to the crux of the problem between Dewey and Wieman was to supply the dialectical recognition that the term "God" refers to a reality which is both one *and* many. He pointed out that when Wieman spoke of "that something of supreme value" he implied a single object, and elsewhere when he used language about "those most important conditions . . . which must have supreme value for human living," he implied a pluralistic reality. This ambiguity, however, is problematic only if one assumes, as Meland did not, that the term "God" must refer to a reality which is *either* one *or* many. Oneness, according to Meland's resolution of the issue, is "reality synthesized" in an act of human imagination, and the many is "reality analyzed."[57] The word "God" is a collective term, referring to a plurality of activities with which human life may cooperate. There is no particular point then in contending for the superiority of either the oneness or the manyness. For purposes of worship, the term God has been understood as a collective representation of a wealth of sustaining activities. For purposes of reflective inquiry, or for practical tasks requiring an analytic method, the term God calls for other expressions of the empirical phenomena encountered. God is worshiped as one and served as the wealth of reality expressed through a plurality of activities. In contrast to those cosmic theists who would postulate that such activities are concretely synthesized as one God, the only conclusions which Meland's observations supported were that (1) "the term 'God' is essentially a religious or contemplative concept" according to which the many conditions of reality are imaginatively synthesized into one; (2) when an empirical, analytic, scientific procedure is

needed in order to gain understanding or make practical adjust-
ments, the method yields to manyness; and (3) the structure, character, or process is a multiplicity of functions, pluralistic in character.
The pattern is abstract.[58]

Wieman's reply, indicative of what Meland was to call a "veiled
absolute" in his thought, was that oneness is just as empirical as manyness. "We truly experience the oneness of God," according to Wieman, "whenever we experience that great goodness that consists in the
unity of many conditions, each of which is indispensible to the goodness experienced. Our experience of the goodness is experience of the
oneness of the operative conditions which sustain and constitute it."[59]
But here Wieman's empiricism betrayed a lingering idealist presupposition from which Meland's was relatively free. Why should it be
supposed that the good is always unitary, one in form and structure,
whereas evil is pluralistic? Like James, Meland took with full serious-
ness the presence of evil in experience and the tragic sense of life,
themes which radical empiricism has persistently used to temper the
bias of absolutistic monotheism.

The Linguistic Gap

Meland's sound critical sense led him to avoid conceiving the
character of lived experience as either collapsing into its forms of
expression, or, on the other extreme, emptying wholly into the dark-
ened well of feeling. Intelligibility, he said firmly, "precludes a mind-
less immersion in the stream of experience, or a reveling in the fantasies of feeling."[60] Meland is in fact an example of a religious empiricist
who has gone out of his way to insist that "we must seek clarity,
meaning, intelligibility, and surety with persistence and with all the
critical facilities at our command."[61] At the same time, Meland insisted that "we live more deeply than we can think."[62] This maxim is
perhaps the best summary and most characteristic motif of his entire
work. It captures his sense of a continual tension between the search
for precise definitions, clear distinctions, definite meanings, and his
recognition, at the same time, of the felt inadequacy of thought and
language to convey the full dimensions of the relations and resources
within which we live.

The peculiar tension which this method generates, however, has
serious consequences for empirical inquiry in religion. It entails that
(1) a gap exists between extralinguistic meaning and its linguistic
expression, and (2) lived experience to some extent always outruns the
capacities of linguistic expression. But by virtue of these very prem-

ises, radical empiricism, I submit, finds itself at a methodological impasse: it cannot but appeal to a prelinguistic or extralinguistic context if its descriptions are to be concrete, but as linguistically expressed, its appeal to this concrete context, or to the depths of lived experience, can at best be oblique. The exact extent to which experience outruns linguistic expression is therefore not a matter that can be stated at all. If it is the case that "we live more deeply than we can think," then we are at a loss to *describe* any awareness which surpasses language or thought without employing language in the very process and thus exhibiting the "more" as intralinguistic after all.

The major import of Meland's maxim that "we live more deeply than we can think" is its implicit requirement of two levels of apprehension and inquiry in the religious life. At one level, there are the linguistic forms, the cultural expressions, and the cultic symbols which have been forged out of lived experience and which are useful as guides in directing inquiry back to the organic field of actual experience. At the other level, there is the concrete creative process itself, burgeoning with a qualitative "More," which functions as a constant critique of any idolatrous tendency to equate the forms with the reality or to coalesce language and the structure of experience. In actual practice, however, this distinction turns out to be an exceedingly equivocal one to make, for reasons which I will discuss next.

Certain problematic methodological issues typically arise at the junction of experience, knowledge, and language. Embedded in Meland's work are crucial methodological decisions about their relations, which at least require explication and at most provoke controversy in today's philosophical and intellectual climate. Specifically, the areas of difficulty concern his apparent adherence to the doctrine of the primacy of perception, and to knowledge-by-acquaintance as a form of prelinguistic and nonconceptual knowledge, as well as the implications of his positing a "primal disparity between language and reality."[63]

In endorsing the idea that "perception is given a primacy as being the 'thicker experience,'" Meland explains that "reason is made secondary as being an abstraction from this richer context, and dependent upon recourse to it for verification and renewal."[64] But the thesis of the primacy of perception is ambiguous. It is most probably correct when it simply means that any conceptual structure has ultimately some empirical sources. This would be as true of myths as of the theoretical constructs of science. In this form, the thesis quite fails to help us take account of the notable differences among such things as myths, observation statements, empirical generalizations, scientific theories, religious symbols, and metaphysical principles, none of which has any simple or straightforward relation to perception "for verification and renewal." The thesis of the primacy of perception is very dubious, however, when it is understood in the sense that experience is prior to conception in each and every concrete act of cognition. Meland seems to recognize the artificiality of primacy as prior occurrence when he warns that "the interrelation of what is bodily experienced and that which is perceived, or that which is *experienced, perceived, and then conceived,* is so complex, subtle, and elusive that it defies ready distinction or analysis. Any decisive separation of them is bound to be purely arbitrary."[65] And yet his assumption here that the datum of experience is, as it were, *first* perceived and *then* conceived is an example of just such an arbitrary distinction. It is a distinction not at all essential to radical empiricism and one which an empirical philosophy of religion today would scarcely know what to do with.

In a related way, it might be asked how Meland's general adherence to the primacy of perception fares with respect to "the myth of the given." Of course, Meland does not subscribe to such nonlinguistic qualities as Lockean ideas of sensation, Humean impressions, or Kantian intuitions—the usual targets of criticism on the part of those for whom "the given" is a "myth." Nor is there any doubt that empirical realism is the very antithesis of that search for certainty and foundationalism in epistemology whose quest in the history of philosophy has been long, laborious, and unconvincing. Nevertheless, there *is* a sense in which Meland's "elementalism" bestows a kind of privileged character on "what is initially this bodily event of being, of existing."[66] It is here, after all, that the dimensional or relational context of experience is immediately felt or "given." Meland's conviction that this bodily event takes "precedence over" and provides a perceptual foundation for "secondary" forms of conceptualization invites the obvious question as to whether the content of this "experienceable base" is itself expressible.[67] His answer takes the form of reminding us that "we live more deeply than we can think," thus giving rise to the kind of dilemma recently summarized by Michael Williams who finds that

> insofar as the content of immediate experience can be expressed, the sort of awareness we have in our apprehension of the given is just another type of perceptual judgment and hence no longer contact with anything which is merely given. But if the content of immediate experience turns out to be ineffable or non-propositional, then the appeal to the given loses any appearance of fulfilling an explanatory role . . . : specifically, it cannot explicate the idea that knowledge rests on a perceptual foundation.[68]

The dilemma is not alleviated by making the distinction Meland sometimes employs between "knowledge-by-acquaintance" and "knowledge-by-description." To the degree that Meland emphasizes the nondiscursive character of knowledge-by-acquaintance, such awareness seems to lack the determinateness needed to enable it to function epistemically in confirming or falsifying his appeals to "a goodness not our own" encountered in experience, or at least in revealing the appropriateness or inappropriateness of certain metaphors such as being cradled, nurtured, sustained, gathered, and received by and into "the matrix of sensitivity." On the other hand, to the degree that knowledge-by-acquaintance is determinate enough to function epistemically in this fashion, it would seem to be in some sense conceptually mediated and thus indistinguishable from knowledge-by-description. Granted that some such term as "knowledge-by-acquaintance" is needed to point to an indispensable moment in the process that eventuates in conceptual knowledge, the controversial claim has to do with calling this prehensive activity "knowledge." By widespread agreed upon definition, "knowledge" refers to a mediating process, involving the use of concepts and language in addition to immediate experience.

Meland, like James before him, claimed for this level of lived experience a kind of knowledge. Agreeing with Wieman that knowledge-by-acquaintance is fraught with possibilities of illusion, prejudice, error, and so forth, he nevertheless found a "soundness about this elemental condition of knowing."[69] Just how much cognitive value Meland would claim for this mode of knowing is unclear. On the one hand, he held that "we know by acquaintance through bodily feeling, or through the sheer act of existing, much that we shall never know in any explicit, cognitive way."[70] On the other hand, he also appeared to hold that knowledge-by-acquaintance is not simply immediate, for it involves "accumulative acts of perception and judgment."[71] In that case, it is not immediate awareness alone that furnishes knowledge, "but this in conjunction with persistent, accumulative acts of awareness by which judgments have been formed."[72] Here the danger is precisely the one that Meland himself described critics as having noted of Wieman's method, namely, that what Wieman observed was "not experience or the data provided by experience, but a pattern of happenings presumed to be implicit in these concrete occurrences, but discernible only to those who shared his vision of reality."[73] As far as I know, Meland nowhere guarded himself against the same criticism, except to appeal to a "richer" understanding of more "unmanageable" data, an appeal which begs this particular question.

The fundamental question to be raised regarding Meland's appeal to the contextual or relational ground of any event is the extent to which it is, as he claimed, "a datum in its own right."[74] While it is easy to agree with Meland that "what appears unassimilated as conscious event or decision is not thereby rendered inactual," the crucial issue concerns the actual yield *for* experience of that which is unassimilated *in* experience.[75] We might suppose, in phenomenological discourse, that what Meland is calling for is a radical noetic reversal or shift of attention from the foreground of clear and distinct sense data to the felt background of the field of temporal causal relations which constitutes a horizon only asymptotically approached in experience. Such a reading would be consistent with James's discussion of the "fringe." But Meland asserted more than this in several passages. He wrote, for instance, that

> the witness [of faith] points simultaneously to what is beyond comprehension, designation, or communication, or even beyond what one can think. This penumbra of an *undesignatable* and seemingly *incommunicable* fringe of meaning will find its way into various modes of creative and imaginative discourse where the intention is not designation, but expressiveness, a way of holding in focus or of pointing to whatever evokes or attends the 'More' of experience conveying the wider field or dimension of living.[76]

Certainly any meaning that is not only undesignat*ed* but also undesignat*able* will be in principle incommunicable. But if such meaning is incommunicable, how then is there any way of "pointing" to the "More?" If there is more directly given in lived experience than we can detect, designate, or communicate, then we cannot know that this is the case except inferentially. But if it is by inference, then it is not directly given, after all, and no appeal to lived experience alone can serve to justify it. I suggest that Meland made matters unnecessarily difficult when he contended that "conceivably, all lived experience participates in a context of relations and resources that exceed and *even elude our perceptual experiences*, not to mention our cognitive formulations."[77] Moreover, when he advised an effort marked by "adequate sensibility as to what is beyond comprehension, conceivably *beyond our apprehension*" he quite shut the gate on us insofar as even marginal apprehension is concerned.[78] But elsewhere Meland stated more accurately that causal efficacy "can only be marginally appropriated as a conscious event"[79] and that faith as the elemental source of our being is "active often only at the level of bodily feelings, but always *potentially expressive* through conscious and assertive acts."[80]

Even so, we might ask whether Meland overplayed the potential yield of causal efficacy even in his more cautious expressions. Certainly the distinguishing feature of radical empiricism and its most significant contribution to empirical theology is the thesis that dynamic relations are experienced as given, thus establishing the continuity of perception with nature, and lending a depth to lived experience that underlies the surface semiotic structures of historical experience. Nevertheless, the inclusion of spatial, temporal, and causal relations in experience does not and cannot preclude the further need to construct even physical objects in the act of perception, as well as conceptual modes in the act of synthesizing data, though obviously not out of independent sense data or qualias. Neither for James nor for Whitehead is it the case that the world is just given in perception in such and such a structure so that we might read it off. Rather, our activity partially creates, sustains, and surpasses the patterns we explicate. Causal efficacy is indeed the vitality and power of life, the living core of any structure of experience, whose energy is always formed or patterned energy. But unless we are content with wordless absorption in the flux of felt qualities, we will want to relate the deeply rooted prepredicative perceptions in the mode of causal efficacy to the predicative patterns of expression. This task, however, faces almost insuperable obstacles in the form of understanding how the dimly adumbrated vector feeling-tones of prepredicative experience are to be raised to clear conscious awareness and finally given expression through symbolism. The inverse relation that process philosophy recognizes between "importance" and "clarity" seems to preclude all but the most marginal conscious expression of the concrete, relational data encountered through physical, bodily prehensions.

This raises the larger question as to whether and in what sense an empirical theology can utilize causal efficacy as a datum at all. To the extent to which causal efficacy is unconscious or semiconscious, its richness and contextual density does not seem to offer any exploitable advantage to *thinking*. Insofar as this mode of experiencing can be made conscious, it fails to provide the full richness and density Meland rightly regards as so elusive to rational forms. In the nature of the case, it is not surprising that Meland could confess in 1969: "there still is lacking in my procedure both a methodical way of focusing these occurrences for religious inquiry, and a method of inquiry suitable to the task of probing their theological import."[81]

The never fully resolved difficulty of Meland's empirical realism, as it is also of James' psychology and Wieman's contextualism, is to reconcile the prereflective flow of the dynamic felt qualities of lived experience with the structures of reflective and linguistic expression. In wrestling with this question over the years, Meland presumed "a primal disparity between language and reality"[82] and repeatedly warned against "the risk of coalescing language and reality."[83] In part, this emphasis may be due to his perhaps unwarranted anxiety that intellectuals cannot quite help getting caught in the snares of their own formalism, mistaking the manageable forms for the unmanageable facts. But more particularly, this emphasis may be the inevitable outcome of Meland's understanding of the nature of language and linguistic meaning as secondary processes of instrumental-expressive value only, apparently playing no constitutive role in the very having of human experiences. Meland did not grapple with all the implications of this position. However, in light of the whole methodological ferment in the humanities in the last two decades which generally has taken language rather than lived experience as the main focus, it may be well to reexamine the thesis of "a primal disparity between language and reality."

Surely Meland meant to assert more than the truism that language is not the world, that the word is not the thing itself, that the signifier is not the same as the signified. The more radical implications of his reasoning are apparent in a passage where he states:

> There are depths of awareness accompanying the bodily event of living and experience that yield conditions of knowing which language may not convey; or, for that matter, cannot convey. Whitehead expressed this point in those memorable words, "Mothers can ponder many things in their hearts which their lips cannot express."[84]

Does this mean, then, that the personal, individuated act of experiencing, and not just the full objective datum of that act, is more than can be said? Other passages could be cited, illustrating Meland's disarming ability to glide imperceptibly from the truism that reality exceeds thought to the more controversial corollary that experience exceeds language. It is hard to escape the conclusion that Meland held not merely to a primal disparity between language and reality, but also, more seriously, to a hiatus between human experiencing and human language. But how far are we to take this? Would Meland hold, for instance, that there is a species of experience unmediated by language and socially learned interpretations? How can that which in principle eludes linguistic expression of some sort ever yield "conditions of knowing?" Are concepts and words simply extracts from experience, merely convenient and economic descriptions of experience and reality? Or are they instead complex systems of signification which, as modern linguistics, semiology, and structuralism have shown, represent a human manner of viewing the world and of generating conventions which codetermine the very possibility of any experience at all?

Needless to say, much of theological significance hinges on the exact relation presumed between experience and expression, especially as this applies to language about the ultimate reality called God. If, for example, experience and expression are thought to be so inseparable as to be indistinguishable in practice, then one can hardly expect to *say* anything about the adequacy or inadequacy of language to experience. The major difficulty with any theory of the indistinguishable interweaving of experience and language is that both the symbolization of experience and the experience symbolized are muddled together in such a way that the meaning of the symbolic structures comes to be sought in the linguistically specified forms rather than in the felt qualities of experience. The resulting tendency is to assume or claim for such forms a certain relevance which can only be established rationally, rather than empirically.

On the other hand, however, if experience and expression are viewed as separated by an unbridgeable chasm, then language about God acquires a merely ancillary status externally related to the felt qualities which prompt its use. Religious language about "the realities of faith" may then come to be considered barren and dispensable, except perhaps for its functional utility or devotional suggestiveness. For if there is no cognitive value to the symbols and assertions of religion, if these remain simply variable expressions of an essentially noncommunicable qualitative experience, then in theory, at least, all religious symbols are equally valid expressions of a reality which is basically unknowable. This theory encourages a dramatic awareness of the limitations of discursive formulation but it also gives rise to the problem of the incommensurability of religious experience with the structures of thought and language.

In contrast to these views, Meland promoted a third model, according to which experience and language are not coextensive factors, since experience is primarily concerned with relational and processive concreteness while language is inherently abstractive. In addition to this, and going beyond what Meland implied is only a unilateral relationship, I would argue that radical empiricism should recognize a reciprocal and even codeterminate relation between experience and language. This recognition would reduce the temptation in the other two theories toward either gnosticism or agnosticism. However, it will also entail a certain inescapable relativity in matters of faith, and especially in connection with any empirical discernment of what is called "God." To attempt to report such a discernment is to acknowledge that the experience is conditioned and limited by the language which is at once both the instrument of expression and largely also the conditioning medium of experience itself. It will become extremely difficult then for radical empiricism to signify to what extent the linguistic structures are either a distillation or a distortion of experience, or to what extent the experience is a function of and determined by the available forms of language. To whatever extent language and experience are reciprocal influences, one way of speaking about God, rather than another, will have profound importance in encouraging attention to certain aspects of experience rather than to others, and even in eliciting certain experiences rather than others.

If this is so, then the complex relationship between qualitative experience and linguistic expression plunges us into a hermeneutical circle which can neither be evaded by the simple correspondence model favored by most realisms nor vitiated by the coherence theory of most idealisms. The range of felt qualities in the lives of individuals is bound up with the level and type of culture, which in turn is inseparable from the distinctions and uses marked by the language people speak. The complexity and intensity of felt qualities in an individual's experience is thus a function of the semantic field of the terms characterizing these qualities as much as of the related energies and valuations of the individual's structure of experience. For this reason, the correspondence model is inadequate insofar as it views linguistic expression as a simple description of prepredicative feelings, a way of abstracting forms which would be there without the words. The inadequacy of this model is evident when we observe that often in achieving, for example, a more sophisticated vocabulary of the emotions, we acquire, also, a more sophisticated emotional life, not just an expanded power of description. Reading a powerful novel may give one the image of an experience of which one had previously not been aware. No neat line can be drawn between the increased linguistic ability to identify or differentiate and the altered capacity to feel certain experiences which this enables. Nevertheless, it does not follow from this that saying or thinking makes it so. Not just any new linguistic usage can be urged on us, nor can we induce it voluntarily in ourselves. The distinctive objectivity of the datum of experience, insisted upon by radical empiricism, exerts its own subtle checks upon our socially mediated sign-systems. Yet there seems no way of getting at the structure of felt qualities, in religious or theological inquiry, independently of one's interpretation of them; for one is woven into the other, and language is in human life the primary agency of the very interweaving.

Bernard Loomer: An Aesthetic Order of Relations

Bernard Loomer's contribution to the development of American religious empiricism was as much by way of the art of concentrated teaching and contagious conversation as by way of his intermittent publications. For many decades one of the leading teachers and lecturers in process theology and philosophy, Loomer had in the last decade of his life come to a startling reappraisal of that movement. As a process theologian, he had long been convinced of the importance of Whitehead's metaphysics for twentieth century theology. First as the young Dean of the Divinity School of the University of Chicago, and later as Professor of Philosophy of Religion there and at the Graduate Theological Union, Loomer defended and promoted the importance of using Whiteheadian process philosophy in reinterpreting Christian theology. Toward the end of his career he was to recommend replacing the title "process theology" with "process-relational theology" or "process philosophy" with "process-relational philosophy." The way he explained this shift emphasizes his gradual movement from a rational empiricism to a radical empiricism within process thought:

> In some place or other Charles Hartshorne generously credits me with possibly having baptized this mode of thought with the name 'process philosophy' . . . As a shorthand form of designation it is popular and convenient—and misleading. It suggests that the defining characteristic of this outlook consists in the ultimacy of becoming in contrast to the classical primacy of being. But the ultimacy of becoming is only half of the story. With equal appropriateness this metaphysical viewpoint may be characterized as a 'relational' mode of thought. Except for the cumbersome quality of the phrase, the more adequate name should be 'process-relational philosophy.'[85]

This emphasis on relationality, applied to a variety of concerns, was to be Loomer's expression of James's radically empirical claim that relations are felt in the flux of experience and felt as given. Relations are constitutive of any process of becoming whatsoever. Process is—or exists, as it were—for the sake of the kinds of relationships that are creative of individuals and societies. So Loomer could say:

> The meaning of 'experience' is grounded upon a Whiteheadian or Jamesian epistemology which stresses the givenness of relations and

the primacy of bodily feelings or causal efficacy from which sense experience is an abstraction. It also involves the notion of experience as a synthetic concrescence of the many into some unity, based upon the discontinuous becoming of ultimate drops of experience or quanta of events.[86]

Within the fundamental pluralism of a radically empirical perspective, Loomer began to wrestle with the question of how this general outlook might be turned into a *living* option; that is, how it could be made an option for the living of life, not simply another adventure of ideas or mode of thought. Inherent in his approach was the conviction that:

> All the heights and depths, the originating causes and final ends, the realities symbolized by the principalities and powers (including the demons and angels) that were formerly thought to inhabit the lower and upper worlds, are now found within the many mansions of this world. This is so for some, at least, even when the inevitable implication is drawn that God must be identified, in whole or in part, with this world.[87]

Loomer had stated often that it is the task of empirical theology "to describe as best it can the God formed within our experienceable world." He had acknowledged Charles Hartshorne's admonition that empirical theology does not and cannot deal with a "necessary" God, but he was not particularly daunted by this as a problem. He had agreed that "an empirical method deals with a God who, from a rationalistic point of view, exists contingently, a God who is perhaps finite, imperfect, and surpassable in all respects." He had even considered that "possibly this kind of God is not intrinsically worthy of man's worship," and that "from the perspective of an *a priori* methodology perhaps an empirical theology is a contradiction in terms." Nevertheless, he took his own stand as an empiricist closer to Meland's "margins of intelligibility" than to Hartshorne's ontological argument.[88]

The Emergence of "Size"

Beginning roughly around 1973, Loomer began to express certain criticisms of the prevailing process rationalism he had in fact helped to engender. Reflecting more deeply on the radically empirical side of process thought, he was led to an increasing emphasis on Whitehead's idea of an aesthetic order of relations. The cash value of this idea in Loomer's more colloquial terms was what he came to call

"size," a theme he was to generalize in a variety of ways, finally extending it even to a conception of "the size of God."

By "size," Loomer explained in 1973,

> I mean the stature of a person's soul, the range and depth of his love,
> his capacity for relationships. I mean the volume of life you can take
> into your being and still maintain your integrity and individuality,
> the intensity and variety of outlook you can entertain in the unity of
> your being without feeling defensive or insecure. I mean the
> strength of your spirit to encourage others to become freer in the
> development of their diversity and uniqueness. I mean the power to
> sustain more complex and enriching tensions. I mean the magna-
> nimity of concern to provide conditions that enable others to in-
> crease in stature.[89]

Implicit in this statement were the themes Loomer introduced the
following year. In the context of a Conference on Process Philosophy
and Biblical Theology, he advocated the principles of ambiguity and
aesthetic order as essential to "the primacy of the actual, the concrete,
the historical."[90] Loomer's break with an important aspect of Whitehead's thought and of process theology first began to show in relation
to the problem of evil.

The evil that deeply concerned Whitehead was the tendency
throughout nature to remain at the level of some achieved good and
to resist further advance. Achieved good then tends to become inertial
and its energy to run down to less creative levels. This is why conceptual novelty is required to counteract inertial power. Loomer noted
this as an important perspective on the problem of evil. But he believed the situation to be even more complex and ambiguous. The
Whiteheadian separation between God and creativity was at least partially a reaction to the church which "rendered unto God the attributes that belong to Caesar," a trap Loomer wanted to avoid, to be
sure. But he wondered whether in fact the pendulum had swung too
far in the opposite direction. In contrast to the aesthetic basis of his
metaphysics, was Whitehead perhaps too anxious to keep God morally
pure and clean? Did Whitehead in this way succumb to that peculiar
temptation of a certain kind of moral passion, the temptation to reduce unmanageable problems to ordinate dimensions?

Loomer's own judgment was leading away from the metaphysical distinction Whitehead made between God and creativity, and toward the point that "the unambiguous character of God is clearly seen
only in abstraction." He argued that indeed "process thought must
not do what Whitehead does," and that the metaphysical distinction

between God and creativity "is fundamentally fatal in the long run."[91] But in asserting his own strong sense of "the primacy of the actual, the concrete, the historical,"[92] Loomer still had to contend with the question of norms for thought and judgment. He left no doubt of the radically empirical basis of his approach to this question when he said:

> There is no conceptual basis for normativeness beyond or independent of the efficient and persuasive power of the empirical and historical. In this sense, the actual is not the realization of a possible norm, conceptual or otherwise. The norm lies within the empirical, the historical itself. The norm conceptually is an abstraction from that which is concrete. There is . . . almost an abysmal difference between possibility and actuality. The force of the normativeness does not derive from that which is conceptual in the first instance. It basically derives from the power of the actual and the historical. The sole reason for thought is the elucidation of concrete experience. It is for the enrichment of concrete experience also; but the reality is the concreteness.[93]

This argument was at the same time directed against certain interpretations of Whitehead's doctrine of God's provision of an "initial aim" to concrescing (individual) occasions, involving particular and specific aims for any concrete individual. Loomer's new denial that there can be any such thing as a "possible individual" was based on the radically empirical point that concrete individuality cannot be fully conceptualized, "not even by God." Pressing this point, Loomer drew the conclusion that an individual can never know for a certainty whether his or her decision was the best relative to that context. He or she "must forever bear the haunting realization that there may have been, not one, but perhaps two or three alternative ways, equally good, of realizing some definite value in that particular situation."[94] If this is so, then in the ordering of forms and possibilities relative to any region within the extensive continuum there is no clear or sure sign which indicates that a decision favoring range, variety, and contrast bordering on chaos, on the one hand, or narrowness with greater intensity, on the other hand, is more appropriate to that particular situation.

Here is where Loomer himself saw the special power of an aesthetic conception of order which is not simply rational, or logical, or moral, or even religious where this implies a standpoint above the battle, the ambiguities, and the strange interwinings of life. Aesthetic order, Loomer claimed, is "that structure of relationships that can deal most adequately with the tensions, conflicts and dynamic processes of societal existence."[95] It is that order most suitable for dealing with the tensions involved in great ambiguities.

Over the next several years, Loomer was to give deepened expression to the relational themes of "size" and aesthetic principles on a number of occasions, generalizing their implications for "Theology and the Arts," "Theology in the American Grain," "Two Conceptions of Power," "Beauty as a Design for Life," and "The Web of Life."[96] The root metaphor of size became his most basic category of value, and the aesthetic principles of compatible range, contrast, and intensity of feeling within some unit of harmony became his measure of value. Size, as a value category, emerges as a function of the range and depth of relationships. The greater the range and depth, the greater the contrast and intensity of experience. The greater the compatible contrast, the greater the size or stature of the individual unity achieved. The largest stature occurs in the process of transforming incompatible elements, or even contradictions, into compatible contrasts, yielding the deepest intensity of experience. Confronted as we are on all levels of existence with complex data calling for creative synthesis, the question we face in every context is how to order relationships so as to maximize value. Loomer came to regard rational and moral categories as more limited, less adequate categories for dealing with the radically empirical ambiguity of life. Sometimes moral considerations are relevant, sometimes not. Sometimes rational considerations are relevant, sometimes not. The same is true for conventionally religious considerations. What Nelson Goodman has said of "truth," Loomer might have said of each of these limited categories: it is "often inapplicable, is seldom sufficient, and must sometimes give way to competing criteria." But aesthetic order, in Loomer's view, is the most *inclusive* and at the same time most *concrete* form of order which is *always* adequate.

It remained only to apply this perspective to the difficult question of theism. Some indication of the direction in which Loomer was moving can be seen in "The Future of Process Philosophy," which foreshadowed his last document on "The Size of God." In the closing pages, after examining this mode of thought from a variety of viewpoints (metaphysical, methodological, epistemological, intellectual, individual, valuational, and relational), Loomer brooded over the possibility of such a philosophical orientation becoming a mode of life—not only a mode of thought. He recalled the remark of John Herman Randall, Jr., that for centuries the naturalists had the correct methodology but the idealists had all the wisdom. He concluded with his own description of the religious wisdom that is available to and appropriate for a radically empirical religious stance within a naturalistic worldview. The religious wisdom of the radically empirical stance is importantly different from the "wisdom of the pilgrim," Loomer said. The pilgrim, in Loomer's description, is one for whom the earth is not truly his home. The pilgrim "is passing through this life on his way to another home and another life and therefore travels lightly. He is concerned about earthly life, but he has no deep attachment to it. He feels that the resources of earth and this life are not adequate for the living of it. The final resources must be derived from outside and beyond. When life comes to one of its many abysses, and meaning seems to have dissolved into nothingness, the pilgrim is not in complete despair because he has his way out, his escape hatch of transcendent meaning. He lives as one who at heart is detached from the processes of this world. His anchorage is elsewhere."[97]

To this Loomer counterposed "the wisdom of the earth." It is not only a deeply naturalistic wisdom but also, I believe, a description of the religious stance entailed by radical empiricism. In Loomer's depiction, "this is the stance of one who is deeply attached to this life, this earth, this world. He believes that this is his home. Like the Jew, he trusts that the kingdom will come and that it will come here and not some place else. Or, rather, he may believe that it is always happening here, although its more complete exemplification lies in the future." Most profoundly for Loomer, the life of attachment meant that one believes that "this life, including its possibilities, contains the resources that are adequate to the meaningful living of it." On this account, "one must live through all the suffering, tragedy, emptiness, brokenness, destruction, and evil; that one must not run from defeat, however deep the hurt; that like the ancient Jew, he must pour the ashes of his emptiness over his whole being and acknowledge what has happened, and wait creatively, openly, and hopefully for a new and deeper vision and understanding to emerge from the ashes."[98]

Finally, for Loomer the wisdom of the earth, in contrast to that of the pilgrim, entails that "one must be wholly present to the specific processes of life; that one is deeply attuned to the concreteness of life; that one does not commit himself to the abstractions that lure us from a discerning immersion in what is most deeply present at hand and concretely at work in our midst."[99] The cultivation of this discernment is precisely what radical empiricism in its religious outreach is all about.

The Size of God

The culmination of these reflections was Loomer's essay, "The Size of God,"[100] a long, dense, and disturbing document. It is disturbing as much for its challenge to certain orthodoxies within process thought as for the way in which Loomer's prose, as one commentator noted, "leans into the wind."

The fundamental argument of "The Size of God" is that if the one world, the experienceable world with its possibilities, is all the reality accessible to human life, then one religious implication is inevitable: "God is to be identified either with a part or with the totality of the concrete actual world." Loomer's own thesis is that "God is to be identified with the totality of the world, with whatever unity the totality possesses." The development of this thesis proceeds through a critical analysis of Hartshorne's *a priori* method of defining the abstract character of God, and Whitehead's conception of the primordial nature of God as the principle of order. In contrast to these approaches, Loomer arrives at the conclusion that the universal web of interconnected events has the unity of a generalized enduring "society," in the Whiteheadian sense of an "organic extensive community . . . that is always passing beyond itself."[101] God as a wholeness is then identified, in terms of Loomer's analysis, with the concrete, interconnected totality of this struggling, imperfect, unfinished, and evolving societal web. "More concretely God is expressed as the organic restlessness of the whole body of creation, as this drive is unequally exemplified in the several parts of this societal web."[102]

A question naturally arises at this point. Inevitably, it is the perennial question for a religious empiricism such as Loomer's. It has been asked fairly and frequently of other forms of religious empiricism, including Wieman's and Meland's. Why deify this interconnected web of existence by calling it "God?" Why not simply refer to the world and to the processes of life? If the being of God is not other than the being of the world, and if to speak of God is to refer to the world in some sense, then what is the point of their semantic identification?

Loomer's own answer to this question took the form of the following peroration:

The justification for the identification is both ontological and pragmatic in the deepest Jamesian sense. In our traditions the term 'God' is the symbol of ultimate values and meanings in all of their dimensions. It connotes an absolute claim of our loyalty. It bespeaks a primacy of trust, and a priority with the ordering of our commitments. It points the direction of a greatness of fulfillment. It signifies a richness of resources for the living of life at its depths. It suggests the enshrinement of our common and ecological life. It proclaims an adequate object of worship. It symbolizes a transcendent and inexhaustible meaning that forever eludes our grasp.[103]

The world is God, Loomer explained, because "it is the source and preserver of meaning; because the creative advance of the world in its adventure is the supreme cause to be served; because even in our desecration of our space and time within it, the world is holy ground; and because it contains and yet enshrouds the ultimate mystery inherent within existence itself. 'God' symbolizes this incredible mystery. The existent world embodies it. The world in all the dimensions of its being is the basis of all our wonder, awe, and inquiry,"[104]

That the world, so conceived, is also inclusive of evil, waste, destructiveness, regressions, ugliness, horror, disorder, complacency, dullness, and meaninglessness, is a fact Loomer did not overlook. But his primary focus was not on these facts so much as on an eros he also discerned, with Whitehead, "in and through, and because of, and in spite of this diversity and these contradictions and this disorder." There persists, he said, "a restlessness or a tropism not only to live, but to live well and to live better (Whitehead)."[105] But even as he was able to speak teleologically of a "passion for greater life and stature" at the "heart" of things, of an "organic restlessness of the whole body of creation," and of "a drive to create certain kinds of relationships," Loomer's discussion never lost sight of the ineradicable presence of ambiguity.

In advancing the thesis that "an ambiguous God is of greater stature than an unambiguous God," Loomer was deliberately working against the traditional idea of perfection rooted in Christian faith and against the dominant tradition of Western religious thought which has valued the resolution of the ambiguous in terms of the perfect and the unambiguous. His thesis cuts against all those who have concluded that the final answer to the ambiguity and evil in the world lies either in a nonambiguous God, or in a transcendental realm which is the domain of a perfected and indivisible whole. It cuts against the powerful and often unconscious presupposition of even much modern thought that, somehow, in some way, "the partial and fragmentary meanings we achieve will be completed, phenomenal appearances in all dimensions of life will give way to god-perceived reality, the obscure will be clarified, the ambiguous will be purified, the contradictions of life will be resolved, and sin and evil will be vanquished by a triumphant goodness."[106]

It cuts against Reinhold Niebuhr's contention that since the power of sacrificial love must be vindicated if life is to be affirmed as meaningful, and since no such vindication occurs in history, there must be a "point beyond history" where justification takes place. It cuts against Kant's presupposition that the fulfillment of the moral imperative should be conjoined with the realization of human happiness, but the *summum bonum* does not occur in this life, therefore we are entitled to postulate the existence of a nonphenomenal realm in which this unambiguous and complete union is realized—else all is finally absurd.

From Loomer's perspective all these are abstract strategies or theoretical vindications which attempt, implausibly, to transcend the ambiguity of the world.

No two thinkers had a greater influence on Loomer than Wieman and Whitehead. Yet he came to regard even their versions of theism as instances of "misplaced concreteness." Wieman's conception of God, in Loomer's considered evaluation, is "a high abstraction from the world of events." Wieman pointed to the process of creative transformation as one kind of process among many kinds, limited in effectiveness, but unambiguous in character and religiously trustworthy. In Loomer's view, however, this is not God as concretely actual, either as a concrete process or as a process with a distinguishable and unambiguous structure. Given the interconnectedness of events, transformative and nontransformative processes are to be seen as interpenetrating and participating in each other, constituting and shaping each other. "The unambiguous character of Wieman's creative event," according to Loomer, "is derived by abstractive separation from the convoluted web of events which in its totality may exemplify a spectrum of kinds and levels of ambiguous dynamics and structures."[107]

Do the several phases of the experience of creative transformation in themselves constitute a concrete process or even a set of processes with a distinguishable structure? Loomer's answer is that they do not. With greater attentiveness to concreteness, one would be led to see with Loomer that the elements Wieman described as factors of creative transformation actually emerge "within the almost infinite number of all kinds of interconnected events, of all sizes and degrees of complexity, that constitute the complex and concrete life of an enduring individual existing over an extended span of time."[108] This makes demarcation virtually impossible.

Another way of putting Loomer's point would be to say that, in the terms of Wieman's analysis, "qualitative meaning" should be seen as highly dependent upon and supported by "instrumental meaning," even though Wieman stressed their distinction. Loomer's criticism effectively blurs the distinction between qualitative value and instrumental value *as concretely experienced.* One theological implication of this blurring is that God may be manifested in structures of experience other than what Wieman discerned as the creative event and without which the creative event would not emerge. But then to see this is to see the temporal and material *extensionality* of the creative event in its concreteness. If this concreteness is restricted too much, the *unity* of the creative event may appear only conceptual, as Loomer charges. But Loomer's own argument also serves to show the full extensiveness of Wieman's creative event, involving interrelations with instrumental values. This is to see the very *ongoingness of life* as creative event.

"The Size of God" concludes with what can only be regarded as a very daring speculation, scarcely even conceivable. Having elevated ambiguity to the status of a metaphysical principle, having defined the creative advance of the world not as an adventure toward perfection, but as a struggle for greater stature, Loomer could still write:

> The conception of the stature of God that is presupposed in this essay may be indicated by the speculative suggestion that the world is an interconnected web endeavoring to become a vast socialized unit of experience with its own processive subjectivity.[109]

Here we may be forgiven if we find not an empirical generalization but purely a statement of faith.

American Religious Empiricism in the Conversation of Humankind

Michael Oakeshott has written of poetry as a "voice in the conversation of mankind," arguing against the disposition to impose a single character upon significant human speech. Adopting the same metaphor, Richard Rorty has described the place he sees for the voice of philosophy in the conversation of humankind, arguing that it is hermeneutics all the way down. The American religious empiricists depicted in this chapter have endeavored to clear a place for *experience* in the religious conversation of humankind, arguing that the field of experience is not a hermeneutical reality we cannot break out of, but a web-like plenum, a creative passage, an inclusive whole which can be given theistic valuation. In notable ways, their combined proposals could be said to parallel the program of neopragmatic American empiricism in recent years. The accumulated critiques of the Wittgensteinians, of Quine, Sellars, Davidson, Rorty and others, have shown that there is no pure sense experience, no clear-cut meaning, no unambiguous use of language, no privileged syntax, no prior philosophical problem. Science cannot be deduced from sense data. Wieman, Meland, and Loomer, extending the range of these recognitions, have argued that there is no *sui generis* religious experience, no clear-cut meaning in historical communities other than the "margins of intelligibility" we sometimes create and other times discover, no un-ambiguous, privileged, or prior *ontological* realm which secures our projects from the possibility of final shipwreck. God cannot be re-duced to simple data.

The future course of religious empiricism, like that of poetry and of philosophy, may depend on its ability to become a conversable voice, one speaking in an idiom of its own but capable of participating in other discourses. In the totality of the ongoing religious conversa-tion about experience, no party of that conversation can be founda-tional to any other, no part more basic than any other. This is so not only for the epistemological reasons recent antifoundationalists have shown, but also for the religious reasons radical empiricists have shown.

As a direct implication of this, one of the contemporary tasks of an empirical philosophy of religion must be to extend its conversa-tional partners to include non-Western religious and philosophical traditions. There are several reasons to expect that American reli-gious empiricism will find its most conversable partner in the Bud-dhist experiential tradition in the East. First, in the work of American religious empiricists such as Wieman, Meland, and Loomer, we can see the beginnings of something very much like a Buddhist epistemol-ogy, serving to deconstruct our normal (Western) views of experience and religious valuation. Similar deconstructionist moves form an im-portant part of the ancient literature of Abhidharma Buddhism, Madhyamika Buddhism, and Zen meditational practices. Insights which have only recently found their way into Western philosophical thinking—antifoundationalism in epistemology, pluralism in cosmol-ogy, and the dismantling of logocentrism in ontology—have been fully at home in Eastern religious philosophies for more than two thousand years.

Second, American religious empiricists in the West have in com-mon with Buddhists in the East a rejection of any theism that posits an ultimate ground of being or substance underlying and relativizing the flux of events, or any static substantial essence transcending the flux of concrete space-time. Radical empiricism's recognition of the non-substantial character of what has been called "God" in the West leads to a revisionary theism that affirms the category of creativity as the most fruitful conception of ultimate reality. In the East, the recogni-tion of the nonsubstantial character of ultimate reality leads to the Buddhist affirmation of "Emptiness." Both can be said to chart a "middle way" between the denial of anything that is holy and the hypostasizing of an ultimate reality that transcends the world. Togeth-er, they are evidence of the fact that a new fourth voice deserves to be added to the conversation in Hume's *Dialogues Concerning Natural Religion.*

Third, both American religious empiricism and Buddhist religious philosophies offer striking resistance to the seductive efforts by Oakeshottians and Rortyians to reduce "the conversation of mankind" to the dimensions of "our" bourgeois liberal European values in the West. Neither religious tradition has much sympathy with ethnocentric apologies for the status quo. Neither tradition has much interest in dialogues that only deteriorate into incommensurable discourses incapable of effecting creative transformation. Each in its own way uses metaphysical analysis to enlighten concrete experience.

If the most promising feature of contemporary philosophy of religion today is the conversation between religious traditions, then the least promising avenue of philosophy, in the minds of most empiricists, is metaphysics. Yet radical empiricism is deeply rooted in an American tradition that is willing to risk metaphysical generalization. From James and Dewey to Wieman, Meland, and Loomer, radical empiricism has pursued a vision of reality as creative social process. The pivotal figure in this history is Alfred North Whitehead, whose process metaphysics drew on the insights of James and Dewey and directly influenced the work of Wieman, Meland, and Loomer.

In the next chapter, therefore, we will revert to Whitehead, whose process metaphysics grounds a radical empiricism. By going forward from the Chicago School back to Whitehead, we can see more clearly the meaning of radical empiricism as a distinctive metaphysical viewpoint, one that also reveals unexpected similarities with experience as understood in classical Buddhist thought. Furthermore, by selectively examining the radically empirical side of Whitehead's philosophy, we can highlight important themes that have been neglected during the theological appropriation of Whitehead's philosophy. Themes that the American religious empiricists left only implicit in their work can now be lifted out and generalized by way of Whiteheadian categories to engage a new conversation with Buddhism, the first philosophy to perceive reality as creative social process.

Chapter Five

Radical Empiricism in Metaphysical Perspective

By now Anglo-American philosophy has long since abandoned the search for a criterion of cognitive meaning that would once and for all distinguish empirically meaningful propositions from those that parade as cognitively meaningful propositions but fail to meet a "rigorous" criterion of empirical meaning. One way to look at the failure of all such attempts and the increasing realization of the futility of the entire project is to describe it as not having been rigorous *enough*. The search was called off before any of the really interesting questions were broached. Submerged beneath logical and semantic questions was the underlying and highly destabilizing question "What is a *fact*?" The only rigorous way to analyze *that* question as far as possible is, of course, to engage in some form of metaphysical analysis, the very thing that many Anglo-American analytic philosophers have considered most disreputable and dubious.

"The final problem," according to Whitehead, "is to conceive a complete fact." Such a conception, he maintained, can be formed only in terms of "fundamental notions concerning the nature of reality." It is precisely those fundamental notions that I wish to consider now. My concern in this chapter is to lay the groundwork for demonstrating that the epistemology of radical empiricism, as summarized and transformed in the direction of a metaphysics by Whitehead, and as represented and reinforced by Buddhist schools of philosophy as well, offers a distinctive key for (1) unlocking the philosophical impasse to formulating an acceptable empiricist criterion, and (2) further developing a radically empirical approach to the question of the justification of theism.

The special relevance of Whitehead in this discussion is the effective way in which he has altered the locus of concreteness as over against the modern tradition of empiricism. Throughout his writings, discernible under multiple treatments, a distinctive theme emerges that undercuts and reverses the method of much modern epistemology in various forms since Descartes. This methodological principle is fundamental to Whitehead's philosophical vision and to the way in which, like James, he broadened the concept of perceptual experience to include a deeper and qualitatively richer form of apprehension in which relations are experienced as given. Most generally stated, this is the principle that the controlling, but uncontrollable, elements of experience are vaguely and obscurely given, while the manageable, and therefore more superficial, aspects are clearly and distinctly present.

The contention that the data of experience which are most important, insistent, and necessary to existence are also vague, uncontrollable, and hard to distinguish carries serious methodological implications for empirical inquiry in religion. If the necessary and fundamental features of life are unmanageable and elusive to analysis, while those which are manageable and well-defined are comparatively accidental and superficial, then the movement toward clarity and precision in perception and conception proceeds in the opposite direction from the movement toward the concrete and causally efficacious. To the extent that empirical inquiry in religion is concerned with the fullness, depth, and richness of concrete experience it must direct attention to those areas where experience itself provides the data. But these data, because they are more complex and inclusive, are also, on Whitehead's thesis, vague and only dimly discerned. Therefore, concrete experience by its very nature poses a severe challenge to clarified understanding and articulation.

Whitehead's remarkable success in articulating a systematic theory of experience is not widely appreciated today. Appraisals of his work normally focus on the fact that *Process and Reality*, his "essay in cosmology," presents an abstract *theory* of experience, thus emphasizing the role of speculative reason in philosophical construction. Less attention has been paid to the way in which the speculative theory is a theory of *experience*, where "experience" is understood along the lines of a radical empiricism. But in acknowledging his intellectual debts in the Preface to *Process and Reality*, Whitehead explicitly wrote: "I am also greatly indebted to Bergson, William James, and John Dewey. One of my preoccupations has been to rescue their type of thought from the charge of anti-intellectualism, which rightly or wrongly has been associated with it."[1] While Whitehead's rescue mission was accomplished with considerable rational apparatus, he nevertheless took the principles of empiricism more seriously than do most of those who claim this name in the history of philosophy. That aspect of Whitehad's philosophy in which an empirical mode was most fully developed, namely, his doctrine of causal efficacy, was a continuation and amplification of James's efforts to analyze the "perceptual flux." The technicalities of this doctrine, not to mention its reliance on a systematic metaphysical scheme, have made it difficult for White-head's thought to have any impact on the hard core of analytic phi-losphy today. But it is here that we can begin to construct a solution to the question of the cognitive content of theistic language.

The special relevance of Buddhist philosophy in this discussion is its prolonged and complex history of sensitively attending to the analysis of concrete experience, with results whose philosophical con-tours strikingly parallel many Whiteheadian themes. As the first pro-cess philosophy in history, Buddhism offers an important cross-cultural comparative source for attesting to insubstantiality, the non-primacy of sense perception, and the religious depths to be found in the aesthetic matrix of life.

In introducing certain similarities between Whiteheadian and Buddhist philosophy, for the purpose of stating and exploring a radi-cally empirical conception of the nature of experience, one should certainly remain alert to the dangers of what Edward Conze com-plained of as "spurious parallels to Buddhist philosophy" and which he thought

> often originate from a wish to find affinities with philosophers recog-nized and admired by the exponents of current academic philos-ophy, and intend to make Buddhist thinkers interesting and respect-able by current Western standards. Since this approach is not only objectively unsound, but has also failed in its purpose to interest Western philosophers in the philosophies of the East, the time has now come to abandon it.[2]

But this is no argument for abandoning comparative study. To the contrary, contemporary philosophers like David Hall, for instance, argue that the enrichment of Anglo-European cultural resources through the pursuit of novel evidences found in Asian culture is one of the more pressing of the responsibilities of Western philosophers today. In Hall's view:

> The vision of the process philosopher is so radically at odds with our received wisdom that we have little choice but to construe philos-ophers of process in terms of our more familiar substance categories, radically distorting their most profound insights. The principal dif-

ficulty is that we do not have a recognized intellectual tradition that allows the proper interpretation of the process perspective. For this reason it is necessary to turn to the East, where a fully developed process tradition does indeed exist, in order to discover a context in which to interpret our process philosophies.[3]

There is little doubt, according to Hall, that Anglo-European process philosophers have much more in common with Taoist and Buddhist thinkers than with extant Western philosophic traditions. Conze's worry that comparative work might merely intend to make Buddhist thinkers "respectable" by Western standards is balanced by Hall's concern that Western philosophical standards tend to construe process thinkers "according to substantialist principles, thus trivializing them while rendering them 'respectable.'"

The themes that I consider in this chapter are common to both Eastern and Western process philosophers; they are neither trivial nor "respectable." From a discussion of causal efficacy in Whitehead and codependent origination in Buddhism, I will turn to the critique of substantialism and sensationalism in each, culminating in an interpretation of the role of felt qualities in an interrelated world of process.

Whitehead's Doctrine of Causal Efficacy

Prescinding from the more technical features of Whitehead's system, the main features of his philosophy of experience can be summarized in the broader, nonsystematic language he uses in developing a theory of nonsensuous perception or "perception in the mode of causal efficacy." According to this theory, the most basic mode of experience is not sense perception but sense reception, or the perception of process. Most modern schools of epistemology have confined their analysis of experience to sense-perception (what Whitehead calls "perception in the mode of presentational immediacy") as the only valid means of deriving and testing empirical knowledge. But underlying the sharp, precise, spatially located experience of contemporaneous sense perception, projected as presentationally immediate, is the receptive nonsensuous experience of causal efficacy with its dim and vague vector feeling-tones.

The exclusive attention to sense perception in other forms of empiricism has served to focus interest on the clear, controllable, and distinct details of experience to the neglect of the vague, unmanage-

Proudfoot Reviews

Zoschke, J A A R 55 N.3
Fall 1987

Friedrichs, Soc Ann 48: S 1987

Gelpi   Horizons 15 Sp 1988

Ontzen   J Th St 38 O 1987

Wainwright   Faith Phil 5 Ap 1988

Frankenberry Reviews

Bracken , Horizons 15 Sp 1988

Cobb   Proc St 16 (4) W 1987

Tilley   Encount 49 Wint 1988

Stone   CTS Register 78 Sp 1988

Stout
West

able and dimly given features of experience. By contrast, Whitehead insisted that:

> We enjoy the detail as a weapon for the further discrimination of the penumbral totality. In our experience there is always the dim background from which we derive and to which we return. We are not enjoying a limited dolls' house of clear and distinct things, secluded from all ambiguity. In the darkness beyond there ever looms the vague mass which is the universe begetting us . . . . We can never disengage our measure of clarity from a pragmatic sufficiency within occasions of ill-defined limitations. Clarity always means 'clear enough.'[4]

Whitehead's doctrine thus inverted the classical view of sense-perception as primary and feeling-tones as derivative. Instead, in his thesis, the primitive data of experience are more complex and inclusive, though dim and vague, while clarity and simplicity are the sophisticated result of later abstraction. Sense-perception is a selective highlighting from more complex experiences, making them handy and manageable.

Discrimination of the mode of experience which Whitehead termed perception in the mode of causal efficacy is the result of rigorous adherence to an analysis of immediate human subjective experience. Fundamental to that act of experience, as Whitehead analyzed it, is its sense of derivation from factors in its immediate past and of anticipation of an immediate future for which it will be a datum. Causal efficacy produces

> percepta which are vague, not to be controlled, heavy with emotion . . . a sense of emotional feeling, belonging to oneself in the past, passing into oneself in the present, towards oneself in the future; a sense of influx of influence from other vaguer presences in the past, . . . modifying, enhancing, inhibiting, diverting the stream of feeling which we are receiving, unifying, enjoying, and transmitting. This is our general sense of existence, as one item among others, in an efficacious actual world.[5]

The basis of experience is at once physical and emotional. "Stated more generally," Whitehead said, "the basic fact is the rise of an effective tone originating from things whose relevance is given."[6] Each of the three features found in this statement is pertinent to a full analysis of the primary mode of experience. "The rise of an effective tone" can be understood more technically as the conformal and vectorial inheritance of the feelings of other past actualities immanent in a present act of experience. "Originating from things" emphasizes that such prehension, though it is an active grasping, is always provoked by the object(s) of experience. "Whose relevance is given" refers to the web of ordered interconnections among individual occasions of experience, in which the perspectives are determined by both the settled weight of the past and by the actual and possible elements ingredient in the environment.

Above all, this mode of perception is an instance of causality. The organic bodily process of nonsensuous perception, through which we feel our being-in-the-world in interaction with other real things, constitutes the network of causal connections. It is inheritance from the past, felt as causally efficacious in the present. It is an affective response, whether attraction or repulsion, to some vague presence dimly felt. Such nonsensuous perception is found in elementary forms throughout nature. The jellyfish advances and withdraws; the plant reaches down into the moist soil; everything throughout the universe "feels" its environment and responds. The primacy of the doctrine of causal efficacy in Whitehead's analysis of experience is the assertion that the world lives physically within the subject, that occasions of experience are constituted by felt transitions from past actualities, and that in every specific instance of experience there is a content that is not exhausted by a description of the formal qualities in virtue of which that instance is repeatable.

Whitehead as much as James recognized that this mode of perception is vague, haunting, and unmanageable. In Whitehead's language, it is experience "heavy with the contact of things gone by, which lay their grip on our immediate selves." It is the perception of the conformation of the present to the past and the future to the present, "whereby what is already made becomes a determinant of what is in the making."[7] This is a stress on the feeling of real connection with real forces, on such insistent though vague experiences as the awareness of a presence in the dark; an immediate attraction or repulsion to or from another person; the apprehension of a "warm" or "sinister" atmosphere of a room; the flow of sympathy towards persons or nature. Whitehead maintained that all such experiences are felt as prior to sensory recognition, and as more compelling and unmanageable in impact.

Due to these features, perception in the mode of causal efficacy can only rarely be realized consciously. There is lacking a clear awareness of sensa or forms of definiteness that would locate and discriminate the various objects prehended. But causal efficacy is not, because of this, a dubious inference made at the causal level about a nonexperienced though hypothetically presupposed ground of conscious awareness. On the contrary, causality is directly experienced when we attend to the ground stream of becoming. This is a direct repudiation of Hume's doctrine that causal feeling arises from the long association of well-marked presentations of sensa, one precedent to the other. If Hume's analysis was accurate, we would expect to find that inhibitions of sensa would be accompanied by a corresponding absence of causal feeling. But the exact opposite is the case, as Whitehead tried to demonstrate by an appeal to ordinary experience:

> An inhibition of familiar sensa is very apt to leave us a prey to vague terrors respecting a circumambient world of causal operations. In the dark there are vague presences, doubtfully feared; in the silence, the irresistible causal efficacy of nature presses itself upon us; in the vagueness of the low hum of insects in an August woodland, the inflow into ourselves of feelings from enveloping nature overwhelms us; in the dim consciousness of half-sleep, the presentations of sense fade away, and we are left with the vague feeling of influences from vague things around us. It is quite untrue that the feelings of various types of influences are dependent upon the familiarity of well-marked sensa in immediate presentment. Every way of omitting the sensa still leaves us a prey to vague feelings of influence.[8]

Perhaps the most compelling example of the experience of causal efficacy is the memory of our own immediate past. Discussions of memory too often concentrate on long stretches of time, in which case we only dimly perceive fragments of our experience. Whitehead's analysis, however, examined our memory of the immediate past. He asked us to focus our attention upon the linkage between two contiguous moments of awareness. Estimating the actual size of such a quantum, Whitehead considered that "roughly speaking, it is that portion of our past lying between a tenth of a second and half a second ago."[9] We are plunged into the paradoxical heart of time: "It is gone, and yet it is here." It is "the continued life of the immediate past within the immediacy of the present."[10] Here we are catching our present moment of awareness taking immediate account of another occasion of experience. We are also observing a *past* occasion directly acting *causally* upon the present; an energizing intention or purpose from the past shaping things in the present. Consider the intentional unity of purpose involved in the simple act of uttering a simple phrase such as "United States." If experience were built up entirely upon the basis of sensa, the presupposed teleological unity would be unintelligible. Why should it just happen that the four syllables U-nit-ed States are pronounced so as to add up to a meaningful symbol, if not because of the *shaping* of each quantum of energy-experience by its immediate past? Whitehead rejected the Humean explanation in terms of "association of ideas," and pointed out that a person inventing a new name for a new business enterprise might well break the ties of association in a creative moment and utter the syllables "United Fruit Company."[11]

A similar appeal can be made to the immediate experience of our bodily organs as directly influencing the shape of consciousness. The body, as the most intimate part of our environing world, presents direct evidence of an objective world. Whitehead appealed to this feeling of bodily efficacy as another instance of causal feeling. One's body is that part of the external world which serves as an amplifying field for experience. We cannot define where a body begins and where external nature ends. There is no definite boundary. "We feel *with the body*," Whitehead emphasized, and "the present perception [sense perception] is strictly inherited from the antecedent bodily functioning, unless all physiological teaching is to be abandoned."[12] We see *with our eyes* and *by* our eyes. Physiology, physics, and common sense combine to indicate an historic route of inheritance from one occasion to another starting from an external environment, moving through the sense organs and nerves into the brain. The alternative interpretation of Humean sensationalism is a doctrine of private psychological fields that flatly fails to render an intelligible account of the procedures of modern science. The physical energy, the precision instruments, the eye and brain of the observer, and the record of the experiment on paper are all reduced, on the Humean view, to narrow bands of color-impressions in the private psychological field of the percipient subject. This series of sense impressions, Hume concluded, "arises in the soul from unknown causes." Unless we are prepared to accept solipsism, we must admit the immediate evidence for direct nonsensuous perception of the causal efficacy of our bodies and of the immediate past moment of awareness.

The major importance of these considerations, aside from possible solutions to the skepticism raised by Hume concerning the grounds for belief in causality, is its illustration of a fundamental fact: the "conformation of feeling," as Whitehead called it, or alternatively, the "flux of energy." Attention to the primacy of causal efficacy involves an important shift in value theory as over against those philosophies and theologies which designate mind or substance or matter as primary categories. The doctrine of causal efficacy also provides an elemental base in human experience for designating the most deeply creative transformations associated with religion. It is an insistence on the centrality of the body and the fact that consciousness, even when dominant in human experience, is in organic association with bodily, visceral, affective processes which either enhance conscious attention or frustrate and attenuate it. It points also to the fact that images, concepts, and theories alone do not enlighten or liberate, redeem or destroy. More profoundly, lives are created and re-created in terms of organic physical energies of nature which are most intimately experienced with the body. The creativity of all existence originates in the realm of concrete relationality, present in physical feelings, for this constitutes the stream of experience, the qualitative flux in which and out of which events have their reality. This is the level of common creaturehood, a level more pervasive than that of mere sensation or refined intellectuality. As we shall see next, for the Buddhist process view, too, what is most real is the flow of experiencing.

The Buddhist Doctrine of Pratītya-samutpāda and Sunyata

The concept of *pratītya-samutpāda* is unique to Buddhism, but exhibits a close affinity to Whitehead's causal efficacy and conception of the processive-relational nature of actuality. *Pratītya-samutpāda* literally means conditioned coarising or dependent coorigination. *Pratyaya* refers to the conditional or auxiliary causes or concomitant factors; *samutpāda* refers to their arising together. While a number of different, and sometimes contrary, expressions of the meaning of *pratītya-samutpāda* exist, both Hīnayānists and Mahāyānists agree that the comprehension of this truth about life is basic to release from suffering.

The heart of the Buddha's claim is that all experience is intrinsically impermanent. The arising, maintenance, and dissolution of existence is an orderly sequence, but it is not to be seen as a universal substance nor simply as a mental projection. Rather, it is a relational process which coordinates the momentary factors (*dharmas*) as they pulsate in and out of the causal process. Formulated as *pratītya-samutpāda*, the teaching is significant religiously as an explanation of the cause of suffering and of the possibility for its dissipation. By perceiving causality as a multiple-directional convergence, the Buddha discards the notion of a one-directional movement of power from a prime substance to another independent substance. The early Buddhist descriptions of dependent coorigination advise against mistaking the common sense experience of "self" for a primal and unchanging source of our experiences.

The Abhidharmists, the Mādhyamika philosophers, and the Yogācārins each had their different renditions of the Buddha's insight.

The Abhidharma literature discussed the co-arising of existence in terms of elemental conditioned dharmas, working out in minute analysis the conditions under which different dharmas would arise together. Theirs was a depth analysis of causation for which conventional formulations were viewed as inadequate. The early Mahāyānists, as expressed in the Prajñāpāramitā literature, rejected the Abhidharma concern to identify the dharmas as the basic constituents of existence. From the Mahāyānists' perspective, the Abhidharmist attempt to identify the "own-being" (svabhāva) and the "own-marks" (svalaksana) of dharmas was a drift back into essentialist thinking. Nāgārjuna, traditionally considered the founder of the Mādhyamika school, identified dependent co-arising with "emptiness" (sūnyatā) and maintained that the Buddhist formulation of "that being, this becomes" could not obtain when either existing things (bhāva) or dharmas were thought to have "own-being."[13] Finally, the Yogācārin tradition offered its own understanding of the principle of pratītya-samutpāda within its particular focus on the working of the human psyche.

In all cases, one thing is clear: pratītya-samutpāda depicts the multifaceted dependent or relational nature of ordinary experiential process, how it is that events come and go or arise and subside. Despite different emphases within Buddhist schools (and perhaps even in order to correctly assess those differences), the emphasis is to be placed on the primacy of the experiential process itself. Only then and within that process can one attend to the dharmas as defining or characterizing that process. If one tries to see the dharmas first and not the process (pratītya-samutpāda), one runs the risk of committing what Whitehead called "the fallacy of misplaced concreteness."

Whether the Abhidharmists did in fact commit this fallacy is probably impossible to tell. Nāgārjuna's polemics against the Abhidharmic views, beginning with the opening chapter on Pratyaya (Relational Condition), seem to be advanced not so much against carving out of dharmas within the causal flux as against giving them independent primacy over against pratītya-samutpāda. In the Prasannapāda, Candrakīrti explained that pratitya is a gerund signifying the phenomenon of "extending over" or "reaching," and samutpāda means manifestation or origination of the momentary event.[14] Viewed together, pratītya-samutpāda refers to the dynamics of momentary experiential process.

Process philosophers familiar with Whitehead's perspective have no difficulty comprehending pratītya-samutpāda in terms of the principle of process and the principle of relativity which, viewed together, point to the principle of creativity, "the ultimate notion of the highest generality at the base of actuality." The Buddhist aesthetic vision of all experiences as a unique process of relational origination, ranging from the microscopic to the macroscopic realm of existence, is nearly identical to the Whiteheadian insight that "creativity is the universal of universals characterizing ultimate matter of fact. It is that ultimate principle by which the many, which are the universe disjunctively, become the one actual occasion, which is the universe conjunctively."[15]

The climax and conclusion of the theory of *pratītya-samutpāda* is often thought to be found in the Chinese Buddhist school of Hwa-yen which is receiving increased scholarly attention. Recent studies by Garma C. C. Chang[16] and by Francis H. Cook[17] explicitly note comparisons between Hwa-yen's doctrine of mutual interpenetration and Whitehead's organic philosophy. Hwa-yen takes to its fully "explicit meaning" (*nitartha*) what it regards as the "implicit meaning" (*heyartha*) in the tradition it received and interprets *sūnyatā* as interpenetration of events, emphasizing the ontological fullness and cosmic togetherness of dharmas. *Sūnyatā*, as a specification of *pratītya-samutpāda*, is then seen to designate the causal process of combining all in all in an extravagant conception of Dharmadhatu Causation. The *dharmadhatu* or all-merging field of Suchness is conceived as a universal matrix of causation. But the precise nature of the mutuality of the causal relations perplexes Whiteheadian scholars. In the most systematic analysis to date of comparisons between Hwa-yen Buddhism and process metaphysics, Steve Odin[18] advances several startling theses. He finds in Hwa-yen the argument that since all dharmas are mutually related, they are mutually penetrating; and because they are mutually penetrating, they are mutually identical. He postulates that for the Hwa-yen school, since each dharma can be exhaustively analyzed or reductively factored into its causal relations to everything else without remainder, each is entirely devoid of substance or unique selfhood; everything "dissolves" into everything else at the level of *sūnyatā*, according to Odin. To this "speculative" theory of mutual interpenetration Odin counterposes Whitehead's process model, involving a metaphysics of "cumulative penetration." Finding the latter to be a more balanced descriptive generalization of experiential immediacy than the Hwa-yen position, Odin charges Hwa-yen with divesting immediate experience of all creativeness, novelty, and freedom.

Many Buddhist thinkers would no doubt be surprised to learn that they have "the deepest ontological commitments" which Odin discerns and, most of all, that these are in tension with creativeness, novelty, and freedom. Furthermore, it is not altogether clear, at least on my reading, that Hwa-yen's *metaphors* of mutual interpenetration (ocean and waves, house and rafters, Indra's Net, Hall of Mirrors, Tower of Maitreya, etc.) function to denote or are expressive of *tempo-*

ral distinctions of nature as Odin claims, thus contradicting "time's arrow" as it has been conceived in the West and elaborated into a doctrine of asymmetrical relations by process philosophers.

At this point, a resolution of some sort can be sought in what we have already seen of Whitehead's doctrine of causal efficacy. This gives us the perspective of temporal transition which is asymmetrical, *i.e.*, the present includes the past but is not itself included by the past to which it is externally related. But when the felt immediacy of the present moment is analyzed as a concrescence, *i.e.*, a growing together of causally efficacious relations, the perspective is nontemporal, symmetrical and unifying in what might be called buddhistically an "eternal now." With something like this in mind, Jay McDaniel and John Cobb explain that: "From the perspective of 'concrescence,' past and future are realized as felt relations. Physical feelings feel the past, anticipatory feelings feel the future; and these feelings are symmetrically unified in the becoming of subjective experience. Thus, from the perspective of transition, time is asymmetrical, from that of concrescence, it is symmetrical."[19] This suggests, if it is at all applicable to the Hwa-yen problematic, a way of understanding the all-merging Thusness which does not contradict the temporal character of physical actuality.

But in any case there is reason to think that *sūnyatā* (whether "dependent cooorigination" or, in Stcherbatsky's suggestive translation, "universal relativity") is sufficiently close to Whitehead's notion of creativity that we may seek its experiential basis in causal efficacy. In other words, the perception of *sūnyatā* through nondual wisdom (*prajñā*) involves perception in the mode of causal efficacy as a most exceptional emphasis within the flux of *pratītya-samutpāda*. Radical empiricism understands the Buddhist practice of compassion and nondual wisdom to imply a mode of perception consisting of feelings which *feel the feelings* of other actual beings conformally, leading to a natural and unobstructed sympathy with all that is actual. In order fully to see this, however, one must first be free of attachment to prevailing forms of substantialism and sensationalism.

Whitehead's Critique of Substantialism and Sensationalism

If Whitehead was right about causal efficacy, and if indeed *pratītya-samutpāda* turns the Wheel of Life, two very fundamental shifts in understanding are required for an adequate philosophical analysis of the nature of experience. In the first place, the notion of actuality as composed of substances is radically subverted. And secondly, sensationalist doctrines of perception are shown to be nonempirical. Important shifts in ontological theory are also involved here, of course, but it is the epistemological implications of the critique of substantialism and sensationalism that I want to highlight next.

The particular view of substance called into question by this analysis can be traced to Aristotle's definition that "a primary substance is 'neither asserted of a subject nor present in a subject'" and to Descartes's corollary that "when we conceive of substance, we merely conceive an existent thing which requires nothing but itself in order to exist." This conception of enduring substances with accidental qualities may be a useful abstract for many purposes of life but it is simply mistaken when taken as a fundamental statement about the nature of things. As Whitehead noted, in a manner reminiscent of William James:

> All modern philosophy hinges round the difficulty of describing the world in terms of subject and predicate, substance and quality, particular and universal. The result always does violence to that immediate experience which we express in our actions, our hopes, our sympathies, our purposes, and which we enjoy in spite of our lack of phrases for its verbal analysis. We find ourselves in a buzzing world, amid a democracy of fellow creatures; whereas, under some disguise or other, orthodox philosophy can only introduce us to solitary substances, each enjoying an illusory experience.[20]

The objectionable influence of the substance-quality conception of actuality in Western thought applies strictly to the interpretation of substance as a static, vacuous substratum of undifferentiated endurance, devoid of internal activity or intrinsic worth, and the interpretation of qualities as accidental relations or universal characteristics inhering in a substance. The chief difficulty with this metaphysical presupposition is that the relations between individual substances constitute what Whitehead called "metaphysical nuisances." Radical empiricism rigorously rejects this doctrine because it entirely leaves out of account the interconnection between real things:

> Each substantial thing is thus conceived as complete in itself, without any reference to any other substantial thing. Such an account of the ultimate atoms, or of the ultimate monads, or of the ultimate subjects enjoying experience, renders an interconnected world of real individuals unintelligible. The universe is shivered into a multitude of disconnected substantial things, each thing in its own way exemplifying its private bundle of abstract characters which have found a

common home in its own substantial individuality. . . . A substantial thing can acquire a quality, a credit—but real landed estate, never.[21]

In addition to the failure of traditional theories of substance to account for anything but accidental relations, a revised concept is also necessary in view of the discoveries of modern science. At one time, and within the limitations of the Newtonian framework, the notion of an inert, passive bit of matter floating around in space may have been adequate, but this simple conception of material substance has received several successive blows at the hands of modern science. To the discovery that a material body was actually a society of molecules in violent agitation, science responded by pushing the concept of substance back in succeeding steps to more primitive elements, first to molecules, and then, when this was discovered to be composed of a society of atoms, the atom was viewed as the material "substance." Soon, however, the atom was likewise found to be a process of activity of sub-atomic entities which are energy-events. By now, the whole idea of a material substance persisting unchanged through change has been deemed useless for science. Whitehead was able to write in 1929 that:

What has vanished from the field of scientific conceptions is the notion of vacuous material existence with passive endurance, with primary individual attributes, and with accidental adventures. Some features of the physical world can be expressed in this way. But the concept is useless as an ultimate notion in science, and cosmology.[22]

As a result, philosophy can hardly remain satisfied with the notion of "static stuff" as a fundamental fact of concrete experience.

In contrast to the theory that the data of experience are representations by universals of underlying substances which are otherwise unknowable and themselves unrelated, radical empiricism posits a theory of internal, as well as external relations, in which the process of the becoming of an "actual entity" replaces the notion of "substance" as the ultimate nature of actuality.

The sensationalist doctrine of perception, which is directly dependent upon acceptance of the substance-quality conception of actuality, has only aggravated the difficulty of analyzing the nature of experience in its most concrete form. The sensationalist theory is the doctrine of *mere* sensation, that is, the assertion that the act of experience is primarily a bare subjective entertainment of a datum, without any affective tone. It has usually been combined, in the history of philosophy, with the assumption that the datum itself can be analyzed adequately solely in terms of universals. This has given rise to representative theories of perception which create the problem of how we can justifiably make inferences from subjective experiencing to the existence of external things. Subjectivist sensationalism underlied Descartes's method of doubt, was shared by the British empiricists, and was basic to Kant's Copernican revolution, as well as to various forms of modern idealism. The combined effect of sensationalism and subjectivism produced an analysis of experience characterized by the view: (1) that all perception is by the mediation of sense-organs; (2) that all percepta are bare sensa, in patterned connections, given in the immediate present; (3) that experience of the social world is an interpretative reaction which is completely derivative from this perception; and (4) that emotional and purposive experience is a reflective reaction derived from that original perception, and intertwined with the interpretative reaction.[23]

In rejecting these assumptions we do not need to deny that perception includes sensations of color, sound, etc. But we will need to repudiate the notion that such definite, clear-cut "sensa" are the *fundamental* elements of experience from which all else is derived either by inference or construction. Exclusive emphasis upon sense-perception as supplying the sole data for examination has promoted the dubious assumption that the fundamental mode of experience is that which appears in consciousness, and that the basic data are immediate, definite, and discrete. Furthermore, on the assumption that we only experience the world in terms of the sense-data qualifying the objects which compose it, there has been the tendency to conceive the world as composed of substances with vacuously inherent qualities. The notion that we only perceive contemporary sense-data, and that these data are not inherent in the objects which we infer from them, promotes a view of the objects themselves as passive recipients of the qualities and hence devoid of intrinsic worth. The perceived world then comes to be regarded as composed of barren substances decorated by universal qualities.

However, if we accept the basic contours of Whitehead's analysis of causal efficacy, the most primitive data of experience will not be identified with distinct, clear-cut, first-person awarenesses that are singular in character. These data are actually the result of reflection and intellectual refinement. Neither will the thesis of radical discontinuity implicit in this approach be accepted. For once experience is deprived of its own constitutive connections and relations, the way is paved for rationalists to reintroduce relations as merely the peculiar contribution of the mind.

This was the move that led directly to the Kantian doctrine of the objective world as a construct from subjective experiencing. Because Kant, like Hume, assumed the radical disconnectedness of impressions *qua data*, he conceived his transcendental aesthetic as descriptive merely of a subjective process appropriating the data by orderliness of feeling. The phenomenalistic reduction of the ordered world of experience was then a direct result of Kant's adherence to subjectivist sensationalism, or the assumption that the datum in the act of experience could be adequately described purely in terms of universals. As a result of these premises, the temporal world emerged from *The Critique of Pure Reason* as dead, phantasmal, phenomenal.[24]

A related difficulty with Kantian philosophy was the way in which its analysis of the act of experience concentrated on mental operations, and entirely neglected the role of physical feelings. For Kant, experience was the product of operations that occur in the higher of the human modes of functioning. On this basis, order in experience was understood as the result of the schematization of *thought* concerning causation, substance, and quality. The limits of experience were thereby viewed as the boundaries of thought and the boundaries of thought were regarded as the limits of knowledge. By thus giving precedence to intellectual cognition, Kant identified structures and forms and order with mental activity. Experiential unity could then only be achieved by *conceptual* functioning which is imposed on, rather than derived from, the data. When all relationships and patterns were thus excluded from the data, and order was attributed to the experiencing subject, it was no wonder that the world was degraded into mere appearance.

From the perspective of radical empiricism, the basic criticism of Kant's philosophy is that it neglected the role of what Whitehead calls "physical feelings," which form the nonconceptual element in experience. Although radical empiricists can agree with Kant that "intuitions without concepts are blind," they want to add, with Whitehead, that this is so for a different reason: there are objects for knowledge in every act of experience, but knowledge arises only when intellectual functioning is included in that act of experiencing, and such inclusion is not always the case. For Kant there was nothing to know apart from concepts, since it was intellectual functioning which introduced order into what was otherwise a mere spatio-temporal flux of sensations. Mental operations were the foundation rather than the culmination of experience in Kant's system.

By contrast, radical empiricism involves an important inversion of Kant's philosophy. *The Critique of Pure Reason* described the process by which subjective data pass into the appearance of an objective world. Radical empiricism seeks to describe the way objective data pass into subjective immediacy, and the way order in the objective data provides intensity in the subjective immediacy. For Kant, the world emerged from the subject; for radical empiricism, the subject emerges from the world. The difference here is crucial as it may lead in the direction of two quite different ontologies. If radical empiricism can correct the Kantian critique of pure reason with a Whiteheadian critique of pure feeling, then in place of a subjective phenomenology of cognitions, it may propose an objective ontology of feelings, in which the felt unity of aesthetic experience will replace Kant's transcendental unity of apperception.

In repudiating the substance-quality doctrine, together with exclusive reliance on sense-perception and the Kantian version of objectivity, it is not necessary to reject either an empirical starting point or the "subjective turn" Descartes introduced into modern philosophy. But whenever philosophers have construed the functioning of the subjective enjoyment of experience according to substance-quality categories, they have tended to regard as concrete fact precisely those elements radical empiricism considers most abstract: immobile objects unaffected by anything else, or sense-data privately perceived but associated with substances other than the perceiving substance, or a conscious enduring subject which, paradoxically, perceives change yet remain unchanged. Radical empiricism, as we have seen, does not view the subject as an enduring thing which requires nothing but itself in order to exist; it does not necessitate consciousness as essential to experience; nor does it require the data to be precise and instantaneous.

In summary, then, the alternative to subjectivist sensationalism, and the substance-quality categories with which it has been associated, is a radical empiricism which accepts experiencing as the primary data for analysis but disposes of the notion of individual substances each with its private world of qualities and sensations. The data for analysis is understood to include more than sensations, or representations by universals of underlying substances, in terms of which an external world is either inferred or constructed.

Buddhist Critique of Substantialism and Sensationalism

Instead of probing, as countless Western philosophers have, for some unknown substratum to which the qualities of experience adhere, Buddhism has concluded to the nonexistence of any such unknown independent substance. In the form of the doctrine of *sūnyatā* or "emptiness," Buddhism entails the most relentless and complete abolition of the notion of *svabhāva* or "own-being." Already contained in the doctrine of *pratītya-samutpāda* is the understanding that there is no unconditioned substance or substratum, no soul or self or Being, or Nature, or Universe-at-Large, or Truth beyond, above, or even within the flux of experiencing.

One of the most famous illustrations in Buddhist literature occurs in a collection of dialogues between a Buddhist sage, Nagasena, and King Menander. In the document entitled "The Questions of King Milinda," Nagasena tells the king that the chariot is made up of wheels and axle and other parts, just as a house or army or tree or city are likewise societies of elements disposed toward one another in the unity of function. If you infer a chariot behind the parts, and a similar entity behind a man or a house, Nagasena explains, you must infer such an entity behind every individual thing, leading to nonsense.[25] The point is that, as Whitehead frames it, "there is no going behind actual entities to find anything more real."[26]

A radical critique of substantialism is of course also entailed by the Buddha's doctrine of *anātman* (no-self), and by the themes of *anitya* (impermanence) and *duhkha* (ill, suffering) as well. In the *Katyayanava-vada Sutra*[27] the Buddha explained that knowing the truth of causality means not fixing the mind on the tendency of involvement in statements that assume independent and self-substantiated reality, such as "This is mine" or "This is not me." Such formulations tend to arrest the flow of experiencing and to coagulate the impermanent and "empty" factors of existence into "things" to which the flux of impermanent energy becomes attached in terms of "I," "mine," "not me, "It is," or "It is not." One objective of Buddhist meditation is to overcome this form of attachment.

A few centuries later this same spirit was captured by Buddhaghosa who wrote:

There is no doer who does the deed;
No one who reaps the content of the deed as such.
The aggregates of being continue to become.
This alone is the correct view.

There is suffering but none who suffers;
Doing exists but none who does
There is cessation but none who ceases
The path exists but not the goer.[28]

If this seems unduly cryptic, one has only to consult the language of modern quantum physics and relativity theories which endorse the

Buddhist-Whiteheadian conception of *anātman* at all levels of the physical universe. "Things" or "selves" alike are "energy-events" in cross-points of collision between vibrating forces. These collisions may set enduring patterns of change for the energies that collide so that things are dynamic processes whose patterns of activity persist through their flux. But the endurance of patterns resides not in simple, elementary entities, but in the wholeness of all the interrelated components together. None of these components can be adequately explained except by their relations to one another.[29]

Like the entities of modern physics, dharmas in the Buddhist analysis lack simple location, independent existence, and static permanence. The formula "all dharmas are empty" succinctly expresses the central Mahāyāna view of "matters of fact."

The formula "all dharmas are empty" came into prominent focus in Nāgārjuna's "Fundamentals of the Middle Way" in which he employed a logic of dialectical negations to radically desubstantialize all reified entities. From Nāgārjuna's perspective, the Hīnayāna school reified dharmas into some sort of absolute, independent, irreducible moments of existence, just as the Yogācāra school hypostatized consciousness (*vijñāna*) into a doctrine of consciousness-only (*vijñaptimatratata*). The Mahāyāna school, in focusing on the conditions relative to the rise and subsistence of the causal process itself, used the image of waves in an ocean. As one interpreter explains: "A single wave or an aggregation of waves is not an isolatable or independent phenomenon. Each has a relational structure as well as a content, both of which are dynamically involved such that the mere sensationalist perception is wholly inadequate in accounting for the nature of things."[30]

Nāgārjuna offered an ingenious explanation of the problem of causality according to which it is pure relativity, synonymous with emptiness (*śūnyatā*). On this basis he maintained:

> Since there is no dharma whatever which is not causally conditioned [*i.e.*, not relative], no dharma whatever exists which is not empty.

> If all existence is not empty [*i.e.*, if it is not causally conditioned], there is neither origination nor destruction. You must therefore wrongly conclude that the four holy truths do not exist.[31]

The argument is clear. Every dharma is relative. Hence every dharma is also empty. There is no dharma that is not relative. Therefore, there is no dharma that is not empty. If there is any dharma that is not empty, it cannot be causally conditioned. "Own-being," like everything else in the world of dharmas, dissolves upon analysis into the indefinite multiplicity of causal conditions that forms the background of the arising and perishing of dharmic events. There is no going back of verbs and adjectives to nouns and substances.

This is the crux of the process-relational perspective as grasped by both Buddhist and Whiteheadian philosophy. When it is grasped, one no longer yearns to push below process to anything more substantial. Until it is grasped, descriptions of existence in terms of process, interaction, and activity cannot help but have a haunting sense of bottomlessness, slipperyness, and incompletion.

Philosophy, however, only interprets the world; the point of enlightenment is to experience it in all its immediacy. For this, strict sensationalist theories of perception are no more to the point in Buddhism than in Whiteheadian philosophy. That is, just as *pratītya-samutpāda* is not comprehensible on the basis of substantialistic theories of being, the practice of *prajñā* (nondual wisdom) leading to an immediate experience of *sūnyatā* is not comprehensible on the basis of sensationalist accounts of perception.

The Buddhist aesthetic vision of the interrelationships of things in their immediate factual character is captured in enlightened perception. *Sūnyatā* is variously described not as a concept but as a field of perception, radically empty of subject and object, center and periphery, and because empty, also full and freely open to all that is immediately experienced. To effect this enlightened perceptivity one must shift one's attachment from the clear and distinct sense-data given in the mode of what Whitehead calls presentational immediacy to the penumbral fringe of causal feelings vectorially transmitted in the mode of causal efficacy. Enlightened perception through Buddhist *prajñā* can be said to involve the most complete cultivation of perception in the mode of causal efficacy. In terms of the traditional Buddhist form/emptiness (*rūpam/sūnyatā*) distinction, *rūpam* signifies the focal core of the perceptual field, and emptiness signifies its penumbral background. The Buddhist position on the indivisibility of form and emptiness is affirmed here by acknowledging that *sūnyatā* is present in and presupposed by every determinate *rūpam*. But enlightened perception is focused on the dynamic field itself, rather than on the "forms" perceived within the field of rising and falling dharmas. Nonattachment to dharmas involves, perceptually, nonfocal awareness in the pure mode of causal efficacy.

The fundamental Mahāyāna doctrine of the nondifference of form and emptiness or of *samsāra* and *nirvāna* affirms, as Nāgārjuna expressed it, that "There is nothing whatever which differentiates the existence-in-flux [*samsāra*] from nirvāna. And there is nothing what-

ever which differentiates nirvāna from existence-in-flux . . . . There is
not the slightest bit of difference between these two."[32] Or, as Whitehead put it: "The reality is the process."[33]

Felt Qualities in a World of Process

If the preceding analysis is convincing, it remains to be seen just
what we are left with for fashioning a metaphysics of radical empiricism. If "substance" and "sensation" turn out to be thoroughly shot
through with aesthetic qualities, as both the Buddhists and the American religious empiricists have maintained, the next step is to look at
what all the shooting is about. What is the status of qualities in a
radically empirical worldview which is characterized by *pratītya-samutpāda* and in which *nirvana* is an experiential possibility?

The term "quality" has represented a variety of confusing things
commonly lumped together in the philosophical grab bag, often with
differing ontological status. The persistent ambiguity of the word may
be one reason why Whitehead rejected the term "quality" in his systematic work and tried to invent a more precise terminology. However, in giving us a category called "subjective form," Whitehead unwit-
tingly endorsed the unwary reader's tendency to view the qualitative
aspects of existence as purely subjective or, worse, merely formal. In
turning now to a consideration of the way in which qualities in a
processive-relational universe are neither abstract universals nor private dispositions, we will be on the way to providing the most concrete
answer to the question "what is a fact?"

To bring out all that Whitehead means by the category of subjective forms, or what I will be calling felt qualities of experience, requires that we suspend the usual commonsense assumption that only
certain events and qualities which contribute to human enhancement
are of value, and that those which do not are mere facts devoid of
intrinsic worth. Such a view can be sustained only by accepting a
bifurcation of nature and a substantialist metaphysics in which the
data of perception are said to be universal qualities accidentally qualifying a world of barren substances. On such assumptions, qualities
remain incurably private, purely subjective vagaries, dualistically separated from the objectivity of description conducted along quantita-
tive lines. But in moving from "substance" to "process" as the primary
metaphysical category, qualities can be understood as constitutive of,
and emergent from, the processive-relational matrix of all experience.
Indeed, according to the radical empiricism common to both White-

head and Buddhism, *there is nothing actual in the world but felt qualities.* What is immediately observable in human experience are variegated, changing qualities in a span of duration. As felt, these dynamic qualities are emergents out of previous events and are tending toward future events. As a determinate creative synthesis of previous events, each complex felt quality is unique, unrepeatable, and spontaneous.

The Whiteheadian category of subjective form refers to felt qualities of existence or particular "hows" of qualitative experience. As modes of feeling, their analysis is best undertaken in terms of the mutual relations (1) between the objective content of a prehension and the subjective form or "affective tone" of that prehension; (2) between the subjective forms of various prehensions in the same occasion; and (3) between the subjective form of a prehension and the spontaneity involved in the subjective aim of the prehending occasion.

In their capacity as modes of reception, felt qualities are a derivation from objective influences external to the act of experiencing. They denote *how* an individual experiences the energy of concrete process. They therefore register the *what*, or objective data, of feeling and they have the character they do because of that data.

In their capacity as modes of response, felt qualities belong to the real internal constitution of the act of experiencing. They do not determine what the individual receives, but they are decisive with respect to what it makes of what it has been given. This fact expresses the unifying activity of the immediate occasion in process of becoming. The felt qualities are contributions to the one fact which is the unified feeling of harmony of the one occasion.

In their final unity at the point of completion of a process of becoming, felt qualities constitute the decision that defines the freedom and individuality of the subject. The unity of any single act of experience is a patterned texture of qualities, always shifting as it passes into the future. This is a complex, never a simple, unity. The qualities of one occasion are many in terms of their data, but one in terms of their subject. This fact expresses the final self-creative freedom of the individual whose reception of many, often conflicting, qualities from its environment must be synthesized into a unified feeling. The exact shape of the synthesis of felt qualities derived conformally is not settled by the antecedent fact of the data. The subject itself supplies the final determination for the synthesis of felt quality.

In summary, radical empiricism understands felt qualities as modal, relational, and individualized. Felt qualities arise in human experience from the coalescence of a whole field of events into a particular momentary unity. Discrimination of felt qualities is to be sought in the network of internal relations through which they are constituted.

This account of quality differs strikingly from the traditional way in which philosophy has construed qualities as universals or accidental adjectives which inhere in primary substances without having any real relational function. The extent to which radical empiricism obviates the problems connected with the more traditional view of quality needs to be emphasized.

Most conspicuously, this formulation is not open to the charge of subjectivism or psychologism. The usual dilemma one encounters in traditional epistemological discussions is predicated on the assumption that qualities must be either objective or subjective. If one holds that quality is strictly objective, pertaining to experience as a given datum, then one is faced with the problematic need to introduce a third term as a medium through which what is essentially objective passes into the subjective experiencing as a reaction to the datum. Or, if one holds that quality is primarily subjective, one is at a loss to explain whether it is really *there* in the world beyond the subject and how statements about felt quality can have cognitive meaning. But the question whether felt qualities are objective, in the sense that they exist in the data of perception, or are subjective, in the sense that they exist only in the observer, presupposes in its very framing an epistemological dualism which radical empiricism repudiates at the outset.

By viewing the subject-object relation as itself within the context of the unity of an act of experience, it is possible to go at the problem in an entirely new way, one which dissolves the Cartesian dualism between thinking and extended substances. In the first place, the notion of subjects and objects is a derivative abstraction from the unity of experience. Contrary to substance modes of thought, there is never, for radical empiricism, a primary quality apart from a so-called secondary or tertiary quality or apart from a subject. The *what* of feeling can be abstracted analytically from *how* it is felt, and described quantitatively, but in its concreteness it can only be felt as inseparable from the qualitative *how* of experience. Apart from the qualitative aspect, the *what* of feeling is an abstraction, like the "substance" of traditional philosophy. And considered apart from the flux of energy, the quality is also an abstraction, or in Whitehead's categories, it is an "eternal object," the form of a felt quality, and not the quality itself.

In the second place, the term "felt quality" embraces both the object of feeling and feeling itself as a unity. It follows that the *how* of the individual's feeling is the best clue to *what* that individual is in its role of shaping the energies of its environment into a new valuation. This valuation is both the "self" at the present moment and a continuation of the antecedent world. When the role of the environment is stressed, this is a process of causation. When the role of active reception is emphasized, the same process can be seen as valuation, or self-creation. Or, if the role of the conceptual anticipation of the future is accented, this dual activity of subjective forming and objective structuring is the teleological aim at some (ideal) value in the future.

This is to say that quality has a processive-relational character, tied as it is, externally, to the inherited dynamic actuality, and, internally, to the concrescing subject. Every act of perception has a quality by virtue of which it is vectorially related to its data in such a way that the structures of the data are given in the processive activity of the subject. Failure to describe the qualitative structures of perception leads inevitably to a psychological reductionism which restricts, and indeed falsifies, the data of experience.

If the *how* and the *what* of perceptual experience are intrinsically connected, then the charge of sheer subjectivism cannot be sustained in regard to the felt qualities discerned in experience. It is not a case of a subject in its interpretation creating or imposing qualities which do not obtain in the basic data of experience. Nor does one begin in the first instance with private certainty and then seek to reach a totally problematic external world by a process of inference. Rather, subjectivity begins its career in a causal way as an emergent from a public past. No element in the universe is capable of pure privacy, although there is, nevertheless, an important individualization or uniqueness of perspective in any actual occasion of experience. Uniqueness of perspective, however, does not plunge one into a Cartesian abyss, a dualism of mind and body with no bridge. Uniqueness of perspective always requires an antecedent, causal public world that one can perspectivalize.

It should be apparent also that in a radically empirical perspective felt qualities are what there is experientially. Enduring sense-receivers and sensibilia are abstractions from the most concrete experience. Hence, both the efforts to bridge a subject-object gap and assertions of the primacy of one over the other are debates about a derivative level of experience. They acquire their importance because they are the loci of the debates people undertake to justify their claims. But an appeal to felt qualities of experience does not make justification simply dependent on a felt difference to the *individual* alone without reflecting any differences in the world of fact. For the world of fact is itself conceived as built up out of just these felt qualities.

Having argued that Whitehead's category of subjective form, or what I am calling felt qualities of experience, provides the most concrete understanding of factuality, I now want to extend this analysis to the Buddhist side. That phase of Buddhism which seems to me to be most suggestive in this connection is found in the Abhidharma literature. My contention is that the Abhidharmists are close cousins to American radical empiricists, although, I must admit, I know of no comparative work or textual study which supports this hypothesis.[34] Just as Whiteheadian scholars have been more appreciative of the cosmological and speculative side of Whitehead's philosophy than attentive to its radically empirical insights, they have also found the highly metaphysical forms of the Mādhyamika and the Hwa-yen schools most congenial to comparative analysis. The empirical insights into the nature of experience which Buddhism has advanced in its long history are frequently bypassed in the same way as Whitehead's are.

Precisely what form of empiricism does Buddhism represent? "Its *own* form," might be the best answer. But Western commentators, intent on cross-cultural understanding, are apt to look for parallels (whether "spurious" or not in Conze's sense) in terms of their own paradigms. British-trained scholars, for instance, have tended to foster the comparison between "early" schools of Buddhism and British forms of empiricism. Among recent studies, one finds a distinguished group of Pali Buddhist scholars, notably Jayatilleke,[35] Kalupahana,[36] and Dharmasiri,[37] interpreting the Buddhism of the five *Nikaya* as an empirical viewpoint. Just which form of empiricism does it resemble most closely? Logical positivism, according to Kalupahana. Gudmunsen[38] goes so far as to find the early Sarvāstivādin Abhidharmists astonishingly close to Bertrand Russell's brand of logical atomism in which particulars, qualities, and relations are so confusingly factored that it is no wonder the Mahāyāna critique, like the Wittgensteinian therapy, was needed to correct the situation. Streng[39] lends important strength to an understanding of Nāgārjuna's dialectical logic of negations as sharing Wittgenstein's deontologizing motives and his inspiration that words are not names that refer to extralinguistic realities.

No doubt there are valid insights here, especially with respect to a Nāgārjunan-Wittgensteinian analysis of language, but I suspect it has been a mistake to read the early Abhidharmists either through the eyes of Bertrand Russell or through the Mahāyānists. The Abhidharmists may not have been such reifiers as the Mahāyānists accused them of being, and they may have had more in common with radical empiricism in the American tradition than with logico-linguistic empiricism in the British tradition. I shall seek a Middle Way between an apprais-

al of the Abhidharmists as narrowly empiricist and a suspect appreciation of them as full-blown radical empiricists.

I find some support for my interpretation in the remarks of
Kenneth Inada:

> The [Whiteheadian] notion of a subjective form, the affective tone,
> strongly suggests a relationship to the Buddhist dharmic analysis of
> experience. For, each dharma is a definite form or mode of being
> expressing a particular event whether in the conditioned or noncon-
> ditioned realm of existence . . . . A dharma, being evanescent, still
> exerts itself long enough to exhibit a certain characteristic to an
> experience or of the percipient.[40]

Inada does not develop this passing insight, other than to suggest that
the Buddhist descriptions of (1) the five *skandhas* (constituents of
being), (2) the twelve *ayatanas* (bases of being), and (3) the eighteen
dhatus (spheres or regions of being) might comprise in part what
Whitehead analyzed as "the genetic structure of experience."

As such, these three sets of classifications tell us no more than
would a simple listing of Whitehead's "Categories of Existence,"
"Categories of Explanation," and "Categoreal Obligations," and they
would certainly take as long to explicate. Without pausing to unpack
all that is involved, I want to call attention to the Abhidharma section
of the Buddhist *Tripitaka* which brings into focus the factors of experience, structurally analyzed according to five *skandhas*. These are: *rūpa*
(corporeal nature), *vedanā* (feelings and sensations), *samjñā* (perceptions), *samskāra* (impulses, volitions, emotions), and *vijñāna* (consciousness). These aggregates are to be seen in terms of continuous
functions. They begin with simple feelings and lead on to highly
sophisticated modes of discrimination. *Rūpa* or corporeal matter is
the initial phase, but its content is passed on to the high-grade activities of consciousness (*vijñāna*) by way of the visceral feeling conditions
(*vedanā*) which persist throughout the experiential process. According
to the further analysis by way of the eighteen realms (*dhatu*) of being
or the dharmic structuring of experience, the sense-faculties are included—but not highlighted—in the analysis. Dominance appears to
be given to the relational structure of existence, out of which sensa are
derived. As there is only *pratītya-samutpāda* as the matrix for the dynamic process, there is no postulation of subject or object prior to the
experiential process, no doer or deed, but only doing in the strictest
sense. The five *skandhas* indicate vital interrelationships within the
total perceptual process.

If the skandhas, ayatanas, and dhatus deal with the genetic structure of the flow of experience, dharma-theory in the *Dhammasanganī* treatise adds an even more elaborate analysis of the factors or forms of the experiential process. We need not be concerned here with the number of dharmas, which range from a classification of seventy-five for the Sarvāstivāda to one hundred for the Vijñānavada. The more important question concerns the several ways of understanding dharmas within both the Hīnayāna and Mahāyāna traditions. Conze[41] distinguishes seven senses of the term "dharma," of which three are most germane to Whitehead's claim that "the final problem is to conceive a complete fact," in terms of "fundamental notions concerning the nature of reality." These senses are: (1) dharmas as the "truly real events," dharmic facts; (2) dharmas as "objective data," whether dharmically true or untrue, and thus referring to any experienced object; and (3) dharma used adjectivally—*i.e.*, dharma as characteristic, quality, property, attribute. In Edgerton,[42] we find that the word "dharma" can serve as a term both for particulars and their qualities, thus ambiguously embracing both (2) and (3) above. Stcherbatsky holds that "to every unit of quality there corresponds a dharma."[43]

The word to watch here is "quality." The other thing to keep an eye on is the way in which dharmas, whatever else is said about them, are factors *within* and *of* the experiential process and so are in no way dominant over the primacy of *pratītya-samutpāda*. With this in mind, we can avoid the mistake of reification which the Mahāyānists charged to the Abhidharmists. But we also need to avoid the mistake of foisting onto dharma-analysis the categories of British empiricism, in which the real objects in the world are reduced to simple particulars which "have" qualities of one sort or another and stand in external relations to each other. Not only does this view lead to logical dead-ends in Western empiricist philosophy, but it also, in the east, would seriously undermine the Buddhist emphasis on dependent cooperation.

There is a middle view which could, I submit, do justice to both the Abhidharmist perspective that "dharmas alone are real" and the Mahāyānist perspective that "all dharmas are empty" if we but alter one aspect of Conze's description and eliminate the ambiguity in Edgerton's. The alteration is small but dramatic: dharmas are <u>adverbial</u>, not adjectival; as concrete facts, they refer to qualitative events, which cannot be described or analyzed exhaustively in terms of universals.

In the Abhidharma, the dharma-list is a list of seventy-five qualities, and of each of them there are numerous examples. The only way of identifying or reidentifying a dharma is by its "marks" (*laksana/ lakkhana*). A mark is a characteristic of a dharma which enables one to say what type it is. Each of the seventy-five dharma-types has a mark to help one identify it as such. Jayatilleke gives some examples:

> 'Greed' has the characteristic [= mark] of wanting . . . . 'Desire' has the characteristic of attachment . . . . 'Absence of hatred' has the characteristic of not harming . . . . Here *lakkhana* is used to denote the 'basic characteristic' of a concept which distinguishes it from everything else, but in the section on *lakkhana*, the term is used in the sense of a 'property' common to members of a class . . . . These two 'senses' are basically the same in that the essential characteristic of a thing is a property common to members of the class to which it belongs.[44]

Jayatilleke is obviously treating names for dharmas as denoting universals. But the idea that dharmas "have" qualities, rather than *are* qualities, throws us back into the ideas of "inhering quality" and "universals," which have often been pointed out as having been firmly rejected by the Abhidharmists. On the assumption that dharmas are "the truly real events" and a mark is a universal-property, we are still faced with the question as to how these truly real events and their properties are *related*. If they are viewed as logically separate, we will be tempted to speak of a dharma's own-being (*svabhāva*) as what "carries" its own-mark (*svalaksana*) and to miss the sense in which a quality, far from being *only* a universal, is a concrete feeling. Perhaps part of the Mahāyāna dissatisfaction with the Hīnayāna assumptions about dharmas is due to confusion between particulars and universals, and between the concreteness of dynamic events and the abstractness of linguistic forms.

The Sarvāstivādins, however, made it clear that they were referring to a particular and not to quality as a timeless universal. They did so by using the phrase "a dharma's own-being" (*dharma-svabhāva*). According to the Sarvāstivādins, a dharma can exist only in the present while it has its mark, yet it can exist "markless" both before and after this. Thus there is a clear distinction between a dharma's own-being, which lasts through time, and its being identifiable at a particular moment by its mark.[45] This suggests a familiar distinction perfectly compatible with a process perspective grounded in *pratītya-samutpāda*, but not with a substance orientation. If that which lasts through time, the *svabhāva*, is only a universal and if this is an abstraction from a dharma's existence at a particular moment, it is because the very particularity is the concreteness that cannot be analyzed exhaustively in terms of universals. On the basis of this distinction, it is also true, as the Mahāyānists urged, that dharmas are "empty of own-being" and are neither existent nor nonexistent. To say that "all dhar-mas are empty" is not to say simply that "there are no dharmas." It is to reject any risk of reification of even these momentary, imperma-nent events.

I am arguing that dharmas are best viewed as felt qualities in the radically empirical sense explicated earlier. As such, they are relation-al, modal, and concrete. The task of fully demonstrating this conten-tion textually is beyond my scope here, but the following two examples may serve to show the possibilities for further comparative study. It is interesting to note, first, that for the Abhidharmists the evaluating of other dharmas is itself made into a dharma. It is put into the category of *vedanā* (feelings). Of course, in all Buddhist schools conditioned dharmas are divided into five *skandhas*, one of which is *vedanā*. But why is *vedanā* made a distinct dharma? Is it because *vedanā* is roughly equivalent to the "affective tone" of feeling which is an intrinsic aspect of the complete analysis of any "fact?"

Consideration of two apparently similar words which fall under two differnt *skandhas* seems to support this hypothesis. The first is *sukha*, variously translated as "pleasure," "happiness," "bliss," "ease." It is listed under the skandha *vedanā*. According to one commentator, "*Sukha* is one of the three possible feelings we can have toward things."[46] The other two modes of feeling are *duhkha* (pain, suffering) and *upeksa* (neither *sukha* nor *duhkha*—indifferent feelings). The sec-ond word is *piti*, translated as "pleasure" or "happiness," or sometimes as "joy," "zest," "rapture," and "interest." *Piti*, although it appears to have virtually the same meaning as *sukha*, falls under the different skandha of *samskaras*.

We may wonder why *sukha* and *piti* are members of different skandhas. Why is *sukha* not subsumed under the "impulses, volitions, and emotions" skandha just as *piti* is? Why, for that matter, are "feel-ings" with all three of their components not subsumed under *sams-karas*? My suggestion is that it is because specific feelings are not viewed here as mental states but as facets of dharmas. *Piti* as one kind of pleasure is a distinct dharma, but *sukha* as another kind of pleasure is one facet of the single dharma "feelings." If to be a facet of a dharma-feeling is to have a certain affective tone, then it is clear that three affective tones—*sukha*, *duhkha*, and *upeksa*—denote species of feelings valued, in Whitehead's terms, "up," "down," or neutrally. The distinction between *piti* and *sukha* can be clarified further by attention to the analytic distinction between the *what* and the *how* of perceptivity. *Piti* would appear to refer to the *what* or the data given to the experiential process, while *sukha* as an affective tone connotes *how* the data are immediately felt. *Piti* is pleasure as an objectified feeling-datum of prehension; *sukha* is pleasure as the mood or mode or qualitative form of prehension.

Furthermore, nirvāna is *sukha*[47] but nirvāna is not *piti*, a conditioned dharma. According to my reading, to say that nirvāna is *sukha*, is to say that is it a complex, unified, fully harmonious felt quality of experience.

This may also shed some light on the meaning of Buddhaghosa's[48] statement that where there is *piti*, there is *sukha*, but where there is *sukha*, there is not necessarily *piti*. Pleasurable data of experience normally give rise to felt-qualities of pleasure, but one can value pleasurably all kinds of data other than pleasurable ones. Buddhaghosa also explains that *piti* is what an exhausted person has when told of water and shade nearby. Images of water and shade would be functioning as a "lure for feeling"; then when one actually experiences the water and shade, one has *sukha*. This is consistent with Buddhaghosa's explanation elsewhere[49] that *piti* is of different kinds: minor *piti* is only able to raise the hairs on the body, but showering *piti* breaks over the body again and again like waves on the seashore. *Piti* is causally efficacious data objectified for immediate feeling in the flux of existence. *Sukha*, as an evaluative mode of appropriating such data, intensifies and harmonizes the associated dharmas.

To understand *duhkha* as, like *sukha*, a felt quality of experience in the valuational mode is to gain further insight into the first Holy Truth of Buddhism that everything this side of nirvāna is *duhkha*. The statement that "all conditioned dharmas are *duhkha*" is a perspectival evaluative felt quality of the enlightened person, from the standpoint of nirvāna. The same facts may be evaluated differently by those unenlightened persons who experience a measure of *piti* and who never appropriate *all* of ordinary experience with the subjective form of *duhkha*.

The very heart of the dharma-theory consists in isolating qualities in experience. But this is not to say that qualities are *themselves* isolated or the dharmas independent and self-existent. It is precisely because, in the experiential flux as *lived*, dharmas are like James's concatenated much-at-onceness, that "mindfulness" is needed. And this is why the Abhidharmists acknowledge the extreme difficulty of "getting dharmas into view." To take dharmas as data which can be "got into view" in the practice of mindfulness may seem to risk reifying consciousness as that which gets dharmas into view. Reification is, in fact, a constant temptation for any process philosophy, but it is avoidable in this instance by recourse to a Jamesian analysis of consciousness as a function, not an entity. Consciousness is not that which gets dharmas into view, but that which *emerges from* a certain emphasis within the flux of experience.

Granted the primacy of *pratītya-samutpāda* within the Buddhist process view, and the ultimacy of the notion of creativity within Whitehead's process view, dharma-analysis can never be a matter of trying, implausibly, to get *back* to quality, *back* to the starting point, *back* to the undistorted datum in Locke's dubious fashion. Rather, it is a question of *getting on* to qualities, not as self-existent starting points, but as eventuations and outcomes of fluctuating events. At the same time, if it be granted that felt qualities are the content of processive experience and the final referent of the term "empirical" in human experience, it is evident that they pose a severe challenge to linguistic expression.

Whether the severity of this challenge will prove finally insurmountable to radical empiricists who would articulate the felt qualities of the religious dimension of experience currently remains an open question. Both Buddhists and radical empiricists have good reason to be struck by Wittgenstein's statement:

> Some things can be said about the particular experience and besides this there seems to be something, the most essential part of it, which cannot be described . . . . As it were: there is something further about it, only you *can't say* it; you can only make the general statement. It is this idea which plays hell with us.[50]

The same idea played hell as well with William James who finally concluded that

> the concepts we talk with are made for purposes of *practice* and not for purposes of *insight* . . . . I must *point*, point to the mere *that* of life, and you by inner sympathy must fill out the *what* for yourselves. The minds of some of you, I know, will absolutely refuse to do so, refuse to think in non-conceptualized terms. I myself absolutely refused to do so for years, even after I knew that the denial of manyness-in-oneness . . . must be false, for the same reality does perform the most various functions at once.[51]

Nevertheless, radical empiricism is not in principle reduced to futility in its linguistic efforts to express the "manyness-in-oneness" which comprises the aesthetic matrix of experience. Despite James's hesitations, and despite Wittgenstein's early injunction "whereof one cannot speak, thereof one must be silent," the felt qualities associated with religious experiencing are no more ineffable than are any other modes of experience. They contain patterns that are ready to be expressed, whether as "God" in the West or as "Emptiness" in the East. In both cases, radical empiricists in the West and Buddhists in the East have always insisted that the conceptual elements utilized in what they are saying are not what they are talking about; what they are talking about is that to which the concepts "God" and "Emptiness" are applied, and by which they are justified.

But if this is so, have we not ended by arriving at the only mode of empirical justification that the preceding chapters would warrant? Felt qualities with all their discriminable modes are what is directly encountered in experience. They form the ultimate evidence by which religious assertions are tested, and they comprise the empirical content of any form of religious experiencing. Justification terminates ultimately not with beliefs about felt qualities of experience but with the felt qualities themselves. And yet, given the particular notion of experience which has been expounded in this book, the termination is always unfinished and there is no permanent or single kind of justification in practice.

[handwritten marginalia, left margin: which or shaped by belief]

[handwritten notes at bottom of page:]

felt qualities — central problem what gets included in this ; realtime, perceptual schemata, but also emotions + more complex religious experiences

The 1st seems okay, ntuge may be not best way to describe, but the 2nd still problematic

cf Johnson

Those tied to body + shared phys nature — emotions one too, yet seem different (up-down) happy-sad

178 — all of these they described about felt qualities shaped by cultural, linguistic, social context ; point of her claim about why not 'subjective'. relationship both in 'natural' + linguistic - cultural world

[handwritten marginalia, left margin: "how" is or are expressed ; problems]

Epilogue

Hardly anyone would want to defend the claim that religion has nothing at all, or very little to do with experience. Most people want to know what role, if any, experience plays in religion and why one should be concerned with religious beliefs that make no difference in experience. Posing the question this way makes it seem disarmingly simple. However, the philosophical sense in which experience is relevant to the vicissitudes of human belief has become a particularly elusive matter, in the field of religion as much as in other areas.

In recent epistemological empiricism, for example, only the most attenuated version of experience appears in the justification-of-belief literature. Debates among contextualists, coherentists, and foundationalists have generated an imposing body of highly technical studies concerning the logic of warrant as a formal relation holding between statements or propositions. The category of experience enters these discussions only as a ghostly shadow—haunting the premises, but unreal. Now that many philosophers in the analytic tradition have come to think that there is no longer any epistemologically interesting distinction to be drawn between propositions and experience, experience is treated simply as a kind of cipher, an indeterminate surd in a linguistic network. Such dereliction is understandable. The phenomenon of experience is one of the most difficult topics to analyze empirically.

In philosophy of religion, many have turned to a study of the conditions for the justifiability of holding basic religious beliefs, rather than to an appraisal of the empirical basis of religious beliefs in experience. But the belief systems typically examined in the rationality-of-belief literature are often troublesome, born of dubious theology or outdated cosmology, and reinforced by suspect paradigm cases ("God is speaking to me"). A great deal of painstaking analysis has been focused on the question "Is it rational for s to believe that p?", only to

189

yield the minimally interesting conclusion that p is a rationally admissible belief to which s is epistemically entitled.

One purpose of this book has been to clear a space for renewed interest in the phenomenon of experience in religion, and to suggest ways in which the problems of justification and theism look different when approached from the standpoint of a radical empiricism. More interesting, I think, than the question "Is it rational to hold that p?" is the radically empirical question "Can p be referred to concrete experiencings?" What sort of experiences would a particular religious belief lead to or lean on, if true? Is there, as William James would want it, a felt difference which *makes* a difference? Is either "God" or "Emptiness," for example, concretely experienceable? Or is the use of such terms in religious language simply an epistemic entitlement not yet proven irrational? What theory best enables the philosopher of religion to comprehend the kinds of experiences that both Western and Eastern religions cultivate?

In the physical sciences, the notorious underdetermination of theory by experience is commonplace. It stems from the increasingly abstractive modes of knowledge scientists pursue, isolated from analyses of intentional and value-laden behavior. In the human sciences, however, where we are concerned with social beliefs and practices, the data are incomparably more subtle and complex, making theory-construction much more difficult than in the simpler systems studied by physics and chemistry. In philosophy of science, Quine can be impressed that there is so much torrential "output" in the form of our theories, when there is so little "input," as he sparingly puts it, from the side of experience. In philosophy of religion, however, we face the very different problem of contending with far more "input" from religious traditions than we are currently able to conceptualize adequately in putting-out our limited descriptive and explanatory models.

One reason for this is that experience itself has been undertheorized. Not only do most of our Western conceptions of experience still reek of remnants of positivist philosophies, but also they are proving inadequate for dealing with cross-cultural religious data.

If radical empiricism, as I have argued, provides the most adequate philosophical theory of experience, it also permits a new theory concerning a set of experiences interpreted as religious. This theory merits attention in its own right and deserves to be recognized as one of the distinctive contributions of American religious empiricism. It is implicit in James's amorphous "More" and Dewey's "consummatory experience." It is present in Wieman's "creative event," in Meland's "appreciative awareness," and in Loomer's "size." It entails, in all cases, a religious application of Whitehead's cosmological axiom that "the many become one and are increased by one."

Summarily stated, the theory is that the distinguishing mark of religious experiencing is a pervasive type of physical and conceptual sensitivity to the aesthetic matrix of relations, leading to the emergence of greater complexity, deeper intensity, and wider range of contrasts within a harmonized unity of feeling. The felt qualities of the religious dimension of experience, like those of art, are a matter of maximizing complexity and intensity in harmony. But religious experiencing, unlike aesthetic experiencing, seeks an unrestricted field of value whose harmony involves an ever-enlarging process synthesis of the widest range and deepest contrasts of relational data. The particular set of experiences interpreted as religious on the basis of this theory are therefore those that pertain to the creative transformation of existing forms of experience, enabling individuals (and cultures) to move from narrower, constricted patterns of perception and feeling to wider and deeper modes of sympathetic inclusiveness.

In radical empiricism, religious experience is thus a testimony to the communal aspect of human experience. The individual is not simply one among many; the many are literally creative of the internal life of the individual who is an emergent from these relations. As Buddhists have recognized, this dynamic process both demands and also effects a freedom from the arresting names we impose on the flux of experience, a purification of the compulsive attachments, illusions, and constricting forms that mark our normal perceptual habits, and an insight into the emptiness of those distinctions that ordinarily set one entity apart from another.

The explanatory categories of this theory are resolutely naturalistic, thereby ruling out explanations in terms of the supernatural, the transcendental, the Wholly Other, or the Sacred. It is precisely the suitability of this type of religious experiencing to naturalistic categories of explanation that frees it from the parochial apologetics of one religion or another and at the same time is the source of the complaint that it seems indistinguishable from what could be said in strictly nonreligious terms. But this is exactly what one should expect from a theory that prescinds from the dichotomy religious-nonreligious. The distinction between religious experience and other kinds of experience is, after all, a poor one. That is why Dewey urged a concern with "religious qualities" rather than with "religions."

Although this theory fits with an entirely naturalistic understanding of religious experience, it does not attempt to offer an explanation that might be appropriate to all religious experiences in all cultures. It neither explains religious experience in general, nor explains it away. Given the bewildering and disparate cultural forms commonly lumped together under the label of "religious experience," it is extremely doubtful that there could ever be any such general explanation. It is even more doubtful, from the perspective of radical empiricism, that any cross-cultural single phenomenon called "religious experience" can be identified, except as an invention of modern scholarship. Just as there is no "essence" of religion for phenomenologists to capture, there is no *general* "phenomenon" of religious experience for empirical philosophers of religion to explain.

William James, who knew this as well as anyone and sooner than most, could pioneer at the turn of the century in a study of the varieties, unities, and insistent particularities of religious experience. In our time, radical empiricists who would fashion a genuinely comparative philosophy of religions, beyond existing formalisms, positivisms, and parochialisms, will attend to James's kind of "full facts" in the full experiential sweep of world religions.

Notes

Chapter One

1. William James, *A Pluralistic Universe* (New York: Longmans, Green, and Co., 1909), p. 314.

2. J. Loewenberg, "What is Empirical?," *Journal of Philosophy*, XXXVII:11 (May 23, 1940), p. 283.

3. James Alfred Martin, Jr., *Empirical Philosophies of Religion* (New York: King's Crown Press, 1945), p. 122.

4. Bernard M. Loomer, "Empirical Theology Within Process Thought," in Bernard E. Meland, ed., *The Future of Empirical Theology* (Chicago: The University of Chicago Press, 1969), p. 160.

5. Bernard E. Meland, *Fallible Forms and Symbols* (Philadelphia: Fortress Press, 1976), p. xiv.

6. Michael Williams, "Coherence, Justification, and Truth," *Review of Metaphysics* 34 (December 1980), p. 243.

7. See William P. Alston, "Has Foundationalism Been Refuted?," *Philosophical Studies* XXIX(1976):287-305 and "Two Types of Foundationalism," *Journal of Philosophy* LXXIII, 7(8 April, 1976):165-85.

8. Anthony Quinton, *The Nature of Things* (London: Routledge and Kegan Paul, 1973), p. 119.

9. Michael Williams, *Groundless Belief* (New Haven: Yale University Press, 1977), p. 83.

10. Otto Neurath, "Protocol Sentences," trans. in A.J. Ayer, ed. *Logical Positivism* (New York: Free Press, 1959), pp. 199-208.

11. Ludwig Wittgenstein, *Philosophical Investigations*, trans. in G.E.M. Anscombe, 2nd ed. (Oxford: Basil Blackwell, 1963), p. 200.

12. Ludwig Wittgenstein, *On Certainty*, ed. G.E.M. Anscombe and G.H. von Wright, trans. G.E.M. Anscombe and Denis Paul (Oxford: Basil Blackwell, 1969), # 559.

13. Ludwig Wittgenstein, *Philosophical Investigations*, # 217, # 654.

14. Ludwig Wittgenstein, *Lectures and Conversations on Aesthetics, Psychology and Religious Belief*, ed. C.K. Barrett (Berkeley: Univ. of California Press, 1966), pp. 53-4.

15. *Ibid.*, p. 58. In depicting the religious attitude in this way, Wittgenstein does not seem to pay sufficient attention to the difference between one who would say "I live as if there were to be a Last Judgment," and one who would say "I live this way because of my belief that certain actual events will happen in the future."

16. D. Pears, *Wittgenstein* (London: Fontana, 1971), p. 174.

17. Norman Malcolm, "The Groundlessness of Belief," in Stuart C. Brown, ed., *Reason and Religion* (Ithaca, NY: Cornell University Press, 1977), p. 152.

18. *Ibid.*, pp. 152, 156.

19. D.Z. Phillips, *Faith and Philosophical Enquiry* (London: Routledge and Kegan Paul, 1970), pp. 14, 17.

20. D.Z. Phillips, *The Concept of Prayer* (London: Routledge and Kegan Paul, 1965), p. 18.

21. *Ibid.*, pp. 50-51, my emphasis. Phillips has reconsidered some of his earlier views in "Belief, Change, and Forms of Life: The Confusions of Externalism and Internalism," in *The Autonomy of Religious Belief* (Notre Dame, IN: University of Notre Dame Press, 1981), p. 60-92.

22. Patrick Sherry, *Religion, Truth and Language-Games* (New York: Harper & Row, 1977), p. 60.

23. See Roger Trigg, *Reason and Commitment* (Cambridge: Cambridge University Press, 1973).

24. See John H. Whittaker, *Matters of Faith and Matters of Principle* (San Antonio, TX: Trinity University Press, 1981), Chapter 1.

25. The essays I am considering are Plantinga's most recent work in the epistemology of religious belief: "Is Belief in God Rational?," in C.F. Delaney, ed., *Rationality and Religious Belief* (Notre Dame, IN: University of Notre Dame Press, 1979); "Is Belief in God Properly Basic?" *Nous* 15(March 1981):41-51; "Reason and Belief in God," in A. Plantinga and N. Wolterstorff, ed., *Faith and Rationality* (Notre Dame, IN: University of Notre Dame Press, 1984). A full account of Plantinga's position would have to take note of the fact that he has offered a version of the ontological argument. His *God and Other Minds* (Ithaca,

NY: Cornell University Press, 1967) takes as its central topic "the rational justification of belief in the existence of God" (vii). In *The Nature of Necessity* (Oxford: Oxford University Press, 1974) he attempts to resolve the problem of evil while providing a sound version of the ontological argument (Chapters IX and X). For responses to Plantinga's work as a whole, see the essays in *Alvin Plantinga*, ed. by James E. Tomberlin and Peter Van Inwagen, Vol. 5, *Profiles*, An International Series on Contemporary Philosophers and Logicians (Dordrecht: D. Reidel Publishing Co., 1985), especially William P. Alston, "Plantinga's Epistemology of Religious Belief," pp. 289-311, which extends and develops Plantinga's position in an original way.

26. "Is Belief in God Rational?," p. 27.

27. "Is Belief in God Properly Basic?," p. 50. Strictly speaking, Plantinga takes to be properly basic the following specific beliefs, each of which he treats as entailing that "God exists":

(6) God is speaking to me,
(7) God has created all this,
(8) God disapproves of what I have done,
(9) God forgives me, and
(10) God is to be thanked and praised.

28. *Ibid.* Here and in other places Plantinga departs significantly from the Reformed tradition that, historically, from John Calvin to Charles Hodge of Princeton University to L. Berkhof of Calvin College, embraced some version of natural theology. Cf. Calvin's *Institutes of the Christian Religion*, Book 1, Chapters 3-5; and Hodge's monumental nineteenth century work, *Systematic Theology*, esp. Volume 1.

29. *Op. Cit.*, p. 46.

30. Roderick M. Chisholm uses this theological analogy in his fundamentalist *defense* of unmoved (or self-moved) movers of the epistemic realm, upon which empirical knowledge is alleged to rest. See his *Theory of Knowledge* (Englewood Cliffs, NJ: Prentice-Hall, 1966), p. 30.

31. Charles Hartshorne, *A Natural Theology for Our Time* (LaSalle, IL: Open Court Publishing Co., 1967), p. 79.

32. Charles Hartshorne, *Creative Synthesis and Philosophical Method* (La Salle, IL: Open Court Publishing Co., 1970), p. 19f.

33. Charles Hartshorne, *Anselm's Discovery: A Re-Examination of the Ontological Proof for God's Existence* (LaSalle, IL: Open Court Publishing Co., 1965).

34. Charles Hartshorne, "Is God's Existence a State of Affairs?" in *Faith and the Philosophers*, ed. John Hick (New York: St. Martin's Press, Inc., 1964), pp. 26-27, 31-32.

35. Charles Hartshorne, *The Logic of Perfection and Other Essays on Neo-classical Metaphysics* (LaSalle, IL: Open Court Publishing Co., 1962), pp. 72, 111, 116.

36. Robert C. Neville has incisively argued this point (and other important criticisms) in his *Creativity and God: A Challenge to Process Theology* (New York: The Seabury Press, 1980).

37. Hartshorne himself addresses this result in "Some Empty Though Important Truths," in *The Logic of Perfection*. My argument in the previous paragraphs is, of course, open to Hartshorne's frequent complaint that his critics have not succeeded in refuting his ontological argument but only in rejecting either the law of noncontradiction or else his particular definition. From the standpoint of radical empiricism, however, Hartshorne appears to have defined ontological possibility as logically necessary possibility and to have reduced ontology to logic (*i.e.*, conceivability).

38. See, for example, William Dean, "An American Theology," *Process Studies* 12/2(Summer 1982):111-28; Bernard J. Lee, S.M., "The Two Process Theologies," *Theological Studies* 45(1984):307-319; and especially, Bernard E. Meland, *Fallible Forms and Symbols* (Philadelphia: Fortress Press, 1976).

39. Charles Hartshorne, *Man's Vision of God and the Logic of Theism* (Chicago: Willett, Clark and Co., 1941), p. 345.

40. *The Logic of Perfection*, p. 15.

41. *A Natural Theology for Our Time*, p. 77.

42. Schubert Ogden, *The Reality of God* (New York: Harper & Row, 1966), p. 1.

43. For a speech-act theory of religious language and convictions, see James William McClendon, Jr., and James M. Smith, *Understanding Religious Convictions* (Notre Dame, IN: University of Notre Dame Press, 1975).

44. Richard Swinburne, *The Coherence of Theism* (Oxford: Clarendon Press, 1977), p.2.

45. J. L. Mackie, *The Miracle of Theism: Arguments For and Against the Existence of God* (Oxford: Clarendon Press, 1982).

46. Terence Penelhum, "Divine Goodness and the Problem of Evil," *Religious Studies*, Volume II (1966), p. 99.

47. J. N. Findlay, "Can God's Existence be Disproved?" in Flew and MacIntyre (eds.), *New Essays in Philosophical Theology* (London: SCM Press, 1956), p. 46.

48. Edward H. Madden and Peter H. Hare, "Evil and Unlimited Power," *The Review of Metaphysics*, vol. xx, no. 2 (December 1966):285.

49. *Ibid.*, p. 288.

50. Reinhold Niebuhr, *The Nature and Destiny of Man*, vol. II (New York: Charles Scribner's Sons, 1964), p. 291.

51. Henry Nelson Wieman, *Religious Experience and Scientific Method* (Carbondale, IL: Southern Illinois University Press, 1971; originally 1926 by The Macmillan Co.), Preface to the 1971 Edition.

52. *Ibid.*, p. 27f.

53. John M. Moore, *Theories of Religious Experience* (New York: Round Table Press, 1938), pp. 225-26.

54. C. B. Martin, *Religious Belief* (Ithaca, NY,: Cornell University Press, 1959), pp. 67-68.

55. Ronald Hepburn, "Religious Experience," *The Encyclopedia of Philosophy*, Volume 7, p. 168.

56. George Bernard Shaw, *Saint Joan* (Baltimore, MD: Penguin Books, 1951), p. 59.

57. John E. Smith, *Experience and God* (London: Oxford University Press, 1968), p. 22.

58. This point has been repeatedly raised over the years by John E. Smith in various works. See especially his *Reason and God: Encounters of Philosophy with Religion* (New Haven, CT: Yale University Press, 1961) and *Religion and Empiricism*, The Aquinas Lecture (Milwaukee, WI: Marquette University Press, 1967). Cf. Eugene Thomas Long, "Experience and the Justification of Religious Belief," *Religious Studies* 17:499-510.

59. Hans-Georg Gadamer, *Truth and Method* (New York: The Seabury Press, 1975), p. 310.

Chapter Two

1. Alfred North Whitehead, *Symbolism, Its Meaning and Effect* (New York: Macmillan, 1927), p. 16.

2. Marjorie Grene, *The Knower and the Known* (New York: Basic Books, Inc., 1966), p. 99.

3. David Hume, *A Treatise of Human Nature*, ed. L.A. Selby-Bigge (Oxford: Clarendon Press, 1888), p. 4.

4. *Ibid.*, p. 180.

5. David Hume, *An Enquiry Concerning Human Understanding*, ed. Eric Steinberg (Indianapolis, IN: Hackett Publishing Co., 1977), p. 13.

6. *Treatise*, p. 6.

7. *Ibid.*, p. 36. Emphasis added. Cf. Alfred North Whitehead, *Process and Reality*, Corrected Edition, ed. D.R. Griffin and D.W. Sherburne (New York: The Free Press, 1978), p. 131f.

8. *Ibid.*, p. 10.

9. *Ibid.*, p. 16.

10. *Ibid.*, p. 233.

11. *Treatise*, p. 1; cf. *Enquiry*, p. 10.

12. *Ibid.*

13. *Ibid.*, p. 11.

14. *Enquiry*, p. 16.

15. *Ibid.*, p. 7.

16. *Ibid.*, p. 162.

17. Cf. *Process and Reality*, p. 176.

18. *Treatise*, p. 89.

19. Cf. *Process and Reality*, p. 176.

20. John Dewey, "The Need for a Recovery of Philosophy," in *Creative Intelligence: Essays in the Pragmatic Attitude* (New York: H. Holt and Co., 1917), by John Dewey, *et. al.*, p. 14.

21. *Ibid.*, p. 32. In this landmark 1917 essay Dewey disparaged "the submergence of recent philosophizing in epistemology" (p. 29) much as Richard Rorty has done more recently in *Philosophy and the Mirror of Nature* (Princeton, NJ: Princeton University Press, 1979). According to Dewey, "the theological problem of attaining knowledge of God as ultimate reality was transformed in effect into the philosophical problem of the possibility of attaining knowledge of reality." Dewey thought the problem was artificial; the question of how self or mind or subjective experience or consciousness can reach knowledge of an external world is "assuredly a meaningless problem." It is meaningless because the assumption that experience is something over against the world is, as Dewey shows, contrary to fact (p. 31f.).

22. *Ibid.*, pp. 7-8.

23. *Enquiry*, p. 93.

24. *Ibid.*, p. 98.

25. *Ibid.*

26. David Hume, *Dialogues Concerning Natural Religion*, ed. Richard H. Popkin (Indianapolis, IN: Hackett Publishing Co., 1980), p. 89.

27. *Ibid.*, p. 88.

28. *Ibid.*, p. 69. All subsequent quotations from Part XI of the *Dialogues* are taken from pages 69-76 of the Hackett edition.

29. A.J. Ayer, *Language, Truth and Logic*, (New York: Dover Publications, 1952), p. 116, 117-18.

30. See, for example, Alonzo Church, review of Ayer's *Language, Truth and Logic*, 2d ed., *Journal of Symbolic Logic*, Vol. 14(1949); Friedrich Waismann, "Verifiability," *PAS*, Supp. Vol. 19(1945):119-50 (reprinted in A.G.N. Flew, ed., *Logic and Language*, First Series (Oxford: Basil Blackwell, 1951); Carl G. Hempel, "Problems and Changes in the Empiricist Criterion of Meaning," *Revue internationale de philosphie*, Vol. 4(1950):41-63 (reprinted in A.J. Ayer, ed., *Logical Positivism*. Glencoe, IL: Free Press, 1959). The last is an exceptionally rigorous and clear analysis of these difficulties by a positivist himself.

31. Antony Flew, "Theology and Falsification," in *New Essays in Philosophical Theology*, edited by Antony Flew and Alasdair MacIntyre (New York: Macmillan, 1955), p. 99. It may be that incompatibility with and counting against are two separate cases, but I will not address that issue here.

32. See Hempel's article on "Empiricist Criteria of Cognitive Significance: Problems and Changes" in C.G. Hempel, *Aspects of Scientific Explanation* (New York: The Free Press, 1965), pp. 103-5.

33. In *Mind, Matter, and Method*, ed. P.K. Feyerabend and G. Maxwell (Minneapolis, MN: University of Minnesota Press, 1966), pp. 354-76.

34. *Ibid.*, p. 355.

35. *Ibid.*, p. 358.

36. Contained in *The Linguistic Turn*, ed. Richard Rorty (Chicago, IL University of Chicago Press, 1967), p. 320.

37. *Process and Reality*, p. 4. Certainly it is fair to say that there has been very little of the sort of analysis which Whitehead was urging when he recommended that philosophical analysis consult the widest possible understanding of the range of experience," . . . experience drunk, and experience sober, experience sleeping and experience waking . . . experience anticipatory and experience retrospective . . . experience normal and experience abnormal." *Adventures of Ideas* (New York: The Free Press, 1967), p. 226. Instead, Anglo-American philosophers in this century have raised to paradigmatic status a most peculiar and singular sort of experience: this-patch-of-red-here-now. This example has been a source of fascination to sense data and anti-sense data philosophers alike. John Austin once used the example of magenta, but, it is reported, "this was thought to be slightly off-color" (*The New Republic*, December 6, 1982, p. 36).

38. This point has also been stressed by Ernest Gellner, *Words and Things*, (Harmondsworth, England: Penguin Books, 1968), p. 235.

39. John L. Austin, "A Plea for Excuses" in *Philosophical Papers*, ed. J.O. Urmson and G.J. Warnock (Oxford: Clarendon Press, 1961), p. 133.

40. *Ibid.*, p. 130. Emphasis added. Here an underlying rationalism seems to be evident in Austin's phrase. Instead of saying "what we *would* say when" or "what we *do* say when," Austin's "should" confronts us with a normative criterion governing what can legitimately be said.

41. *Ibid.*

42. See for example Raeburne S. Heimbeck, *Theology and Meaning: A Critique of Metatheological Skepticism* (Stanford, CA: Stanford University Press, 1969) where the author notes at the outset the new options provided by existentialist theology and process theology, but passes over these in favor of vouching for the cognitive meaningfulness of "classical Christian theism" on the grounds that" . . . the metatheological analysis of classical Christian theism is rightfully, it seems to me, the most pressing business in this area of philosophical work" (p. 44).

43. John Passmore, "Review Article: Christianity and Positivism," *Australasian Journal of Philosophy* 35(1957):125.

44. See John Hick, "Religious Faith as Experiencing-As," in G.N.A. Vesey, ed., *Talk of God* (London: Macmillan, 1969); Donald Evans, *The Logic of Self-Involvement* (London: SCM Press, 1963), Chapter 3; Ian Barbour, *Myth, Models and Paradigms* (New York: Harper & Row, 1974).

45. Ludwig Wittgenstein, *Philosophical Investigations*, p. 193.

46. *Ibid.*, pp. 186, 197.

47. *Ibid.*, p. 197.

48. *Ibid.*, pp. 208-9.

49. *Ibid.*, p. 227.

50. John Wisdom, "Gods," in *Philosophy and Psychoanalysis* (Berkeley, CA: University of California Press, 1969), p. 154. Wisdom did not suppose that the difference between theists and atheists is *sheerly* attitudinal and noncognitive and therefore serving to state nothing factual. On the contrary, religious language functions to direct our attention to patterns in the facts.

"And though we shall need to emphasize how much 'There is a God' evinces an attitude to the familiar we shall find in the end that it also evinces some recognition of patterns found in time easily missed and that, therefore, difference as to there being any Gods is in part a difference as to what is so and therefore as to the facts, though not in the simple ways which first occurred to us." (*Ibid.*)

51. *Ibid.*, p. 158.

52. John Hick, "Religious Faith as Experiencing-As," p. 23.

53. *Ibid.*, p. 27.

54. See for example, Steven T. Katz, "The 'Conservative' Character of Mystical Experience," in *idem*, ed., *Mysticism and Religious Traditions* (New York: Oxford University Press, 1983). See also, Katz, ed., *Mysticism and Philosophical Analysis* (New York: Oxford University Press, 1978).

55. Mary Hesse, *Revolution and Reconstructions in the Philosophy of Science* (Bloomington, IN: Indiana University Press, 1980), *verbatim* pp. 172-73.

56. Wilfrid Sellars, "Empiricism and the Philosophy of Mind," *Minnesota Studies in the Philosophy of Science*, Volume 1, Herbert Feigl and Michael Scriven, eds. (Minneapolis, MN: University of Minnesota Press, 1956); reprinted in Sellars, *Science, Perception and Reality* (New York: Humanities Press, 1963). All references are to 1956 edition, pp. 293, 300, 293, 298-99 *seriatim*.

57. W.V.O. Quine, "Two Dogmas of Empiricism" in *From a Logical Point of View* (New York: Harper Torchbooks, 1963). All references are to this reprint, pp. 42, 43, 43, 46, 44 *seriatim*. By concentrating on the early Quine, I am leaving out of account other aspects of his philosophy which are, as his critics claim, in tension with his holism and pragmatism. A curious feature of Quine's empiricism is the number of ways in which he suggests a view of experience no less attenuated than that of positivism. Where earlier empiricists talked of sense-data, Quine talks of nerve endings. In proposing that the epistemological burden shouldered by philosophy should be surrendered to psychology, Quine asserts that "the stimulation of his sensory receptors is all the evidence anybody has had to go on ultimately in arriving at his picture of the world." *Ontological Relativity and Other Essays* (New York: Columbia Univ. Press, 1969), p. 75. The positivist program, of explaining how our individual bits of knowledge of the external world can be reconstructed from sense-data by logic, was a failure. Quine would replace it, however, with something equally ambitious: a new program of explaining how our knowledge of the world generally, and theoretically, can be developed from sensory stimulations of homologous nerve endings by socially controlled devices of reinforcement of desired response. With this, he thinks, epistemology "simply falls into place as a chapter of psychology and hence of natural science." (*Ibid.*, p. 82). In the context of his behaviorist account of language, Quine is thus led to a difficult description of observation sentences in terms of "stimulus meaning," which is not easily reconciled with the kind of evaluational account of our web of beliefs required by Quine's theory of evidence. For an argument that "observation sentences" in Quine's work lead a conflicting double life, in which two quite different parties (Stimulus Sentences and Periphery Sentences) masquerade as the hardworking but schizophrenic observation sentences, see Sandra Harding, "Making Sense of Observation Sentences," *Ratio*, Vol. 17, no. 1 (June 1975):65-71.

58. Donald Davidson, "On the Very Idea of a Conceptual Scheme," in *Inquiries into Truth and Interpretation* (Oxford: Clarendon Press, 1984). All references are to pp. 193-94, 198 *seriatim*. Richard Rorty recommends giving up the world as the Thing-in-Itself, that which we might never get right, in "The World Well Lost," *Journal of Philosophy* 69(1972):649-666.

59. Richard Rorty, *Philosophy and the Mirror of Nature* (Princeton, NJ: Princeton University Press, 1979). All references to pp. 182, 178, 179, 186, 361 *seriatim*. See also his *Consequences of Pragmatism*, (Minneapolis, MN: University of Minnesota Press, 1982).

60. Rorty alludes to Michael Oakeshott, "The Voice of Poetry in the Conversation of Mankind," in *Rationalism and Politics* (London and New York: Methuen, 1962), pp. 197-247.

61. Both Richard Bernstein and Cornel West have offered important critical perspectives on Rorty's work. See Bernstein, "Philosophy in the Conversation of Mankind," *Review of Metaphysics* 33(1980):745-76, and *Beyond Objectivism and Relativism: Science. Hermeneutics, and Praxis* (Philadelphia: University of Pennsylvania Press, 1983); for West, see *Prophesy Deliverance! An Afro-American Revolutionary Christianity* (Philadelphia: Westminster Press, 1982).

62. Jeffrey Stout, *The Flight From Authority: Religion, Morality, and the Quest for Autonomy.* (Notre Dame, IN: University of Notre Dame Press, 1981). Stout's work is to date the single best source for appraising the impact of postpositivist American philosophy on religious epistemology.

63. *Ibid.*, p. 63.

64. *Ibid.*, pp. 35, 20.

65. *Ibid.*, pp. 147, 146.

66. *Ibid.*, p. 146, quoted by Stout. MacIntyre accuses liberal theologians of offering the cultured despisers of religion "less and less in which to disbelieve." I think he misconstrues the motivation of liberal theology and the pathos of the liberal theologians who have labored to reinterpret traditional theism as much for their own sake and that of their communities as for the culture at large. Cf. Van A. Harvey, "The Dilemma of the Unbelieving Theologian," *American Journal of Theology and Philosophy* 2/2(May 1981):46-54; "The Alienated Theologian," in Robert A. Evans, ed., *The Future of Philosophical Theology* (Philadelphia: Westminster, 1971), pp. 85-113; "The Pathos of Liberal Theology," *Journal of Religion* vol. 56, no. 4 (1976):385-86; David Tracy, *Blessed Rage for Order* (New York: Seabury Press, 1975), and *The Analogical Imagination* (New York: Crossroad, 1981).

67. *The Flight From Authority*, p. 97.

68. *Ibid.*, p. 133.

69. *Ibid.*, e.g., pp. 10, 118, 149, 150.

Chapter Three

1. This is the way Nelson Goodman introduces his dismissal of epistemological foundationalism as well as the "given" element in experience, advising that now "we face the questions how worlds are made, tested, and known," in *Ways of Worldmaking* (Indianapolis, IN: Hackett Publishing Co., 1978), p. 7.

2. Rorty, *Consequences of Pragmatism*, p. xviii.

3. John E. Smith, *Reason and God* (New Haven, CT: Yale University Press, 1961), p. 179f.; cf. also *Purpose and Thought: The Meaning of Pragmatism* (New Haven. CT: Yale University Press, 1978), Chapter 3. Although I mention Peirce as partaking in a radical empiricism, my attention in this chapter is confined to James and Dewey.

4. William James, *The Meaning of Truth* (Ann Arbor: University of Michigan Press, 1970), pp. xxxvi-xxxvii.

5. *Ibid.*

6. *Ibid.* The same point is made more vividly in *Essays in Radical Empiricism* (Cambridge, MA: Harvard University Press, 1976), pp. 46-7:

> The conjunctions are as primordial elements of 'fact' as are the distinctions. In the same act by which I feel that this passing minute is a new pulse in my life, I feel that the old life is continued into it, and the feeling of continuance in no wise jars upon the simultaneous feeling of a novelty. They, too, compenetrate harmoniously. Prepositions, copulas and conjunctions, 'is,' 'isn't,' 'then,' 'before,' 'in,' 'on,' 'besides,' 'between,' 'next,' 'like,' 'unlike,' 'as,' 'but,' flower out of the stream of pure experience, the stream of concretes or the sensation stream, as naturally as nouns and adjectives do.

7. James, *The Meaning of Truth*, p. xxxvi-xxxvii.

8. William James, *A Pluralistic Universe* (Gloucester, MA: Peter Smith, 1967), p. 309.

9. For an interesting exception, one which ably clarifies both continuities and discontinuities in James's religious thought, see H.S. Levinson, *The Religious Investigations of William James* (Chapel Hill, NC: The University of North Carolina Press, 1981).

10. William James, "Pragmatism's Conception of Truth," *Pragmatism and the Meaning of Truth* (Cambridge, MA: Harvard University Press, 1978), p. 97.

11. William James, *The Principles of Psychology*, Volume 1 (New York: Dover Publications, 1950, first published by Henry Holt and Company in 1890), p. 258n.

12. *Ibid.*, pp. 258, 472.

13. *Ibid.*, p. 258.

14. *Ibid.*, p. 254.

15. *Ibid.*, p. 222.

16. *Ibid.*, pp. 245-46.

17. *Ibid.*, p. 221.

18. Rorty, *Consequences of Pragmatism*, p. 214, quoting Hans Reichenbach, *The Rise of Scientific Philosophy* (Berkeley: University of California Press, 1951), pp. 121-22.

19. William James, *The Varieties of Religious Experience*, (Cambridge, MA: Harvard University Press, 1985), p. 66.

20. *Ibid.*, p. 67.

21. *Ibid.*, p. 400.

22. *Ibid.*

23. *Ibid.*, p. 386.

24. *Ibid.*, p. 403.

25. *Ibid.*, p. 405.

26. *Ibid.*, pp. 406, 407, 408.

27. *Ibid.*, pp. 409, 410, 411, 412, 413, 414.

28. James H. Leuba, "Professor William James's Interpretation of Religious Experience," *International Journal of Ethics* 14(April 1904):322-39.

29. Anthony O'Hear, *Experience, Explanation, and Faith* (London: Routledge and Kegan Paul, 1984), pp. 43-4.

30. *The Varieties of Religious Experience*, p. 401.

31. William James, *Essays in Radical Empiricism* (Cambridge, MA: Harvard University Press, 1976), p. 13.

32. *Ibid.*, p. 4.

33. *Ibid.*, p. 14-5.

34. A.J. Ayer, *The Origins of Pragmatism* (San Francisco, CA: Cooper and Co., 1968), pp. 310-17.

35. D.C. Mathur, *Naturalistic Philosophies of Experience* (St. Louis, MD: Greer Publishing, 1971), pp. 13ff.

36. Bruce Wilshire, *William James and Phenomenology* (Bloomington, IN: University of Indiana Press, 1968) *passim*; John Wild, *The Radical Empiricism of William James* (Garden City, NJ: Doubleday & Co., 1969), pp. 159ff.

37. C.I. Lewis, "A Pragmatic Conception of the A Priori," in *Pragmatic Philosophy*, ed., Amelie Rorty (New York: Doubleday and Co., 1966), p. 361.

38. R.B. Perry, *The Thought and Character of William James*, Vol. 2 (Boston, MA: Little, Brown & Co., 1935), p. 666.

39. Charlene Haddock Seigfried, *Chaos and Context: A Study in William James* (Athens, OH: Ohio University Press, 1978), p. 51.

40. *Essays in Radical Empiricism*, p. 22.

41. Seigfried, *op. cit.*, p. 6.

42. *Ibid.*

43. *Essays in Radical Empiricism*, p. 69.

44. Seigfried, p. 44.

45. *Essays in Radical Empiricism*, p. 13.

46. John E. Smith, *Themes in American Philosophy* (New York: Harper & Row, 1970), p. 31.

47. *The Varieties of Religious Experience*, p. 405.

48. *Essays in Radical Empiricism*, p. 29.

49. *Ibid.*

50. *Ibid.*, p. 17.

51. *Ibid.*, p. 18.

52. *Ibid.*, p. 72.

53. *Ibid.*, p. 73.

54. *Ibid.*, p. 75.

55. *Ibid.*, p. 74.

56. *Ibid.*, p. 99.

57. *Ibid.*, p. 27.

58. *Ibid.*

59. *The Varieties of Religious Experience*, p. 407.

60. *Ibid.*, p. 393.

61. *Ibid.*

62. John Dewey, *A Common Faith* (New Haven, CT: Yale University Press, 1934), p. 9.

63. *Ibid.*, p. 14.

64. *Ibid.*, pp. 18-9.

65. *Ibid.*, p. 19.

66. *Ibid.*

67. *Ibid.*, p. 33.

68. *Ibid.*, p. 50f.

69. *Ibid.*, p. 48f.

70. With William M. Shea and Stanley Grean, I share the conviction that Dewey's understanding of aesthetic experience yields a better understanding of the religious than is found in *A Common Faith*. Cf. Shea, *The Naturalists and the Supernatural* (Macon, GA: Mercer University Press, 1984), Chapter V; and Grean, "Elements of Transcendence in Dewey's Naturalistic Humanism," *Journal of the American Academy of Religion*, L11/2(June 1984):262-88.

71. Cf. John Dewey, *Art as Experience* (New York: Minton, Balch & Co., 1934), pp. 27, 41-2, 108, 119, 120, 192-95, 259, 293; and *Philosophy and Civilization* (Gloucester, MA: Peter Smith, 1968), pp. 93-117. My comments are not intended to canvass or to present wholesale all that Dewey wrote on the subject of quality. The ambiguities and even inconsistencies of Dewey's conception of quality are well-known to anyone who has spent much time with his writings. Roland Garrett has catalogued these in his article, "Dewey's Struggle with the Ineffable," *Transactions of the C.S. Peirce Society* 9(1975):95-109. Cf. Richard J. Bernstein, "John Dewey's Metaphysics of Experience," *Journal of Philosophy* LVIII(1961), pp. 5-6.

72. John Dewey, "Qualitative Thought," *Philosophy and Civilization*, p. 105-6.

73. *Art and Experience*, p. 72.

74 *Ibid.*, p. 572.

75. *Ibid.*, pp. 193-95.

Chapter Four

1. Robert W. Bretall, *The Empirical Theology of Henry Nelson Wieman*, ed. Robert W. Bretall (Carbondale, IL: Southern Illinois University Press, 1963), p. X.

2. Henry Nelson Wieman, "Intellectual Autobiography," in *The Empirical Theology of Henry Nelson Wieman*, p. 3.

3. *Ibid.*, p. 4.

4. Henry Nelson Wieman, *Is There a God? A Conversation* (with Douglas Clyde MacIntosh and Max Carl Otto, (Chicago: Willet, Clark, 1932), first in *Christian Century*, 1932-3, p. 276.

5. Henry Nelson Wieman, *Religious Experience and Scientific Method* (New York: Macmillan, 1926), p. 9.

6. "Intellectual Autobiography," in Bretall, *op. cit.*, p. 4.

7. *Religious Experience and Scientific Method*, p. 33.

8. *Ibid.*, p. 15.

9. *Ibid.*, p. 38.

10. *Ibid.*, p. 39.

11. *Ibid.*, p. 343.

12. *Ibid.*, pp. 344, 346.

13. *Ibid.*, p. 206. Wieman was here quoting from A.N. Whitehead's *The Concept of Nature*.

14. *Ibid.*, p. 218.

15. *Ibid.*, p. 207.

16. *Ibid.*, pp. 320-21.

17. *Ibid.*, p. 371.

18. *Ibid.*, p. 381.

19. *Ibid.* Wieman was later to become critical of any "appeal to religious experience" as having normative status in the philosophy of religion. By 1936 he could write that certain Christian liberals had "bungled . . . in misunderstanding and misusing the empirical method" when they identified empirical theology with the appeal to religious experience. (See Wieman, "God is More Than We Can Think," *Christendom*, I:3 [Spring 1936]:438.) One year later he could see in the critical tone of the essays by former students of D.C. Macintosh the signs that "the day of certainty of religious experience has passed . . . . Here is a smashing blow at that method of religious inquiry." (Review by Wieman of *The Nature of Religious Experience*, ed. J.S. Bixler, R.L. Calhoun, and H.R. Niebuhr [New York: Harper and Bros., 1937], in *Christendom*, II:3, Summer 1937, pp. 497-501.)

20. Henry Nelson Wieman, *The Source of Human Good* (Carbondale, IL: Southern Illinois University Press, 1946), p. 302.

21. *Ibid.*, p. 303.

22. *Ibid.*, p. 305.

23. *Ibid.*, p. 18.

24. *Ibid.*, p. 298.

25. *Ibid.*, p. 58. Wieman later added to this analysis a fifth subevent, increase of "freedom." Cf. *Intellectual Foundation of Faith*, pp. 61-2, 125-26.

26. *Ibid.*, pp. 77n, and 264.

27. Carl G. Hempel, "The Logic of Functional Analysis," *Symposium on Sociological Theory*, ed., L. Gross (Evanston, IL: Row, Peterson, 1959), pp. 271-307; reprinted in Hempel, *Aspects of Scientific Explanation* (New York: Free Press 1965); I. C. Jarvie, *Functionalism* (Minneapolis: Burgess Publishing Co., 1973); Robert K. Merton, *Social Theory and Social Structure* (Glencoe, IL: Free Press, 1957); Ernest Nagel, "A Formalization of Functionalism" in *Logic Without Metaphysics* (New York: The Free Press, 1957). These critiques all deal with functionalism in the social sciences and are applicable to explanations of religion in the anthropological and sociological disciplines. For the best criticism of functionalism as a methodology in the study of religion, see the articles by Hans H. Penner, "The Poverty of Functionalism," *History of Religions* 11:91-97(1971-72); and "Creating a Brahman: A Structural Approach to Religion," *Methodological Issues in Religious Studies*, ed. Robert Baird (Chico, CA: New Horizons Press, 1975), pp. 56-9. I know of no critique of functionalism as an implicit or explicit theory in the philosophy of religion or in theology.

28. Hempel, *Aspects of Scientific Explanation*, p. 310.

29. *Ibid.*

30. *Ibid.*, p. 313.

31. In this connection, Hans H. Penner has detected an error in Hempel's presentation of the revision, curiously overlooked by Hempel himself. The revised model, as Penner shows, is "invalid on the same basis as the first" (Penner, unpublished working manuscript). Even though Hempel thinks that the suggested revisions make the argument formally valid, although its conclusion is either tautologous or trivial, Penner points out that the argument remains formally invalid, regardless how many revisions, unless conditional premise (c) can be shown to be a *necessary* condition.

32. See *The Source of Human Good*, pp. 79-82.

33. For Hartshorne's recent speculations about the "seemingly strange and somewhat polytheistic idea" which he is "not prepared to accept or reject" as a way of reconciling his neoclassical theism with the absence of cosmic simultaneity, see his "Creative Interchange and Neoclassical Metaphysics,"

Creative Interchange, ed. John A. Broyer and William S. Minor (Carbondale, IL: Southern Illinois University Press, 1982), pp. 118-19.

34. Langdon Gilkey, "New Modes of Empirical Theology," *The Future of Empirical Theology,* ed. Bernard E. Meland (Chicago: University of Chicago Press, 1969), p. 348. In addition, the Hempelian criticism of the functionalist fallacy should shed light on the conclusion of William Hynes's fine study of the socio-historical method as practiced by Shirley Jackson Case, one of Wieman's predecessors at Chicago. According to Hynes, "the greatest weakness of the method would seem to be its persistent lack of philosophical circumspection," specifically, I would add, its use of functionalist reasoning. See William Hynes, *Shirley Jackson Case and the Chicago School* (Chico, CA: Scholars Press, 1981), p. 128.

35. Karl Popper, *The Logic of Scientific Discovery* (New York: Harper and Row, 1959), p. 42.

36. Cf. W.W. Bartley, Ill, "Non-Justificationism: Popper versus Wittgenstein, in *Epistemology and Philosophy of Science* (Vienna, Holder-Pichler-Tempsky, 1983), p. 260, and *Retreat to Commitment,* 2nd ed., (LaSalle, IL: Open Court Publishing Co., 1984).

37. In order to appreciate fully what Meland means by empirical realism, it is necessary to consult in particular the masterful essay on "Evolution and the Imagery of Religious Thought" in *The Realities of Faith* (New York: Oxford University Press, 1962); the chapters on "Clues to Reconstruction" and "Structure of Experience" in *Faith and Culture* (Carbondale, IL: Southern Illinois University Press, 1953); "The Appreciative Consciousness" in *Higher Education and the Human Spirit* (Chicago: The University of Chicago Press, 1953); and especially the essays on "The New Realism in Religious Inquiry" and "The Mystery of Existing" in *Fallible Forms and Symbols* (Philadelphia: Fortress Press, 1976).

38. Bernard E. Meland, "Response to Inbody," *American Journal of Theology and Philosophy,* Vol. 5, No. 2 and 3 (May and September, 1984), p. 72-3. See also Meland's "Response to Frankenberry" in the same journal, pp. 130-37.

39. Bernard E. Meland, *Fallible Forms and Symbols. Discourses on Method for a Theology of Culture* (Philadelphia: Fortress Press, 1976), p. xiii.

40. *Ibid.,* p. 54.

41. Bernard E. Meland, "Can Empirical Theology Learn Something from Phenomenology?" in *The Future of Empirical Theology,* ed. Bernard E. Meland (Chicago: University of Chicago Press, 1969), p. 297.

42. *Ibid.,* p. 290.

43. Bernard E. Meland, "The Root and Form of Wieman's Thought," in *The Empirical Theology of Henry Nelson Wieman,* ed. Robert W. Bretall (New York: Macmillan, 1963), p. 63.

44. Meland, "Can Empirical Theology . . . ," p. 297.

45. Alfred North Whitehead, *Science and the Modern World* (New York: Macmillan, 1926), p. 90; *Process and Reality*, Corrected Edition, ed. D.R. Griffin and D.W. Sherburne (New York: The Free Press, 1978), p. 17.

46. Alfred North Whitehead, *Adventures of Ideas* (New York: Macmillan, 1933), pp. 158-59.

47. *Ibid.*, p. 222.

48. Meland, *Fallible Forms*, p. 54.

49. *Ibid.*, p. 56.

50. *Ibid.*, p. 51.

51. *Ibid.*, p. xiii.

52. *Ibid.*

53. Bernard E. Meland, "Grace: A Dimension of Nature?" *The Journal of Religion*, 54(1974):134.

54. Meland, *Fallible Forms*, p. 45.

55. *Ibid.*, p. 150-52.

56. See the exchanges between Wieman and Dewey in *The Christian Century* in 1933, occasioned by Dewey's review of the book *Is There a God? A Conversation* (Chicago: Willett, Clark, 1932). The three-way conversation was among D.C. Macintosh, Max Carl Otto, and Wieman. Dewey and Wieman proceeded to address the questions which divided them in subsequent issues of *The Christian Century* on February 8, March 1, March 22, and April 5, 1933.

57. Bernard E. Meland, "Is God Many or One?" *The Christian Century*, L(May 31, 1933): 725.

58. *Ibid.*, p. 726. Cf. also William S. Minor's discussion of Meland's role in this debate in his dissertation, published as *Creativity in Henry Nelson Wieman* (ATLA Monograph Series, Metuchen, NJ and London, 1977).

59. Henry Nelson Wieman, "Is God Many or One?" *The Christian Century* L(May 31, 1933):727. For Meland's reference to the presence of a "veiled absolute" in Wieman's empiricism, see *The Future of Empirical Theology*, p. 36.

60. *Fallible Forms and Symbols*, p. 115.

61. "Grace: A Dimension of Nature?" *The Journal of Religion*, 54(1974):123.

62. *Fallible Forms and Symbols*, p. 24.

63. *Ibid.*, p. 23.

64. "Can Empirical Theology Learn Something from Phenomenology?," p. 13.

65. *Ibid.*, p. 38. Emphasis added.

66. "Grace: A Dimension of Nature?," p. 121.

67. *Ibid.*, pp. 121-22.

68. Michael Williams, *Groundless Belief* (New Haven, CT: Yale University Press, 1977), p. 31.

69. "The Root and Form of Wieman's Thought," p. 67.

70. *The Realities of Faith: The Revolution of Cultural Forms* (New York: Oxford University Press, 1962), p. 223.

71. "The Root and Form of Wieman's Thought," p. 66.

72. *Ibid.*, p. 67.

73. "Can Empirical Theology Learn Something from Phenomenology?," pp. 37-8.

74. Meland, *Fallible Forms*, p. 56.

75. *Ibid.*, p. 188.

76. *Ibid.*, p. 175. Emphasis added.

77. *Ibid.*, p. 174. Emphasis added. This unnecessarily invites the Wittgensteinian query, would not a nothing do as well as something about which nothing can be said? (Cf. *Philosophical Investigations*, #304.)

78. *Ibid.*, p. 141. Emphasis added.

79. *Ibid.*, p. 188.

80. *Ibid.*, p. 181. Emphasis added.

81. Meland, "Can Empirical Theology Learn Something from Phenomenology?," p. 297.

82. Meland, *Fallible Forms*, p. 23.

83. Meland, "Grace: A Dimension of Nature?," p. 122.

84. Meland, *Fallible Forms*, p. 29.

85. Bernard M. Loomer, "The Future of Process Philosophy," *Process Philosophy: Basic Writings*, ed. Jack R. Sibley and Pete A.Y. Gunter (Washington, DC: University Press of America, 1978), p. 518.

86. Bernard M. Loomer, "Empirical Theology Within Process Thought," *The Future of Empirical Theology*, ed. Bernard E. Meland (Chicago: University of Chicago Press, 1969), p. 160.

87. *Ibid.*, p. 151.

88. *Ibid.*, pp. 168-69.

89. Bernard M. Loomer, "S-I-Z-E," *Criterion*, 13(1974):5-8. Reprinted in *Religious Experience and Process Theology*, ed. Harry James Cargas and Bernard Lee (New York: Paulist Press, 1976), pp. 69-76.

90. Bernard M. Loomer, "Response to David R. Griffin," *Encounter*, 36(1975):361-369.

91. *Ibid.*, p. 364.

92. *Ibid.*,

93. *Ibid.*, p. 365.

94. *Ibid.*

95. *Ibid.*

96. Bernard M. Loomer, "Theology and the Arts," a public lecture, Graduate Theological Union (March 1974): 15pp.; "Theology in the American Grain," *The Unitarian-Universalist Christian* 30(1975-76):23-34; "Two Conceptions of Power," *Process Studies* 6(1976):5-32; first presented as the Inaugural Lecture of the D.R. Sharpe Lectureship on Social Ethics at the University of Chicago, October 1975; "Beauty as a Design for Life," a public lecture at the Minneapolis College of Art and Design and at the University of Montana, (1978):38pp; "The Web of Life," *The Nature of Life*, ed. William Heidcamp (Baltimore, MD: University Park Press, 1978), pp. 93-109.

97. Loomer, "The Future of Process Philosophy," pp. 536-37.

98. *Ibid.*, p. 537.

99. *Ibid.*

100. This document was the subject of two separate special sessions at the annual meetings of the American Academy of Religion in 1978 and 1979. It was published posthumously in a special issue of the *American Journal of Theology and Philosophy*, guest editor, William Dean, who supplied a preface and introduction, with responses from John Cobb, Delwin Brown, Bernard Lee, Larry Axel, and myself. It is reprinted in *The Size of God: The Theology of Bernard Loomer in Context*, eds., William Dean and Larry E. Axel (Macon, GA: Mercer University Press, 1987). All page citations are to this volume.

101. Whitehead, *Process and Reality*, p. 289.

102. "The Size of God," p. 41.

103. *Ibid.*, p. 42.

104. *Ibid.*

105. *Ibid.*

106. *Ibid.*, p. 44.

107. *Ibid.*, p. 49.

108. *Ibid.*

109. *Ibid.*, p. 51.

Chapter Five

1. Alfred North Whitehead, *Process and Reality*, Corrected Edition, ed. D.R. Griffin and D.W. Sherburne (New York: The Free Press, 1978), p. xii.

2. Edward Conze, *Thirty Years of Buddhist Studies* (Columbia, SC: University of South Carolina Press, 1968), p. 229.

3. David L. Hall, *The Uncertain Phoenix* (New York: Fordham University Press, 1982), p. 181f.

4. Alfred North Whitehead, *Science and Philosophy* (Paterson, NJ: Littlefield, Adams, & Co., 1964), p. 132.

5. *Process and Reality*, p. 178.

6. Alfred North Whitehead, *Adventures of Ideas* (New York: Macmillan, 1933; reprint ed., New York: The Free Press, 1967), p. 176.

7. Alfred North Whitehead, *Symbolism* (New York: Macmillan, 1927; reprint ed., New York: Capricorn Books, 1959), pp. 44, 46.

8. *Process and Reality*, p. 176.

9. *Adventures of Ideas*, p. 18.

10. *Ibid.*

11. *Ibid.*, p. 182.

12. *Process and Reality*, pp. 311, 312.

13. *Mulamadhyamakakarikas.* Esp. chapters I and XXIV; trans. F.J. Streng, *Emptiness: A Study in Religious Meaning* (Nashville, TN: Abingdon Press, 1967).

14. *Prasannapada*, 5.1. Cf. also, Th. Stcherbatsky, *The Conception of Buddhist Nirvana* (Leningrad: Publishing Office of the Academy of Sciences of the USSR, 1927), p. 85.

15. *Process and Reality*, p. 21.

16. See Garma C.C. Chang, *The Buddhist Teaching of Totality: The Philosophy of Hwa-yen Buddhism* (University Park, PA: Pennsylvania State University Press, 1971).

214 RELIGION AND RADICAL EMPIRICISM

17. See Francis H. Cook, *Hwa-yen Buddhism: The Jewel Net of Indra* (University Park, PA: Pennsylvania State University Press, 1977).

18. See Steve Odin, *Process Metaphysics and Hua-yen Buddhism: A Critical Study of Cumulative Penetration vs. Interpenetration* (Albany, NY: State University of New York Press, 1982).

19. Jay McDaniel and John B. Cobb, Jr., "Introduction: Conference on Mahayana Buddhism and Whitehead," *Philosophy East and West* 25/4(October 1975):402.

20. *Process and Reality*, pp. 49-50.

21. *Adventures of Ideas*, pp. 132-33.

22. *Process and Reality*, p. 309.

23. *Adventures of Ideas*, pp. 177-78.

24. *Process and Reality*, p. 190.

25. Quoted in Louis de la Vallee Poussin, *The Way to Nirvana* (London: Cambridge University Press, 1917), p. 42f.

26. *Process and Reality*, p. 18.

27. *Samyutta Nikaya*, II, 17ff.

28. *Visuddhimagga*, trans. Nyanamoli as *The Path of Purification* (Colombo: A. Semage, 1964), XIX.602; XVI.513.

29. From his work in the field of high energy physics, Henry Peirce Stapp offers the following description, which could also serve as a succinct summary of the aesthetics of Buddhist and Whiteheadian process thought:

> One finds in the realm of experience essentially the same type of structure that one finds in the realm of elementary-particle physics, namely a web structure, the smallest elements of which always reach out to other things and find their meaning and ground of being in these other things. Since this same type of structure is suitable both in the realm of mind and in the realm of matter, one is led to adopt it as the basis of an over-all worldview.
>
> An experience is an integral part of some web of experience. Experiences cannot be analyzed into ultimate unanalyzable entities. The component parts invariably reach out to things outside themselves. To isolate an experience from its references is to destroy its essence. In short, experiences must be viewed as parts of webs, whose parts are not defined except through their connections to the whole.

(in "S-Matrix Interpretation of Quantum Theory," *Physical Review* D3[March 1971]:1319.)

30. Kenneth K. Inada, "The Metaphysics of Buddhist Experience and the Whiteheadian Encounter," *Philosophy East and West* 25/4(October 1975):479.

31. *Mulamadhaymakakarika*, p. 24.

32. *Ibid.*, p. 25, trans. Streng, *op. cit.*

33. *Science and the Modern World*, p. 72.

34. David Dilworth has argued that Whitehead's "process realism" bears a close resemblance to the Abhidharma and as such is subject to the Mahayana criticism. See his "Whitehead's Process Realism, The Abhidharma Dharma Theory, and the Mahayana Critique," *International Philosophical Quarterly,* 18/2(June 1978):151-69. Robert Neville's reply to this argues that Whitehead stands with the Mahayanists because of the common belief that nothing, not even actual occasions, has "own-being." See his *The Tao and the Daimon* (Albany, NY: State University of New York Press, 1982), pp. 173-77.

35. See K.N. Jayatilleke, *Early Buddhist Theory of Knowledge* (London: Allen and Unwin, 1964).

36. See D.J. Kalupahana, *Buddhist Philosophy* (Honolulu, HI: University of Hawaii Press, 1976).

37. See Gunapala Dharmasiri, *A Buddhist Critique of the Christian Concept of God* (Colombo: Lake House, 1974).

38. See Chris Gudmunsen, *Wittgenstein and Buddhism* (New York: Barnes and Noble, 1977), chapter 1.

39. See Frederick J. Streng, *Emptiness: A Study in Religious Meaning* (Nashville, TN: Abingdon Press, 1967).

40. Kenneth Inada, *op. cit.*, p. 480.

41. Edward Conze, *Buddhist Thought in India* (Ann Arbor, MI: University of Michigan Press, 1967), p. 93f.

42. F. Edgerton, *Buddhist Hybrid Sanskrit Grammar and Dictionary* (1953), Volume II, p. 276.

43. Th. Stcherbatsky, *The Central Conception of Buddhism and the Meaning of the Word 'Dharma'* (Delhi, 1970; first published 1923), p. 26.

44. Jayatilleke, *op, cit.*, section 485.

45. Gudmunsen, *op. cit.*, p. 7.

46. *Ibid.*, p. 11.

47. *Anguttara Nikaya* (trans. F.L. Woodward and E.M. Hare as *Gradual Sayings*, 5 volumes, London and New York, published for the Pal. Text Soci-

ety by Oxford University Press, 1932-6), IV, p. 414; *Milindapanha* (trans. I.B. Horner as *Milinda's Questions*, 2 volumes, London, Luzac, 1963-4), p. 313.

48. *Visuddhimagga*, trans. Nyanamoli as *The Path of Purification* (Colombo, A. Semaze, 1964) IV, p. 100.

49. *Ibid.*, IV, pp. 94-8.

50. "Wittgenstein's Notes for Lectures on 'Private Experience' and 'Sense-Data', ed. R. Rees, *Philosophical Review*, LXXVII (1968); reprinted in *The Private Language Argument*, ed. O.R. Jones, 1971, p. 233.

51. William James, *A Pluralistic Universe* (Gloucester, MA: Peter Smith, 1967), pp. 290-91.

Index

mysticism — // p. 140 provided w/ Melms
experience as ineffable or incommunicable

language + experience
pp 142-4